THE CONQUEST OF FAMINE

THE CONQUEST OF FAMINE

by

W. R. AYKROYD

"From lightning and tempest; from plague, pestilence and famine; from battle and murder, and from sudden death, *Good Lord, deliver us.*"

Book of Common Prayer
The Litany

1974
CHATTO & WINDUS
LONDON

Published by
Chatto & Windus Ltd
42 William IV Street
London WC2N 4DF

*

Clarke, Irwin & Co. Ltd
Toronto

© W. R. Aykroyd 1974

ISBN 0 7011 2047 9

Printed in Great Britain by
Butler & Tanner Ltd, Frome and London

CONTENTS

ILLUSTRATIONS

Plates

Line Drawings

ACKNOWLEDGEMENTS

I am grateful to my daughter Juliet for invaluable help in collecting and reproducing illustrations.

Oxfam not only provided some striking photographs, but also gave me access to files containing descriptions of recent famine and famine relief operations.

FAO and other UN organisations, as well as IPPF (the International Planned Parenthood Federation), supplied much relevant documentation.

Thanks are due to Mrs Constance Reed for typing and retyping the book most efficiently.

Dr Laming Macadam, formerly Reader in Egyptology, Durham University, kindly helped me with the chapter on "Famine in Ancient Egypt".

The sources of the Plates are as follows: Plates 1a, 1b, 5, 7, 8a and 8b, Oxfam; 2b, The Royal Commonwealth Society, London; 3a, the editor of *The Statesman*, Calcutta; 3b, Magnus Pyke, Secretary of the British Association for the Advancement of Science, from his book *Man and Food*; 4a and 4b, The United Nations Relief and Works Agency (UNWRA); 6a, Associated Press; 6b, *The Times*, London, and Associated Press. Plate 2a is in the author's possession.

The sources of the line drawings are as follows: Fig. 2, *The Illustrated London News*; Figs. 3, 4 and 5, Population Program Assistance, Office of Population, Bureau for Technical Assistance, Agency for International Development, U.S.A.

The chart showing the increase of sugar production during this century (p. 152) is reproduced from the Bulletin of the British Nutrition Foundation, No. 8, March 1973, by kind permission of the Director-General of the Foundation.

To all these sources grateful acknowledgements are made.

Introduction

WHAT is famine, from which, in the Anglican Litany, we beseech the Good Lord to deliver us? The word came into English through Norman French from the Latin *fames*—hunger—but hunger and famine are not the same thing. The *Encyclopædia Britannica* defines famine as "extreme and general shortage of food causing distress and death from starvation among the population of a district or country", which is not unlike a simple definition put forward in 1867 by an early Indian Famine Commission, namely: "suffering from hunger on the part of large classes in the population". A major work on starvation and famine, *The Biology of Human Starvation* by Ancel Keys and others, proposes: "Famine denotes the semi-starvation of many people—a substantial proportion of the population of some sizeable area."[1]

All these definitions recognise the fact that famine is a catastrophe afflicting large numbers of people. The earlier historical records usually expressed numbers affected in terms of deaths, rather than in terms of the starving, some of whom may survive. Estimates of the number of deaths often ran into many millions; they were naturally exaggerated rather than minimised. But if a figure of 5 million deaths should properly be cut down by, say, one half, famine leading to 2·5 million deaths is still a terrible calamity.

Unlike an earthquake, a famine is rarely a sudden emergency. It is usually a long-drawn-out calamity in which supplies of food dwindle for months or more from restriction to scarcity and in due course to complete dearth. The period when famine is at its height, in terms of suffering and death, may last a year or more, and a few famines said to have lasted for several years are on record. Recovery, when food for the survivors becomes available again, is by no means immediate. Bodily weakness and psychological traumata persist for some time.

We sometimes call an *averted* famine a famine, a well-known example of an averted famine being Joseph's famine in Ancient Egypt, described in the Book of Genesis (see below, Chapter 3).

I

Until recently there have been few famines which threatened to occur but never did. But now we are beginning to catch up with Joseph, and in the future *no* threatened famines should be allowed to happen. Within the last decade or so several major famines have been successfully prevented.

The word "starvation", which can be simply defined as the result of lack of food, has a good deal in common with the word "famine". In fact "mass-starvation" and "famine" mean much the same thing. But usually the word "starvation" is more limited in its range. As commonly used, it admits of degrees: "I'm starving" may mean nothing more than "I've a keen appetite", but it can also mean "I'm dying because I've nothing to eat". Complete starvation brings death, in perhaps ten weeks, to a previously healthy man. "Half-starved" and "semi-starvation", which may be applied both to individuals and groups, usually denote a fairly advanced degree of starvation, though of course the fraction has no physiological significance.

We think, then, of famine as something which strikes large populations over a large area, while starvation, on the other hand, afflicts individuals or small groups of people as well as whole populations. Starvation occurs in a great variety of circumstances and has numerous causes. It is a manifestation of many wasting and lethal diseases; medical terms for it include "cachexia" and "marasmus". It may be self-imposed, brought about by the voluntary act of an individual, as in a "hunger-strike" undertaken with political motives. It has been induced in human volunteers for experimental purposes, providing information of scientific value; much of our more exact knowledge of the bodily effects of starvation has been obtained in such circumstances, rather than through descriptions of famines with many thousands of victims, giving a broad picture of suffering and death, but few clinical details. The verb "to starve" can be transitive as well as intransitive. People have often been deliberately starved, intentionally and horribly, in ghettoes and concentration camps. Famine, as we shall see, is all too frequently "man-made", but the word does at least convey the suggestion of an Act of God and not of the wickedness of man.

"Hunger" is an emotional word associated with fundamental bodily sensations which impel living things to seek for food in a multitude of curious ways. Whether these sensations are pleasant or unpleasant depends on their duration and the immediate prospects of qualming them. Famine victims are indeed hungry, especially in the early stages of famine, but the obsession with food which accompanies established famine is something deeper than mere hunger. In the ordinary sense of the terms, "hunger" and "famine" are far from being synonymous.

Palaeolithic man, primarily a hunter, must often have been hungry. His dependence on successful hunting is shown by the spirited pictures of animals he drew on the walls of dark caves, apparently intended as magical spells to bring about the death of his quarry. If his quarry proved elusive or difficult to despatch, he was in danger of dying of starvation. But we can scarcely apply the word famine to the hunger of small bands of primitive huntsmen. Famine, as defined above, did not occur until the neolithic revolution had transformed man from a hunter and a food gatherer into a farmer, dependent on the weather for the cultivation of crops and the rearing of livestock. The early civilisations in the Fertile Crescent and the Nile Valley were based on the wheat and barley produced by numerous small agricultural communities, making use of simple technology and linked by barter. No doubt other civilisations based on rice or maize evolved in much the same way. Famine, due mainly to drought, made its first appearance at this stage in human development.

Catalogues have been drawn up of the major famines of the world, extending back into the first millenium B.C. or further. The *Encyclopædia Britannica* lists 31 famines, beginning with one in Rome in 436 B.C. when thousands of starving people threw themselves into the Tiber; Keys[1] enumerates 241 famines outside India, and 81 in India itself. All of these were serious famines, remembered for some years by succeeding generations. Europe has been less prone to famine than Asia, but it is said that between the birth of Christ and A.D. 1800 there are records of famine occurring in Europe in 350 different years, while in England, during the same period, there was a food shortage in one year out of ten. An historian has estimated that famine occurred somewhere in France every six years between A.D. 1000 and the 19th century.[2] Loveday,[3] writing of India in 1914, says that "it would probably be possible to find proof of direct failure of crops and ensuing distress in some part of India, in every year in the last two centuries". Somewhat similar statements have been made about China. Such estimates cannot, of course, be taken very seriously in the quantitative sense, but they serve to show that the food supply of mankind throughout history has been highly precarious.

The most extensive famines, leading to the greatest number of deaths, have taken place in India and China. Great famines, usually due to a combination of natural and human causes and almost on the Asiatic scale, have occurred in European Russia in recent as in earlier times. Special attention is given in this book to famine in India, which is well documented; much less information is available about famine in China. West Asia, i.e. the lands between the Tigris and the Mediterranean, has also suffered severely from famine; the references to famine in the Bible usually relate to this part of the world. In Egypt, watered by the Nile, famine has been less frequent, though the earliest account of successful famine relief comes from Egypt. In Africa, territories lying to the east and west of the Sahara have been prone to famine; at the time of writing four newly-established West African countries are suffering from drought and calling for relief.

Since man became dependent on cultivated crops for most of his food, famine has caused severe suffering and high mortality in many parts of the world. Until recently, counter-measures have been largely ineffective. But during the present century, particularly since the second world war, great progress has been made in relieving famine, and in preventing hunger in refugee groups. "Surplus" foods in abundance have been produced in certain fortunate countries, and modern transport makes the carriage of foods across the oceans to famine areas a comparatively easy matter. Within such areas the local transport and distribution of food presents few difficulties. New knowledge of the nutritional needs of children has been obtained by research during the last forty years, and this knowledge, effectively applied, has done much to save child life during famine. Organisations and people with experience of famine problems and relief measures have become available to promote the counter-attack. In this field an impressive lead has been given by the United Nations and its agencies.

This book carries the story of famine and famine relief into the current decade. Much of it, of course, relates to the past; without knowledge of the past history of famine it would be difficult to evaluate the present situation. But the adoption of the historical approach in much of the book should not convey the impression that famine has simply been a disastrous episode in human history, to be relegated, like the Black Death, to the history books. At the time of writing (1973), the world food situation is precarious and causing serious anxiety.

All that has been said so far concerns the catastrophe of famine as defined in the *Encyclopædia Britannica*—"extreme and general shortage of food causing distress and death from starvation among the population of a district or country". But now a new and larger monster is looming up—world-wide famine due to overpopulation, i.e. too many mouths and too little food. This has become a major preoccupation with those who have come to be called prophets of doom. It is easier to write about the concrete calamity of famine as it has cursed mankind since the dawn of history, than about a still more terrible calamity which has not yet happened. But the threat cannot be ignored in a book about the conquest of famine.

Chapter 1

The Causes of Famine

THE most important natural cause of famine has been drought due to insufficient rainfall, preventing crops from being sown and harvested, and killing off domestic animals. Most of the great famines of history have been precipitated by drought. When the Bible says, as it does quite often, "the famine was sore in the land", this means failure of the rains. The failure is frequently gradual; for example, two years of poor rainfall may be followed by a third year without any rain at all. It is then that famine makes its appearance, with no new crops growing, and stocks of food and other resources exhausted. The land takes on a lunar aspect, dry, hard and sunbaked, with nothing green to be seen—"a dry and thirsty land, where no water is". Plate 1a shows a famine landscape in India, with nothing growing because of drought. The dead cow and the watching vultures are typical of such a scene. Cattle are likely to die before human beings. Plate 1b shows the trickle of water remaining in the bed of what is usually a big river. Such drought is characteristic of subtropical latitudes between 10° and 30°, but not of the tropics themselves or of the temperate zone, where rainfall is normally regular and sufficient.

Land may be protected against drought by irrigation systems which use water brought by rivers from distant mountains where rainfall rarely fails. Excess water, often controlled by dams, is diverted through canals, channels and feeder ditches to irrigate the fields over a wide area. Egypt, as everybody knows, is for practical purposes rainless and depends for water on the annual overflow of the Nile. In India irrigation now protects more than one quarter of the cultivated area. Irrigation channels and artificial ponds or lakes— called "tanks" in India—were perhaps the first large-scale engineering works of man, and some of the earliest mechanical devices he invented were concerned with irrigation. Wells, if they are deep enough to tap subsoil water, are often of great importance in times of drought as a source of water, which may be needed not only by the crops but by people.

7

(But large-scale irrigation in hot countries carries risks, of which the most serious is salination. The precious water evaporates in the sunshine, leaving behind a deposit of salts and white sterile soil. This has happened conspicuously in the Indus basin, where the problem is now being mastered.)

Drought leads to great loss of domestic animals. In some Indian famines the whole stock of cattle and horses perished. The skeletons of cattle picked clean by vultures and other scavengers are a common sight in famine areas. Before mechanical transport was invented effective famine relief was often prevented not only by the normally slow pace of animal traction but also by the weakness and death of draught animals. Goats (see Chapter 6) are more resistant to drought than other livestock, and seem to be able to secure enough food to keep them just alive in arid wastes. Loss of meat and milk accentuates the physical weakness of famine-stricken populations.

The opposite of drought—flood—has been a less frequent cause of famine, though there are parts of the world, for example South Bengal and Central and South China, where the inundation of arable land can lead to the widespread destruction of crops on the ground or in storage. In China mighty rivers, fed by heavy rains, have regularly burst their banks and drowned huge tracts of productive land, and with them many thousands of people. It is said that in 1887–89 2 million people in the province of Honan lost their lives either from drowning or starvation. In Bengal danger lies in typhoons or cyclones arising in the Bay and generating tidal waves which sweep across the flat and fertile alluvium of the deltas of the Ganges and the Bramaputra. A great typhoon played an important part in provoking the Bengal famine of 1943.

Exceptionally heavy rains usually follow a period of drought lasting for one or more years, and may provide more water than the thirsty soil needs, so prolonging a famine. But this has not been a common sequence. Mention should also be made of unseasonable, freakish hail-storms which can do a great deal of damage to crops, but rarely afflict large areas.

Earthquakes are sometimes listed among the causes of famine. This is an error. A great earthquake, if it happens to strike a town or a city, may kill thousands of people, but does not destroy much food. The survivors need succour in the form of tents, blankets, building materials, medicines and other things, to carry them through the relatively short period before they can resume normal life again.

They will also need emergency rations, but large supplies of food are likely to be wasted.

The destruction of a staple food crop by a microscopic parasite has not been a common cause of famine throughout history. The terrible Irish famine by 1845–52, due to the destruction of the potato crop by the blight *Phytophera infestans*, is almost unique in this respect. The story of this famine will be told later. But passages in the Bible show that destruction by small parasites was not unknown in ancient times. In Amos 4, 9 the Lord says aggressively to his Chosen People:

"I have smitten you with blasting and mildew; when your gardens and your vineyards and your fig trees and your olive trees increased, the palmer-worm devoured them."

Joel 1, 17 also gives a picture of parastic infestation:

"The seed is rotten under their clods, the garners are laid desolate, the barns are broken down: for the corn is withered."

One larger and most dangerous parasite needs special mention— the locust. A swarm of locusts can leave the countryside as barren as a protracted drought, consuming not only tender growing crops but also the leaves on the trees. Locust eggs, laid in clusters on dry soil, hatch in ten to twenty days in the right conditions of warmth and moisture. After a destructive period as "hoppers" the insects grow wings and fly off in swarms, sometimes for thousands of miles. The direction of the flight of the swarms and where they land are determined by wind, temperature and humidity. When swarms converge, the biblical phrase about locusts is justified: "They covered the face of the whole earth so that the land was darkened."

Locusts seem to have contributed to famine rather by prolonging than by initiating it. (It is, however, recorded that locusts were the primary cause of a famine in East India in 1787.) Swarms are likely to attack the fresh green crops appearing when the rains have broken the drought. But now this most unpleasant insect is in rapid retreat. Modern biological science has alucidated every phase of its life-cycle and migrations, and modern technology has perfected con-centrated insecticides which can be sprayed by plane or helicopter. Co-ordinated international control measures, initiated as long ago as 1934, have been developed. The cost of anti-locust campaigns has been greatly reduced. Before the second world war it cost £100 to kill one ton of locusts. Now it costs under £2.

B

According to tradition, war precedes famine, and famine is followed by pestilence. Examples of famine, or near-famine, caused by war can be found in all ages; in fact, as has been said, war helped to bring about most of the worst famines in history. The starvation of the enemy may be a major weapon of war, as in sieges and blockades; the siege of Paris in 1871 and the siege of Leningrad in 1942 produced all the phenomena of famine in the beleaguered garrisons. There are also "scorched earth" operations which lay waste the countryside. A community may be pitilessly exterminated by starvation, like the Jews in the Warsaw ghetto. In the two world wars of this century both groups of belligerent countries sought hopefully to starve the other into submission by blockade, and at times nearly succeeded. But apart from such direct action, war, particularly civil war, has often by its mere presence reinforced the effects of natural calamities and turned food shortage into famine. Civil disturbance short of war has had similar consequences. War interrupts the sowing and reaping of crops; it takes labourers, domestic animals and means of transport away from farms; it disrupts communications and impedes famine relief. Armies themselves rarely starve; they manage to obtain enough food to the detriment of non-combatants. But in great retreats, like the retreat from Moscow, armies and non-combatants starve together.

Occasionally ill-conceived action on the part of a government may precipitate food shortage. One thinks, for example, of the premature efforts of the Soviet government, early in the 1930s, to establish collective farms, a policy which involved the liquidation of the most competent independent farmers, called Kulaks. As a result Russian agriculture was handicapped for several decades. The food shortage which ensued caused much suffering and indeed extensive famine.

Whatever its cause, food shortage will increase the cost of food. The process may run wild through panic and greed, so that people cannot buy the food that is still available and die of starvation before stocks of food are exhausted. They may die in the street in front of locked stores full of grain. The price of wheat or rice may rise ten or more times; in a famine in England in 1437 the price of wheat per quarter rose from four to twenty-six shillings. In early records the severity of a given famine is sometimes indicated by quoting increases in the price of grain. The food-hoarder flourishes and speculatively-purchased stocks may accumulate on a large scale. Famine throughout history has generally been "class" famine, in the sense that the poor died while the rich secured enough food for survival. It is indeed reported that in a famine in India in the 14th century the emperor of the day could not obtain enough food for his household. But chroniclers more often tell of abundant meals behind the palace walls, with the king's ministers making fortunes by buying grain and selling it at huge prices.

While the main cause of famine is a scarcity of basic foods, this scarcity may be small in degree in relation to the total needs of the population. A short-fall of not more than 20 per cent may be enough to set prices sky-rocketing beyond the means of the poor. We shall see later how this happened in the Bengal famine of 1943.

Other potential causes of famine besides those mentioned in this chapter may emerge in the future. Some new parasitic blight may suddenly arise by mutation and destroy crops on a wide scale before a scientific counter-attack can be launched. Some synthetic poison, like the poison used by the Americans to destroy foliage during the war in Vietnam, may get temporarily out of control. The hopeful theme of this book is that periodic famine, as it has occurred in the past, is outdated as a human catastrophe. But such hopes may be jeopardised by new agents of destruction and extremes of human folly.

Chapter 2

The Effects of Lack of Food

Books about wars can and have been written with little recognition of the fact that soldiers are made of flesh and blood. Armies advance and retreat, they attack and counter-attack, they outflank the enemy or are out-flanked. Strong-points are "softened up" by bombardment before assault. Heavy losses in killed and wounded are reported, usually heavier on the enemy's side. The victorious commander-in-chief is hailed as a great soldier with some of the genius of Napoleon, worthy of an honoured place in his country's history. The reader can sit comfortably in his armchair and appreciate the technical pattern of the campaign and the character sketches of generals on both sides. It would spoil his appreciation if at each point in the story he was reminded of the terror and agony of individual soldiers on the field of battle, the sufferings of the wounded and the crippling disabilities which remain after the war has been won or lost.

Famine can be recorded in terms of area, duration, the size of the population affected, the scarcity and cost of food, the death rate and other features. But essentially it means a lot of miserable people suffering from starvation, and physically and mentally damaged as the result. A book on famine like this one may appropriately describe, at an early point, some of the realities of starvation, however unpleasant these may be. People without food do not simply lie down quietly and die. The way to death is nasty and brutish and often not short. A few years ago I was asked to give a paper at a symposium entitled "The Threat of Famine" which was in effect a discussion of the theme of food supplies, population growth, family planning and their interactions. The participants were healthy well-fed members of the British intelligentsia. Feeling that the word "famine" was being too lightly used, I opened my contribution with something I had written twenty-five years before about the Bengal Famine of 1943*:

> "Many of the patients in the famine hospitals were picked up in a state of extreme weakness and collapse, often on the point of

* See Chapter 8.

death. They were for the most part emaciated to such a degree that the description 'living skeletons' was justifiable. Many suffered from mental disorientation, showing a very marked degree of apathy and indifference to their surroundings. When taken to hospital, such patients made very little effort to help themselves and received medical attention with an indifference which some times amounted to passive obstruction. They did not care how dirty or naked they were. Those with famine diarrhoea would repeatedly soil their beds and pay no attention to the protests of the attendants. In a few cases maniacal symptoms were present. The mental state of many starving destitutes indeed sometimes disconcerted workers in famine hospitals, who were not aware that it was a pathological condition induced by starvation. There was some tendency to regard starving cases as needlessly dirty and unco-operative, and, since they made little effort to help them-selves, not worth helping."[1]

I added in my paper at the symposium that this was a glimpse of the sort of things that happen during a famine, but that there were many worse things to be seen.

One result of starvation is loss of weight which in the absence of food progresses steadily until an extreme degree of bodily wasting or emaciation is reached. In most circumstances some food, quite inadequate for needs, is available, and this will obviously affect the speed of wasting. Up to 10 per cent of normal weight can be lost without serious impairment of physical energy and fitness, a provision of nature which induces search for food while the body is still capable of vigorous action. Imperative hunger characterises this stage, which must have been all too familiar to our hunting ancestors in the palaeolithic age. As slimming due to lack of food proceeds beyond this point, the body weakens and begins to adapt itself in various ways. There is a marked decrease in spontaneous activity and the victim takes longer periods of rest. What is called the "cell-mass" of active living tissue is reduced, so that less energy (fuel) is needed to main-tain vital processes and to move the lighter body. When 15 to 20 per cent of normal body weight is lost the victim passes into a state of semi-starvation and is no longer good for much. Mental depression and apathy make their appearance, together with growing weakness and physical signs of starvation other than loss of weight.

For information about fatal degrees of weight loss in famine, we may turn to Alexander Porter, a member of the Indian Medical Service, who was Principal of the Medical College, Madras, in the 1870s. During a severe famine in 1877–78, Porter took charge of "famine sheds" in Madras City which provided shelter for famine victims, many of whom were at the point of death when admitted. Porter performed 459 autopsies on men and women dying of starvation, a rather curious thing to do since there was no doubt of the cause of death and a smaller number of autopsies would have sufficed for observing and recording pathological changes due to starvation. But his industry provided some useful data. The normal weight of Tamil men, he says, was 110–120 lb; omitting a number of dropsical cases, the average weight of the famine victims at death was 77 lb. For women the corresponding figures were 95–105 and 77 lb, i.e. the women had lost a somewhat smaller percentage of their body weight when they died. "The majority", Porter says, "had wasted until they were barely two-thirds of their normal weight, and when emaciation has reached this degree life is held by a slender thread which the least untoward circumstance is sufficient to snap."[2]

Porter's data give us the extreme, showing approximately the limit of weight loss which the human body can tolerate and remain alive. A smaller percentage loss can be serious enough. In the remarkable studies made in Minneapolis by Ancel Keys and his associates,[1] young healthy male volunteers were submitted to a degree of under-feeding which reduced their weight by 15 to 25 per cent. This extent of deprivation was enough to enable a great deal of valuable physiological and pathological information on the effects of too little food to be obtained. Keys called the state of his young men "semi-starvation". In the early months of the Dutch famine of 1944–45 due to the cutting off of supplies to Western Holland by the occupying Germans (see Chapter 10), additional rations were given to people who had lost 25 per cent of their normal weight. As the food situation worsened, the percentage loss of weight calling for supplementary rations had to be raised to 33 per cent, and at this point people began to die of starvation. When the loss reached 40 per cent, death was almost inevitable. It seems that the stalwart Dutch could hold out a little longer against lack of food than the small South Indian Tamils, not well-covered even in normal health. The reserve stores of the body naturally influence resistance to starvation; a man deprived of food may obtain, from his stores, about 3 kg of protein and 6·5 kg of fat, enough to keep him going, at a low level of calorie expenditure, for forty-five days or a little longer. Such a period of survival depends, of course, on having plenty of fluid to drink. Absolute thirst kills in a few days. The public has sometimes been surprised at the long survival of political prisoners undergoing a "hunger strike". This is possible because the prisoner is completely at rest in bed in warm surroundings and has an unrestricted fluid intake.

With continuing lack of food, the pulse rate is slowed, the blood pressure falls and the heart muscle atrophies. The brain is the last organ in the body to lose weight. In the Minneapolis investigations, intelligence tests gave results within the normal range, though the volunteers themselves found it difficult to concentrate and felt that their powers of comprehension had declined. Speech is usually lucid, though a little slow; starving people almost at the point of death can often answer questions clearly. Hearing remains unimpaired; in fact there are reports that it becomes especially acute in starvation, an impression probably arising from increased sensitivity to noise and general irritability. But while, in the physiological sense, the brain continues to function, the psychological effects of deprivation of food are distressing. An obsession with things to eat—what has been called "the persistant clamour of hunger"—takes charge of the mind. This obsession was described, perhaps rather fancifully, by Mr Malcolm Muggeridge, in his early days before he became a television star. The passage quoted below is from his excellent book *Winter in Moscow*, published in 1934.

"Famine is something quite peculiar. It concentrates all effort and thought and feeling on one thing. It makes everyone a frustrated glutton. In a famished town, as in a cheap restaurant, there is always a flavour of food in the air. Everybody brooding on food makes a smell which hangs about them like the smell of gravy and cabbage about a dirty tablecloth. Somehow famine goes beyond hunger and puts in each face a kind of lewdness; a kind of grey unwholesome longing. People's white gums and mouldering flesh suggest rather a consuming disease like leprosy than appetite. They seem diseased, even evil, rather than pathetic. Their eyes are greedy and restless, and linger greedily, it sometimes seems, on one another's bodies. Their skin gets unnaturally dry and their breath parched and stale like dry air in a cellar."

Muggeridge's passage reflects the early stages of famine. If hunger persists further, the canons of normal behaviour are relinquished and the personality disintegrates. The victim sleeps for long hours and wakens to worry about his growing weakness, and to brood on futile schemes for getting food. Though normally honest, he is ready for pilfering and thieving; ready, indeed, to steal food from a blind man's plate. A characteristic attitude is indifference to the sufferings of others; mothers may ignore the clamour of their children for food and abandon them to die of hunger. There are many grim historical accounts of social and family disruption during famine. A passage written by a country doctor about the Irish famine of 1846 is illustrative:

"Another symptom of starvation, and one that accounts for the horrible scenes that famine usually exhibits, is the total insensibility of the sufferers to every other feeling except that of supplying their own wants. I have seen mothers snatch food from the hands of their starving children; known a father to engage in a fatal struggle with a son for a potato; and have seen parents look on the putrid bodies of their offspring, without evincing a symptom of sorrow. Such is the inevitable consequence of starvation."[3]

In India, "wandering" has been officially regarded as evidence that a famine was getting out of hand. It meant that people were leaving their villages *en masse* in response to a vague hope that food was being distributed in some neighbouring town. During food shortages in Europe in modern times, the exodus has been the other way round; famished city-dwellers have made their way to the countryside where some happy farmer might have a few turnips to sell at an exorbitant price.

Stories of cannibalism during famine have come from many countries. Its occurrence is not surprising. It may mean the eating of dead bodies, or it may mean murder for the pot. But in either form it has been remarkably rare, and largely confined to renegades and delinquents. In famine domestic dogs and cats are eagerly devoured, and rats are a delicacy, but the taboo against eating human flesh is strong enough to withstand the urge of extreme hunger in the vast majority of human beings. But sometimes human flesh has been minced, disguised in the form of sausages, and profitably sold.

Oedema or dropsy is a constant phenomenon in all famines, and there are early accounts of the "bloating" seen in famine victims. In starvation water accumulates in the tissue spaces outside the cells, these spaces being larger than normal because the cells themselves are shrunken. Fluid also accumulates inside the cells to some extent, but most of it is "extra-cellular", as is shown by the fact that it *flows*; for example it flows down to the ankles and feet when the sufferer is upright and back to other parts of the body, including the face, when he lies down. According to a classic hypothesis, the concentration of protein in the blood plasma controls the passage of fluid from the blood to the tissues, and in starvation the concentration is usually low. But this hypothesis does not fit all the facts. The kidneys may be involved, though there is nothing obviously wrong with the kidneys in starvation. A great deal of research has been done on famine oedema, much of this in central Europe during the Kaiser's war, when there was acute food shortage in Germany and Austria. But the condition is not yet completely understood.

The prevalence and degree of famine oedema give a rough indication of the severity of a famine, and also, since it appears rather slowly, of the period of starvation to which the victims have been subjected. In the Irish famine which began in 1845, famine oedema was at its worst in 1847. Woodham-Smith[4] quotes a somewhat exaggerated contemporary visitor's account in which it is described as "that horrid disease—the results of long continued famine and low living—in which the limbs and then the body swell most frightfully and finally burst". Another visitor to Ireland, writing at about the same time, said that while three-quarters of the population were skeletons, nevertheless the swelling of limbs was universal; and a philanthropist from the United States was shown a boy of twelve whose body was swollen to the size of an adult, though the arms were "like pipe-stems".

Such extreme degrees of oedema have not been observed in most famines; Alexander Porter, for example, did not see them in the famine sheds in Madras. A cause contributing to dropsy in the Irish famine may have been the setting up, by Act of Parliament, of "soup kitchens" in most parts of the country. The soup contained various ingredients and no doubt looked sustaining and nutritious, but at first was mainly hot water. The daily consumption of a bowl may have contributed to the water-logging of the sufferers. This was at a time when it was difficult to obtain maize meal from America.

Later, supplies of maize became plentiful and the soup was thickened into a porridge.

Possibly something similar happened in Germany during the first world war. To eke out their limited food supplies, the Germans consumed a great deal of soup made from turnips, parsnips and other root vegetables. A voluminous German literature on famine oedema remains. It is noteworthy that the British did not suffer from oedema in either of the two world wars; they must have been close to it towards the end of the first of these, though not in the second when available food supplies were scientifically husbanded and distributed.

The enzymes and hormones which control living processes are nearly all complex proteins. Since the starving body lacks dietary protein, it cannot manufacture these in sufficient quantities. This has various results. For example starving men rapidly lose sexual desire and become impotent, because of failure to secrete enough of the hormone testosterone. In the environment of real famine, this deprivation may be positively advantageous, but Ancel Key's young men, living on an American university campus, found it depressing. Normal sexual desire and potency returned slowly when the experiment was over and the subjects had plenty to eat again. In women menstruation tends to disappear and puberty is delayed. Failure of digestive enzymes is one of the causes of the intractable diarrhoea which, as we shall see, is perhaps the worst thing that happens to famine victims.

The eyes of starving people stick out because of wasting of the tissues around the orbits. The skin is dry and inelastic and often hangs in loose folds on the body. Sometimes patches of dark pigmentation appear on the face and trunk, an irreversible phenomenon probably due to glandular disturbance; these patches may have been exaggerated by the author of the Book of Lamentations 5, 10 into: "our skin was black like an oven because of the terrible famine". Another not uncommon feature is abnormal growth of hair over the arms and back, occurring mainly in children, and probably also due to disturbance of endocrine glands.

A common, almost universal manifestation of famine is diarrhoea, usually called "famine diarrhoea". This may occur early in the course of starvation, but when severe it is more often a terminal event, presaging death. Alexander Porter noted what he called "alvine* fluxes" in 75 per cent of those dying in the famine sheds in

* alvine = intestinal.

Madras. Several causes are recognised. Famine victims, in their desperate search for food, will swallow all sorts of things which cannot be digested and absorbed—leaves, stalks, grass, roots, mixed refuse, even sawdust. These irritate and excoriate the intestinal walls and are rejected. A more basic cause lies in the state of the intestines themselves. Like the rest of the body the intestinal walls lose substance; they become thin as paper, and so transparent that morsels of undigested food can be clearly seen, as in a test-tube; can be seen, that is, by anyone who, like Alexander Porter, performs autopsies on people who have died of starvation. The mucous membrane of the intestine ulcerates, and the glands concerned with digestion atrophy. All these changes lead to severe diarrhoea which further weakens the sufferer. It has long been known that the resuscitation of the starving must proceed slowly; a full meal will finish them off. Given the usual effects of famine on the intestines, this is only to be expected.

In diseases such as cholera and dysentery, the diarrhoea is due to the presence in the intestines of micro-organisms which can readily be seen and identified under the microscope. These infectious diseases, and others localised in the intestines, occur in famine victims. But numerous attempts to find the micro-organisms responsible for the most common type of diarrhoea accompanying famine have failed. It has other causes, as indicated above. A similar kind of diarrhoea also occurs frequently in normal times in badly-fed infants and young children whose intestines come to resemble those of famine victims.

Anaemia of varying degree is almost universal in populations suffering from famine, since their food does not provide them with enough iron and other substances needed for making blood in the bone marrow. For recuperation, they can with great advantage be given a daily dose of blood-forming agents. But this should not be confused with the distribution of "multi-vitamin" tablets, which are sometimes handed out to famine victims by the hundred thousand because this is an easy thing to do and thought to be beneficial. Moreover, pharmaceutical companies usually have obsolescent stocks on their hands which they are glad to dispose of cheaply as a charitable gesture. Actually, multi-vitamin pills are of dubious value. Doctors unfamiliar with famine are sometimes surprised because certain well-known deficiency states do not occur in spite of the gross deficiency of the diet. If the disease beriberi is due to lack of vitamin B_1 or thiamine, then one would expect that people who lack the vitamin because they lack food would suffer from it. The reason they do not is that vital processes in the body cells are reduced because of starvation, and requirements for the vitamins which help to regulate these processes are also reduced. But for some reason one familiar deficiency disease—scurvy—does occur during famine. It sometimes makes its appearance when foods devoid of vitamin C are given for relief: this happened in the Irish famine when the victims were given imported maize meal which lacks vitamin C to replace the potatoes which are quite rich in this vitamin. I have myself seen an outbreak of scurvy during a famine in Central India, appearing after the people had been living for a year or so on cereal grains and almost nothing else.

A reference to vitamin D deficiency in famine victims will be found in Chapter 9.

Unusual circumstances *can* arise in which lack of vitamins is as important as lack of food. This happened in Japanese prison camps during the second world war. The prisoners were not starved; they were given a small ration of milled rice, but almost nothing else. As a result they suffered grievously from beriberi and other vitamin-deficiency states.

In the Litany, "plague and pestilence" precede famine. But history does not seem to provide any example of a major famine being caused directly by epidemics of communicable diseases. Even the Black Death, which was bubonic plague and killed from one-third to one-half of the population of England in the 14th century, did not lead to food shortage among the survivors. A high prevalence of malaria during the planting season in Africa may seriously reduce the subsequent harvest, though rarely to the point of famine. But there is no doubt that famine and pestilence—in that order—have been evil partners through the ages, and that outbreaks of disease in the course of famine have sometimes killed more people than starvation itself. They are not quite inseparable. In a community protected from infectious diseases by modern public health measures, it is possible to have famine without pestilence, as in Holland in 1944 (Chapter 10). In the averted Bihar famine of 1966, there were no epidemics for the same reason—very unlike the situation in the Bengal famine twenty-three years earlier.

Famine and epidemics are associated for two reasons. First, undernutrition may impair the body's defences to the invasion of noxious organisms and prevent it from dealing with them effectively once invasion has taken place. To give an example, the anti-bodies which give protection cannot be formed for lack of specific substances, normally supplied by food. Secondly, the disruption of society which has almost invariably accompanied famine facilitates the spread of diseases from person to person, leading to major epidemics. The second of these has been the more important. In the Western world typhus has been the most formidable famine disease and has indeed been called "famine fever"; in a later chapter an account will be given of its ravages during the Irish potato famine, when the environment was ideal for its spread. Serious malaria epidemics have followed famine after the rains have come, because mosquitoes, like plants, need moisture and multiply when there is plenty of it.

Relationships between under-nutrition and physiological resistance to infection and defence mechanisms are, however, somewhat complicated. A recent publication of the World Health Organisation called *Interactions of Nutrition and Infection*[5] lists some 1440 references. This vast literature records numerous observations on man and experiments in animals. It is, however, more concerned with deficiency of the diet in the qualitative sense than with sheer lack of food, as in famine. Much attention has been given to vitamin deficiency states and infection. The very extent of the literature indicates the complexities of the subject and the difficulty of drawing clear conclusions. Commonsense suggests that in a starving community disease of all kinds will flourish, the ill effects of starvation accentuating those of disease, and vice versa. The pundits call this a "synergistic relationship". But under-nutrition can sometimes inhibit the attack of a specific disease and prevent its advance when it has gained a foothold. Some veterinarians have claimed that "foot and mouth" is particularly likely to occur in well-fed and healthy animals.

An example may help to illustrate this aspect of the subject. It has long been known that respiratory tuberculosis—consumption— tends to increase in prevalence during periods of food shortage. It became most common in Europe during both world wars when the diet was restricted and living conditions bad. There has been, of course, a close association between consumption and poverty and malnutrition in normal times. The main conclusions drawn from such facts were: feed people well and they will not get T.B.; if they have got T.B. feed them well and they will have better prospects of recovery. But T.B. can now be arrested by appropriate antibiotic drugs, notably streptomycin and isoniazid, without relieving poverty and improving the diet. There is no longer need for expensive sanatoria where patients are kept at rest and given a rich diet. They can be effectively treated at home by suitable drugs, even in India. Further, the appearance of the disease in children can be prevented by B.C.G. vaccination, now used all over the world. The old idea that the prevalence of respiratory tuberculosis depends largely on the diet turns out to be misleading, though there is no doubt that it is common in malnourished populations.

One terrible, though rare, consequence of a long period of semi-starvation is *cancrum oris*—gangrene of the mouth—which occurs mainly in children whose tissues are dehydrated because of diar-rhoea and who are living in filthy surroundings. Large areas of the face—the mouth, lips and cheeks—rot away before death takes place. It is sometimes possible to save the victim's life by good feed-ing and cutting away most of the gangrenous tissue, but inevitably gross deformities and hideous scarring persist. Not so many years ago neglected and starved slum children suffering from *cancrum oris* were to be seen in city hospitals in Europe.

One of the earliest Indian famine enquiry commissions, reporting in 1868, made a brave attempt to produce a rational statement about famine and epidemic disease[6]

"We think it is quite impossible to distinguish between the mortality directly caused by starvation and that due to disease, directly or indirectly connected with starvation, want and bad food. Not only do our remarks regarding the want of statistics apply to this subject also, but in truth want and disease run so much into each other that no statistics and no observations would suffice to draw an accurate line. The death of the emaciated and exhausted from cold, exposure and bowel disease, either before re-ceiving or on receiving food (the last is a very common form) may in fact be considered the direct result of starvation. The principal disease of a destructive character in respect of which it is often impossible to say whether it has been caused by want, is cholera.* We believe we are correct in saying that, even where there is no epidemic cholera very generally spread, it has con-stantly happened that the famine-stricken have been carried off

* The cholera vibrio was not discovered until 1890.

by that disease, or by something presenting similar appearances. The truth we take to be simply this, that the ordinary outbursts of cholera (in Bengal and Orissa) were aggravated and extended by want and bad food. The first effect of the scarcity, universally, was to drive the people to subsist on unusual and unwholesome food, jungle roots and such like, and we find that cholera constantly accompanies want."

Much of what has been said in this chapter relates to the effects of starvation at all ages. But a salient fact about famine is that, in terms of mortality, it has pressed most heavily on the very young and the old. Old people tend to be helpless in famine times and no one cares much about them. They cannot forage for food or fight vigorously for their share of what little food is available. They cannot masticate and digest unfamiliar foods. They are more inclined than younger people to lie down and die. Children, especially those under five, have exacting needs for protein and when food is short may suffer almost as much from lack of protein as from lack of calories. Later we shall see that what is nowadays called "protein-calorie malnutrition" is common in young children during famine. This fact, which has been recognised only recently, has given a new turn to famine-relief operations. It means providing the children, not just with food, but with the necessary protein—a life-saving operation.

Chapter 3

Famine in Ancient Egypt

AGRICULTURE in Egypt does not depend on rain falling on fields and crops, and in fact most of the country is rainless. It depends on the overflow of the Nile which is fed by heavy monsoon rains in the distant mountains of Abyssinia. These rains have a regular annual peak, followed by the rising of the river and the flooding of the land. But they vary in volume like rains anywhere in the world, and at times the river may not rise to the level needed to fill dependent canals and irrigation channels. Partial or complete failure of crops ensues.

The main cereal of Ancient Egypt was wheat, and it is believed that the Ancient Egyptians invented the process of making bread by fermenting and baking wheat flour—among the most important of human inventions. The New World cereal maize, the main crop of modern Egypt, did not reach the country until early in the 19th century.

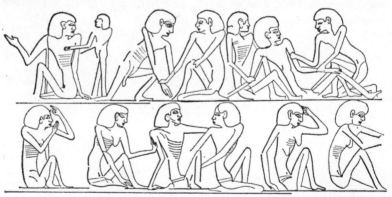

1 Ancient Egypt. *Famine victims shown in bas-relief on the Causeway, Pyramid of Unas, Sakkara.*

The Ancient Egyptians kept careful records of the height of the river in flood-time at Elephantine Island near the First Cataract,

24

where the Aswan dam now stands; the measuring scale they used is still visible on the rocks of the island. There were other scales further down the river; one, for example, at Gizeh beside the great pyramids. But Egypt was better assured against lack of water than Canaan and other lands of Western Asia which relied on local rainfall and, as we shall see, the people of these lands turned to Egypt for food in times of dearth. Ancient Egyptian inscriptions refer to years of scarcity but rarely to famine. There are, however, records of famine in the Old Kingdom, as long ago as the first half of the third millennium B.C. A relief showing emaciated famine victims survives on the causeway of the Fifth-Dynasty Pyramid of Unas in Sakkara.[1] A remarkable inscription on a tomb on the island of Sihêl, dated in the reign of Djeser during the Third Dynasty, was restored and re-written many centuries later, in the time of the Ptolemies. This inscription has been rendered as follows:[2]

"I am mourning on my high throne for this vast misfortune because the Nile flood in my time has not come for seven years. Light is the grain; there is lack of crops and of all kinds of food. Each man has become a thief to his neighbour. They desire to hasten and cannot walk. The child cries, the youth creeps along, and the heads of the old men are bowed down; their legs are bent together and drag along the ground, and their hands rest in their bosoms. The counsel of the great ones in the Court is but emptiness. Torn open are the chests of provisions, but instead of contents there is air. Everything is exhausted."

This ancient inscription mentions many of the phenomena of famine and its effects on the body and mind and the apathy and despair it engenders. Throughout most of history the advice of the great ones at court has indeed been empty.

The first mention of famine in the Bible is in Chapter 12, verse 10, of the Book of Genesis:

"And there was a famine in the land, and Abram went down into Egypt to sojourn there; for the famine was grievous in the land."

The date of this "grievous famine" was probably about 1870 B.C., towards the end of the Middle Kingdom.

The last fifteen chapters of the Book of Genesis are devoted to the story of Joseph, one of the Hebrew patriarchs. The central episode

c

is the prevention of famine in Egypt by measures organised by Joseph in the capacity of chief adviser to Pharaoh. Much of the story tells of the steps by which he attained that exalted position. He was disliked by his elder brothers for boastfulness and a habit of recounting dreams in which they made obeisance to him, and also because he was the favourite son of their father Jacob. From his tent in Canaan Jacob sent Joseph to report on the state of the family in Shechem. The brothers seized the opportunity of disposing of Joseph by selling him to a company of Ishmaelite traders en route for Egypt. These in turn sold him to Potiphar, the Captain of Pharaoh's Guard.

For a time Joseph throve in Potiphar's house, but he came to grief when accused by Potiphar's wife of attempted seduction. He was put into a special prison where Pharaoh's prisoners were kept. Here he was able to interpret correctly the dreams of his fellow-prisoners, the Chief Butler and the Chief Baker. Then Pharaoh had his ominous dream in which seven "well-favoured and fat-fleshed kine" came up out of the river and began to feed in a meadow, followed by seven "poor and ill-fleshed" kine the like of which, as Pharaoh said in recounting the dream, he never saw in all the land of Egypt for badness. The bad cattle ate up the good cattle, but were still lean-fleshed as at the beginning. In a second dream, similar rôles were played by ears of corn. Pharaoh called upon the magicians and wise men of Egypt to interpret his dreams, but they failed. Then the Chief Butler, released from prison, remembered that Joseph, a young Hebrew fellow-prisoner, had accurately explained his dream, and recommended that Joseph should be sent for. After being shaved he was brought into the presence of Pharaoh and promptly interpreted the seven fat and lean cattle of Pharaoh's dream as seven years of good and bad harvests. Joseph added that the years of dearth after the years of plenty would be grievous. There was only one thing to be done, he said. Pharaoh must immediately appoint a discreet and wise man, with a body of officers under him, to take over one-fifth of the land during the seven plenteous years. Their task would be to gather up corn and store it in the cities under Pharaoh's seal.

The plan appealed to Pharaoh and his court. But it was necessary to find a discreet and wise man to take charge of the operation—a man, Pharaoh said, in whom the spirit of God was. He then turned to Joseph and gave him the assignment, setting him at one stroke, with plenary powers, over all the land of Egypt, second in rank only to Pharaoh himself. He took his ring from his hand and put it on Joseph's hand, had him dressed in fine linen clothes, and put a gold chain around his neck.

The next few years were years of preparation. We catch a glimpse of Joseph moving about the land in Pharaoh's second chariot, with outriders crying "bow the knee". There were abundant crops in these years, and grain was "like the sand of the sea". Joseph and his staff collected the surplus and stored it in the cities. Granaries which he built are still pointed out to tourists, but the identification is unlikely. Storage of grain is easy in the dry climate of Egypt. Barley in Tutankamun's tomb was recognisable as barley when the tomb was opened after 3500 years, though tests showed that it had lost its vitamins.

The bad years arrived as predicted and before long the people were hungry and cried to Pharaoh for bread. He replied, "Go to Joseph and do what he says." Joseph opened up the storehouses and sold corn to the Egyptians and also to people from other countries who came to Egypt to buy it, the famine being "sore in all lands". Nothing is said in the Bible about the amount of corn in storage and how its sale and distribution were controlled. Presumably there was some simple system of rationing.

During the first year or so of the emergency, the Egyptians, and applicants from adjacent areas, had enough money to buy Joseph's corn. Joseph put the money they paid into Pharaoh's house. Soon, however, the money ran out and the people came to Joseph and said, "Give us bread or we will die." Joseph answered, "I will give you bread in exchange for your horses, asses, cattle and sheep." The proceeds of this transaction kept them going for another year, but a further approach to Joseph then became necessary. They told him that their money and cattle had gone, and all that remained was their bodies and their lands. "Buy us and our lands for bread," they said, "and we and our lands will belong to Pharaoh." Joseph accordingly bought the land, which became Pharaoh's, and made it a law that after the drought one-fifth of its produce should be handed over to the state. We are not told what was involved by the sale of the people's bodies, but one verse says:

"And as for the people, he removed them to cities from one end of the borders of Egypt even to the other end thereof."

This suggests that Joseph took advantage of the situation to make himself a dictator, and that as a result of the seven years' drought the Egyptians lost some of their independence.

We are told nothing about the aftermath of the emergency and about what would today be called the "rehabilitation" of the country. But Joseph himself seems to have retained a great position in Egypt; he died there at the age of 110 and was embalmed, and buried in his native Canaan.

This well-told biblical narrative seems to be the earliest account of timely action to prevent famine. On some later occasions the building up of stocks of foods (Chapter 20) has been an important measure against famine, and during and after the second world war the expression "Operation Joseph" was sometimes used to describe such action. Pharaoh and Joseph had indeed the advantage of a warning, conveyed by Pharaoh's dream, that bad years were coming, but in later times the destruction and disruption caused by war often made this all too obvious.

Given Joseph's picturesque and positive character, it is surprising to be told by modern scholars that he never existed, or rather that no clear record of him has been found in the form of Egyptian documents or monuments.[3,4,5] One would expect Pharaoh's grand vizier to be buried in a fine tomb, with frescoes showing his principal activities during life; in this case, the building of granaries and the distribution of grain would be suitable themes for pictorial representation. From about 3000 B.C. onwards the names of Pharaohs, the succession of dynasties and the erection of temples and palaces, are recorded. But there is a gap after the Old Kingdom when the pyramids were built (ending about 2200 B.C.), and the Middle Kingdom which lasted until about 1700 B.C., and was later regarded as the Golden Age of Ancient Egypt. An Egyptian Dark Age ensued which lasted until the New Kingdom came into existence about 1575 B.C. The Dark Age was in part due to the invasion of Egypt by the so-called Hyksos, a semitic people from Canaan. Possessing horses and chariots, the Hyksos over-ran and conquered northern Egypt in a few years and set up their own king in Memphis, near modern Cairo. The Jewish historian Josephus (contemporary with Julius Caesar) maintained that the warlike Hyksos were Jews. The ordered civilisation of Ancient Egypt did not revive for 150 years, though an Egyptian king continued to reign in the south at Luxor. It seems possible that during this period the Nile dwindled and famine threatened, and that the Hykson king of the day employed a clever young Hebrew from Canaan to advise him about famine prevention and relief. This in turn gave rise to a story used many centuries later by chroniclers of the Hebrew patriarch, with Joseph becoming a great figure in the Dark Age of Egypt as King Arthur did in the Dark Age of England.

Chapter 4

Famine in Ireland

A CENTURY and a quarter has elapsed since the great Irish famine began in 1845. But it does not seem a remote catastrophe, at least in Ireland itself, where many relics of it are still to be seen by the discerning and instructed eye. It has also had broad historical consequences which affect the world today.

Much has been written about the Irish famine. Recently it has become a favoured theme of Irish economists and historians. Two books should be mentioned which provide invaluable information on the famine itself, and on its causes and sequelae. The first is *The Great Famine: Studies in Irish History, 1845-50*,[1] published in 1956, which consists of chapters on different aspects of the famine written by competent Irish authorities. The second is *The Great Hunger* by Cecil Woodham-Smith, published in 1962;[2] Mrs Woodham-Smith followed up her study of Lord Lucan, an Irish landlord, in *The Reason Why*,[3] with her monumental book on the famine which has proved a best-seller. In writing this chapter, I have made much use of these books, as well as of Freeman's *Pre-Famine Ireland*.[4]

The Irish famine had some remarkable and indeed unique features. Its "natural" cause was the almost total destruction of a staple crop—the potato—by a parasite, and not the failure of crops because of drought, the most common cause of famine throughout history. There is no record elsewhere of famine on a large scale being brought about by a microscopic parasite. Again, many famines have been "class famines", in the sense that they have afflicted mainly the poor. The Irish famine was very much a class famine, largely confined to the poor of the countryside, but it was also confined to people of one religion, Roman Catholicism. Another feature was the high mortality rate; during the years 1845-51 about 1·5 million people starved to death in Ireland or were killed by famine diseases. This is about 18 per cent of the population previous to the famine, enumerated at 8 million by the census of 1841. During the famine years about 1 million emigrated to Canada and America and 600,000 to England. Many of the trans-atlantic emigrants died

30

of fever and starvation on board ship or soon after reaching North America. Through death and emigration the population was reduced by about 25 per cent, and this fall has not been made good; in 1940 the number of inhabitants was about half that of 1840. Ireland today is among the most sparsely populated countries in the world, as any visitor can see. The demographic effects of the Irish calamity are unique in the history of famine.

Travellers were agreed that the Irish peasants, previous to the famine, were the poorest in Europe. They had tiny holdings, of two acres or less, and the windowless single-roomed mud cabins in which they lived usually contained no furniture except a few stools, and were shared with the family pig. Most had no household utensils beyond a vessel for boiling potatoes. Sometimes small quantities of vegetables—cabbages, peas, beans, turnips—were grown on a patch of land beside the cabin. The cultivation of crops other than the potato, for example, oats, depended on the size of the holding and varied in different parts of the country; such crops were usually sold to pay the rent. The south and west produced little except potatoes. In parts of the north-east the peasants, probably because of Scottish ancestry, grew and consumed oats rather than potatoes; these suffered less severely during the famine years. Large coarse potatoes, often called "lumpers" or "horse potatoes", were generally grown, on the same plot year after year. Potatoes were easy to grow, no work being needed beyond putting the seed potatoes in the ground in the spring and digging up the crop in the autumn.

The peasants did not suffer from cold. Cabins were kept warm and smoky by turf (peat) fires and by their numerous inhabitants.

A rough grading of the population dependent for existence on the potato is possible. The least wretched were occupiers of cabins with land holdings of two to four acres. Then there were cottiers living on the land of farmers for whom they worked, with a cabin and a small plot of half to one acre. At the lowest level were landless labourers, with no fixed employment, living in hovels and usually allowed the temporary possession of a small plot of land on which to grow potatoes.

A vivid picture of Ireland just previous to the famine is given by Thackeray in his *Irish Sketch Book*.[5] Thackeray was pestered everywhere by swarms of beggars and noted many signs of population density; in country houses, for example, the number of idling

servants, each assigned a small job, was extraordinary. Another
visitor, again just before the famine, was Asenath Nicholson, from
Vermont, U.S.A., who went to Ireland in 1844 to distribute bibles and
was hospitably received in cabins all over the country. Her book,
The Bible in Ireland,[6] the work of an agreeably dotty middle-aged
spinster, is among the curiosities of literature and most informative.

With this abyss of poverty, it is not surprising that a large proportion of the peasants were on the brink of starvation at the best of
times. According to the Irish "Poor Enquiry" of 1835, about 2·4
million people were hungry every year in July and August before
the new potato crop was ready to be eaten. What is surprising is
that the population survived and increased in such circumstances—
from 5 million in 1780 to 8 million in 1841, both of these figures
being rough but not grossly inaccurate estimates. Potatoes were,
however, usually plentiful for most of the year; and in good years
were so abundant that some were thrown away. It has been said
that a man would eat 14 lb a day in periods of plenty, which is
quite impossible since this amount would provide over 6000
calories—far beyond the needs of a not very active peasant. Less
than half this amount would suffice. A somewhat puzzling question
is how infants and young children managed to survive and grow in
the circumstances. Abundant breast milk, and a usual interval of
two years between births, are among the reasons for this.

Visitors, appalled by the poverty and squalor, were struck by the
good looks of the children. Adam Smith, whose economic principles,
as we shall see, seriously misled some of the authorities trying to deal
with the Irish famine, and also caused much trouble in India, has a
curious and interesting passage on potatoes and the Irish:

> "Experience would seem to show that the food of the common
> people in Scotland (oatmeal) is not so suitable to the human con-
> stitution as that of their neighbours in England (wheaten bread).
> But it seems to be otherwise with potatoes. Porters and coal-
> heavers in London, and those unfortunate women who live by
> prostitution, the strongest men and the most beautiful women
> perhaps in the British dominions, are said to be the greater part
> of them from the lowest rank of people in Ireland, who are gener-
> ally fed with this root. No food can afford a more decisive proof
> of its nourishing quality, or of its being particularly suitable to the
> health of the human constitution."[7]

What were the underlying causes of the situation in Ireland in the 1840s, just previous to the famine? To answer this question it would be necessary to recount the history of Ireland since the time of King Stephen. The Irish were a conquered people and their land belonged to alien landlords to whom it was a source of money, often spent outside Ireland. Ownership of land was commonly regarded as an immediate source of income rather than as a long-term investment involving social responsibility. Many of the landlords were absentees, living in England and rarely visiting their Irish estates, leaving their agents in charge. They could divest themselves of all responsibility by sub-letting their land on a long lease to middlemen who could exploit smaller tenants at will. These tenants had no security of tenure and any improvements they made in their holdings became the property of the landlord should they be evicted. It is thoughtless to blame the Irish peasant for relying too heavily on the potato. The whole iniquitous system, maintained by military occupation, depended on a crop which gave large returns from small plots of land. Without it, the people would have starved, as indeed they did during the famine.

The fungus which destroyed the potatoes first lodges on the leaves. It puts out filaments, with "spore containers" at their tips, which rapidly permeate the whole of the plant. The spores are carried to other plants by the wind and infestation spreads rapidly, particularly in damp weather. The fungus also infects the tubers which may be rotten when they are dug up or become rotten later in storage. In 1845 the rapid progress of the disease was frightening; crops which had promised well withered in a few days and turned into a mass of corruption, so that the fields became black and stank of decay. Actually the blight had visited Ireland on previous occasions and caused hunger in some districts, but its ravages had been limited in extent. In 1845, it appeared during the summer in the Isle of Wight and later in Kent. It was not until October that widespread failure of the Irish crop took place. This was followed by complete failure in 1846. In 1847, the blight, for some reason, did not infest the fields, but since few seed potatoes had been planted, only a small harvest was gathered. It returned in full strength in 1848 and destroyed the crops as completely as in 1846. About three-quarters of the population were deprived of their staple food for four years or more.

The responsible authorities largely failed to save the victims of the blight from starvation. The famine was not a brief emergency, but went on for years. There was ignorance of the realities of Irish life, ignorance of elementary economic facts, and ignorance of human physiological requirements for food. Outside a few coastal towns, Ireland in the mid-19th century was a remote and little known country. Ignorance of economics perhaps showed itself most banefully in undue reliance on the principles of Adam Smith. Charles Trevelyan, the British Civil Servant in the Treasury in London, who for practical purposes was responsible for famine relief policy and measures,* was imbued with *laissez-faire* economic doctrines. He saw Ireland as a country into which food and other commodities would "flow" in response to demand and in accordance with the laws of economics, regardless of the fact that in Ireland there was no money and few merchants to promote such movement. He instructed his subordinates to avoid "disturbing the market", though in fact there was no market. On one occasion his chief officer in Ireland, Sir Randolph Routh, known as the "Commissary General", was goaded into telling him: "You cannot answer the cry of want by a quotation from political economy." Trevelyan was a distinguished man with many good qualities, who subsequently helped to establish the modern British civil service and did sound work in India, but in relation to the Irish famine he was an opinionated and obstinate bureaucrat. He was caricatured as Sir Gregory Hardlines by Trollope in *The Three Clerks*. But Trollope was interested mainly in his association with compulsory examinations for the civil service and was apparently unaware of the part he played in the famine.

One of the first things the government did was extremely sensible. Peel, the Prime Minister, ordered maize or Indian corn, to the value of £100,000, to be bought in America and shipped to Ireland, part of this to be sold immediately and part to be kept in store as reserve. Maize was the cheapest cereal grain available. This action involved Peel's resignation since it ran counter to the Corn Laws, but he was soon reinstated as Prime Minister. There were, of course, complications. At first whole unground maize was shipped, large hard grains which could be softened only by prolonged boiling, and were difficult to chew and swallow. The authorities discovered with surprise that there were scarcely any mills in Ireland capable of grinding the Indian corn. Later, ground maize was shipped from

* He was 'Assistant Secretary to the Treasury', in effect the head of the Department.

America, becoming known in Ireland as "Peel's brimstone" because of its yellow colour. This proved quite popular. There was not enough of it to replace the vanished potatoes, but it helped to keep starvation at bay.

The loss of the potato crop, not complete, was not immediately calamitous. Potatoes even became plentiful for a short time because of eagerness to sell those which had escaped the blight but might turn bad at any moment. But in five or six months every edible potato, or fragment of a potato, was eaten. Meanwhile a Relief Commission was appointed consisting mainly of Irish government officials, and including one Catholic. Pushed by Peel, the Commission drew up a relief programme depending primarily on local effort through local committees, which would raise money to buy food for resale to distressed people, or even for free distribution in cases of extreme necessity. Landlords were to be encouraged to give increased employment on their demesnes. In accordance with earlier practice in times of food shortage, the Board of Works was also to create extra employment through making new roads. Since "fever" was likely to occur, more fever hospitals were needed, and orders were issued that separate fever hospitals were to be constructed in the grounds of workhouses.

During May and June 1846, the weather was warm and the potato plants grew vigorously. But in July the blight reappeared, and by August every potato field was black and every potato rotten. The stench was worse than in the previous year. The people were now at the end of their slender resources. By September many were altogether without food, and deaths from starvation became frequent. By cruel mischance, the winter of 1846–47 was the coldest within living memory; north-east winds blew steadily across the country, as they rarely do, and snow fell in many areas. The most horrifying accounts of the famine, to be quoted in later times, were written during this winter. For example, a famous letter, subsequently used for collecting money in America, was sent to the Duke of Wellington on 17 December 1846, by N. M. Cummins, J.P., of Cork. In a town in West Cork he was surrounded by 200 starving phantoms, "such frightful spectres as no words can describe. By far the greater number were delirious, either from famine or from fever. Their demoniac yells are still ringing in my ears, and their horrible images are fixed upon my brain. My heart sickens at the recital, but I must go on . . ." "My Lord Duke," he finishes, "in the name of starving thousands, I implore you, break the flimsy chain of official etiquette and save the land of your birth . . ."

At this time children began to die in large numbers. Visitors noted that few were to be seen in the open air. Fifty per cent of the children admitted after 1 October to a workhouse in West Cork died, the workhouse doctor correctly ascribing their deaths to "diarrhoea working on an exhausted constitution".

The programme of public works initiated in the spring of 1846 continued through the earlier part of the winter, and at one point some 500,000 men were employed. But the operations performed were generally useless and the wages given were too small to enable the men to feed themselves and their families. Moreover, they had become incapable of physical effort. Early in 1847 the government decided on a new measure. The works were to be gradually closed down, and the famine victims fed free through "soup kitchens". An Act popularly called the "soup kitchen Act" was passed by Parliament on 25 January 1847, by which local committees were charged with setting up the kitchens, with financial help from the government and from charitable subscriptions.

Well-meaning people honestly thought that a sure way of relieving the famine had been found. But unfortunately little was known in the mid-19th century about food values and human nutritional requirements. "Soup" means hot water in which heterogeneous ingredients have been boiled, but it is mostly hot water. There were many different recipes for the soup doled out to the starving, including some devised by the famous French chef, Alexis Soyer, then employed in London, who set up a demonstration kitchen in Dublin. Among the ingredients were oxheads (without the tongue), maize, carrots, turnips, cabbages, onions, peas, leeks and other things. A bowl of such soup* was no doubt warm and comforting, but it probably provided less than 200 calories to people needing up to 3000 calories daily. Famine oedema or dropsy, described in Chapter 2, became widespread in 1847, and it is possible that the soup, by a "water-logging" effect, contributed to its occurrence. Not everybody, indeed, was convinced of the value of the soup. A Protestant clergyman, the Reverend F. Trench, commented as follows:

"Soup may be anything, everything, or nothing; it may be thin gruel or greasy water and I have tasted it of both descriptions;

---

* A pint (0·568 litres) was the quantity usually issued to an adult.

2 Irish famine. *Searching for potatoes in a stubble field.*

or it may be the essence of meat, and very wholesome where there
is some substantial food taken with it." He adds: "There can be
no doubt about a meal of substantial Indian meal stirabout or
porridge . . . one meal daily given to the poor has preserved life
and health to a great degree and does not cost more than 1½d
a day."

An English doctor, writing anonymously to the press from the
Athenaeum, described Soyer's recipes as "preposterous". "Any person," he said, "in the slightest degree acquainted with the principles
of organic chemistry could see, at a glance, that the soup was utterly
deficient in the due supply of those materials from which the human
frame can elaborate bones, tendon, blood, muscle, nervous substance, etc."

Somewhat later, imported maize became more abundant, the
soup was thickened and became more like a meal of porridge. But
supplies of maize were short during the worst period of the famine.

Soup for the starving was made in the big houses of the gentry, as
well as in the kitchens set up by local authorities. The daughter of
one of these houses wrote later:

"One day I saw a poor woman sitting on the footpath surrounded by her starving children. I at once ran back to the house,
and brought a jug of soup and tin mugs. But she was dead when I
returned. I laid her on the footpath and sent the children in a
cart to the workhouse."

The soup made in this particular house was a generous brew. It
contained not only maize meal but also oatmeal, pea flour and
onions, and even a few pieces of salt pork. It was ready for distribution at 7 a.m.[8]

A great epidemic of "famine fever" broke out during this terrible
winter, reaching its height in April. The fever was mainly typhus,
which is caused by an organism transmitted by the louse. Conditions
were ideal for contagion; the people had sold their bedding and
could not obtain fuel to heat water to wash themselves or their rags.
They huddled together for warmth by night and day. Lice were also
transmitted in the jostling crowds waiting for money payments,
food or soup.

The incubation period of typhus after the victim has been bitten
by an infected louse, is about fourteen days. The clinical manifesta-

tions of the disease are revolting. The patient has a high temperature
and is usually delirious; the face is dusky and swollen and on the
fourth or fifth day a dull red rash appears all over the body. Nervous exhaustion increases and the victim lies helpless on his back,
with his eyes half-open and fixed. He stinks horribly. Death comes
about the fourteenth day, though in some cases there is a crisis at
this point and sudden improvement occurs. Typhus is more common
and severe in middle-aged and elderly people than in children.
When infected, healthy people are as likely to die as the weak
and starving.

Relapsing fever, included in the broad category of "famine fevers"
and also transmitted by the louse, took its toll during the Irish famine,
but was less prevalent than typhus. As its name indicates, it tends
to recur at intervals after the first attack.

Medicine was useless in famine fever, a fact which perhaps accentuates the courage of doctors responsible for looking after the
sick in the so-called fever hospitals. The great traditions of the
medical profession held good. Forty doctors died of typhus in the
Province of Munster alone. There were also many deaths amongst
others in contact with the sick, for example the clergy, nuns, relief
officers and policemen. James Martin, a benevolent landlord in
County Galway—the grandfather of Martin Ross who with E. Œ.
Somerville delighted readers fifty years later with stories of Ireland—
caught typhus when visiting tenants in Clifden workhouse and died
of it. So did the Reverend Townsend, a large landlord in West
Cork, who ministered to the starving in Skibereen and its environs.
The peasants themselves were so terrified of contagion that they
would not go into a cabin in which someone lay sick with fever,
and often burnt and broke up cabins in which deaths from fever
had occurred. Helping famine victims is not an agreeable task
today; it is trying work and demands earnest devotion. But it is no
longer desperately dangerous.

It was observed that well-to-do people who died at home from
typhus did not pass on the disease to their families. Quite recently
this fact has been explained in terms of interactions between the
virus, the louse, and the human victim; so have curious anomalies in
the transmission of gaol fever (typhus) from stinking prisoners to
the lordly occupants of the bench.

Scurvy, due to deficiency of vitamin C, appeared as the famine
went on; normally it did not occur in Ireland because of the

abundance of potatoes, which are a good source of the antiscorbutic vitamin. "Land-scurvy", as it was sometimes called because of the usual connection between sea-faring and the disease, produced the familiar signs and symptoms—ulceration of the gums, purpuric patches on the skin, painful effusion of blood into muscles and joints. One Dublin doctor noted the preventive effect of the soup issued by the Quakers (Friends), which, he said, "was well-seasoned with vegetables".

During the decades before the famine there was substantial emigration from Ireland to large cities in Great Britain, to London, Glasgow, Liverpool and Manchester. Emigrants also went to the United States, Canada and Australia. But in 1847 famine and fever prompted emigration on a different scale; it became a mass exodus, a flight from a doomed land. Crossing the Atlantic in a sailing ship was usually an unpleasant experience for prosperous and healthy passengers; for many famine victims, lying on boards in dark and foul holds and given (by law) seven pounds of provisions per week, it proved lethal. One of the worst hardships was lack of enough water. Numerous ships were available because at this period there was a large import of timber from Canada to Great Britain, and on the return journey to Canada ships sailed empty or in ballast. Human beings for whom even small sums were paid were preferable to ballast. The fare of £2 to £3 was found somehow, being often supplied by relations already in America. Many landlords were eager to get rid of miserable peasants encumbering their estates, and found that encouraging and supporting emigration was preferable to eviction. Moreover, in January 1847, the government announced that the destitute population was to be maintained by the Irish Poor Law, i.e. out of local rates largely at the expense of property owners, which meant that the payment of fares would save landlords money. Some landlords offered free passages and provisions to people willing to emigrate. Lord Palmerston, the Foreign Minister, had extensive estates in County Sligo which he had never visited. With his approval, his agents chartered nine old and badly-equipped vessels to accommodate some 2000 people from these estates. The passengers suffered intolerable hardships and many died at sea. When the survivors reached St John, New Brunswick, the citizens there registered a protest at such negligence on the part of one of Her Majesty's Ministers; this was taken up by the Governor-General of Canada, Lord Elgin, who wrote officially to Palmerston asking for an explanation. Palmerston's jaunty reply, sent through his agents, offered no apologies.

It was reckoned that about 17,000 emigrants died during the crossing. An American emigration official wrote:

> "If crosses and tombs could be erected on the water, the whole route of the emigrant vessels from Europe to America would long since have assumed the appearance of a crowded cemetery."

The story of what happened to the refugees in Canada and the United States, and in England, is part of the history of the famine, but will not be told here. It is admirably told by Cecil Woodham-Smith. It will be sufficient to quote an inscription on a monument on Grosse Isle, the quarantine station beside the St Lawrence, below Quebec, where the "coffin ships" landed:

> "In this secluded spot lie the mortal remains of 5,294 persons, who, flying from pestilence and famine in Ireland in the year 1847, found in America but a grave."

Many Canadian officials, doctors and priests contracted fever and died, among them the Mayor of Montreal.

Meanwhile in Ireland the famine dragged on. No potato blight appeared in 1847, but only one-fifth of the usual acreage had been planted. Large charitable donations for relief were made. An organisation known as "The British Association" was founded to supply food, clothing and fuel to "the very numerous class of the sufferers who are beyond the reach of the government". It collected £470,000; Queen Victoria headed the subscription list with a donation of £2000. In the United States an "Irish Relief Committee" was set up in the principal cities, and money, food and clothing for Ireland collected on a large scale. Woodham-Smith comments: "A modern United States authority estimates the total value of gifts at $1,000,000, a sum worth many times its value today." The Society of Friends acted as trustees for the money contributed, helped to arrange the transport of clothing and provisions, and was also the principal channel for the distribution of the donations in Ireland. In the early phases of the famine the Friends did excellent work, tackling relief problems in their realistic and efficient way— as indeed they have done in famines and other disasters down to recent times. A "Central Relief Committee of the Society of Friends", consisting of Irish Quakers many of whose names are

D

familiar in Ireland today, published in 1852 the Transactions of the Committee in 1846 and 1847. Members of the Committee address each other, and correspondents in America, as "thee" and "thou", and refer to months by numbers and not by their pagan names. In the Preface the compiler says in dignified language:

"Although some of the operations undertaken by them (the Committee) were not attended with the hoped-for success, it was nevertheless incumbent on them to endeavour to rescue the famishing from death. It is not for man to command success; but it is his Christian duty, under circumstances of doubt and difficulty such as those presented by the recent famine, to labour from day to day, acting for the best according to his judgment, and willing to leave the event to Him who sees the end from the beginning and who alone can bless the work."[9]

At the end of 1847 the Friends found they had taken on too much. They had begun by making a realistic survey of the situation in different areas; they had stimulated the generosity of people outside Ireland, especially the American public, and these efforts had added substantially to the funds available for relief; they had undertaken direct relief in some of the worst areas. But, as the Transactions grimly comment:

"The exertions made during the past year were evidently too great to last. The sensitive had become habituated to the constant sight of misery; the energetic were wearied of the sacrifices which the distribution of relief involved; the sanguine were discouraged by the hopelessness of the task. Some who had administered relief had become fit objects for receiving it. The necessary attention to their private affairs—an attention which the general depression rendered still more imperative—deprived us of the services of others. Death had taken from us many of our best and most trusted assistants. We saw that the great difficulty with which we had from the first to contend, the want of suitable agents, would be indefinitely increased; and we felt that direct relief by a private association, contemporaneously with the amended Poor Law [i.e. the change from the system of providing food only in exchange for wages earned on public works], was not likely to be useful. It was therefore determined to reserve our funds for other purposes."[9]

The Friends decided to withdraw from direct relief—which they called "almsgiving", at the end of 1847, and devote whatever energies they could muster to less immediate assistance. Seeds were distributed for bringing the land laid waste by the potato parasite under cultivation again. For example, turnip seeds were issued in generous quantities. A model farm was established in County Galway. They gave assistance to industrial schools and encouraged the local manufacture of flannel and lace. New tackle was provided for fishermen, a group which suffered severely during the famine. But it does not seem that these and other constructive projects produced substantial and lasting results.

As time went on deaths from starvation became less frequent. The "soup" became more substantial, incorporating a pound of maize meal, and sometimes biscuit or flour. (Maize had again become cheap and fairly plentiful in Ireland.) Children under nine were given half this ration. Previously, cooked food was supplied only to people actually resident in workhouses, but in the middle of 1847 Parliament, after heated debate, passed the Irish Poor Law Extension Bill, which made "outdoor relief" possible. But one pound of meal daily, supplying about 1600 calories, was not nearly enough to rehabilitate starving people, and the victims remained thin and weak. As Ancel Keys has shown, by clear-cut scientific observations, a very large intake of food is needed for complete rehabilitation even from semi-starvation, and that rehabilitation is remarkably slow. His young men wolfed some 5000 calories daily and asked for more.

The destruction of the potato crop by blight in 1848 brought intense suffering and despair, but not death from starvation and disease on the same scale as in 1847, though corpses could still be seen on the roadside. Evictions went on and over large areas cabins were "tumbled", leaving their wretched inhabitants to live in ditches and holes, and to survive if possible on outdoor relief. Emigration also continued, and it was observed that substantial farmers were now leaving, escaping from a country which seemed to have been laid under a curse. Land was unsaleable and much of it became uninhabited waste. Landlords had lost most of their rents, and some smaller landlords, it was reported, were reduced to shooting rabbits on their demesnes for meat. Stories that landlords continued to live luxuriously and entertain extravagantly were probably circulated by rare visitors from England; as the famine went on,

Irish landlords were cursed almost as bitterly in England as in Ireland. The average degree of deprivation may be as shown in the following passage:

> "Everybody diminished their home expenses and their food. We gave up two horses, retaining one and a donkey. Dogs were also killed, and many persons gave up wine or any stimulant. Our teachers, governess, butler and other dependants were parted with, and the house was reduced to a very low ebb in every way. Indian meal became a common food and many persons made it their breakfast."[8]

Some small towns were altogether deserted. In Dublin many of the shops in the principal streets had their shutters up, and broken windows were stuffed with paper. The city looked so dilapidated that some of the streets between Westland Row Station and Dublin Castle, along which Queen Victoria drove on her state visit in August 1849, were boarded up on both sides to prevent royal observation of decay. The boardings bore welcoming inscriptions such as "Hail Victoria, Ireland's hope and England's glory". The Queen herself greatly enjoyed her visit and does not seem to have noticed that anything was wrong with the country. Early in 1849 nearly 800,000 people were still on relief.

After 1850 slow recovery began, but the long-term effects of the famine were far-reaching. The numbers of small peasants were greatly reduced and land holdings increased in size as they did in England in the 13th century after the Black Death. The proportion of land under tillage gradually declined; the potato remained a principal crop, but the cultivation of wheat, barley and oats gave place to green pasture. Cattle, pigs and poultry became the farmer's main source of income. Emigration continued, though naturally on a smaller scale than during the famine. Close ties were maintained between the Irish refugees in America and their relations in the motherland, and remittances from America contributed substantially to the resources of those left behind. But the most important sequelae of the famine were not in the spheres of agriculture and economics; they were the persistent bitterness and hatred which it generated, partly due to the conviction that there was abundant food in the country which was exported in spite of the desperate hunger of the people. In Bernard Shaw's *Man and Superman*, published in 1903, the returned Irish American, Malone, insists on calling the famine "the starvation".

"Me father died of starvation in the black '47. Maybe you've heard of it?"

"The famine?"

"No, the starvation. When a country is full of food and exporting it, there can be no famine. Me father was starved dead and I was starved out to America in me mother's arms."

Among those starved out to America by the famine, like the Malones, were the forebears of Henry Ford, the founder of the modern motor industry, and of John Kennedy, thirty-fifth President of the United States.

During the worst phases of the famine, in 1846 and 1847, considerable quantities of grain, both oats and wheat, were exported from Ireland. In some seaport towns troops had to be used to quell riots and safeguard the loading of ships. Hungry and enraged mobs threatened merchants and shopkeepers holding stores of food ready for transport to the quays. According to Thomas P. O'Neill,* the import of Indian corn and meal, between September 1846 and July 1847, was three times as large as the total Irish export of cereals, but during the winter, when supplies of maize from America were retarded, the procurement of home-grown cereals for famine relief would have saved lives. To Trevelyan such a step was unthinkable, a gross infringement of basic economic laws. His deputy, Routh, on the spot and seeing the growing hunger with his own eyes, pleaded unavailingly with Trevelyan to do something to prevent or reduce food exports. The fact is that no government can allow the export of food from a famine-stricken area without incurring obloquy, both at the time and later. To prohibit export is often the first official action taken. Whether such action would have seriously influenced the course of the Irish famine is open to question.

There was much else to leave bitter memories. The system of relief based on tenuous payment for useless labour operated harshly and soon proved unworkable. The soup kitchens kept people just alive, but humiliated the beneficiaries. Ruthless evictions, with the "tumbling" of cabins, were not confined to the famine years, but they were more frequent and shocking during the period of dearth.

* Chapter on 'The Organisation and Administration of Famine Relief' in *The Great Famine*.[1]

Perhaps worst of all were the coffin ships with their cargoes of hungry and fever-stricken refugees and the daily disposal of corpses overboard. Apart from the fact that food was taken out of a starving country, there was plenty to explain the hatred for England felt by the Irish refugees and their descendants in America, hatred which lasted for three or four generations. The failure of the potato crop might have been an Act of God, but most of the suffering caused by the famine could be ascribed to the oppressor. Memories of the famine, transmitted from parent to child, were of political importance as recently as the first world war. The modern American-Irish, a vigorous, hard-headed and successful community, have now almost forgotten the famine and the many woes of Ireland; if they think of Ireland they think of it sentimentally as a green and romantic country offering enjoyable holidays to Americans with Irish names and plenty of dollars to spend. But in 1912 one of the founders of Sinn Fein, Arthur Griffith, could say that the British government deliberately used "the pretext of the failure of the potato crop to reduce the Celtic population by famine and exile". During the famine there were indeed people in England, students of Malthus, who said that deaths from starvation and disease were to be welcomed because they reduced the surplus population of Ireland. But they said this behind closed doors. Such an idea would, I think, have shocked Trevelyan. In an article in the *Observer* of 7 February 1971, Mr A. J. P. Taylor says that the Irish famine was "actively promoted by the Treasury officials of the time", which would, of course, especially incriminate Trevelyan as administrative chief. As far as he is concerned, this is to exaggerate obstinate folly into great wickedness.

The measures taken by the government to offset the loss of the potato crop and feed the starving were inadequate, harsh and often ill-conceived. Sensible and humane action was frequently obstructed by belief in the doctrine of *laissez-faire* and the danger of "pauperisation". But in the 1840s little experience of famine relief was available. It was not until the 1860s that the problem of famine in India began to be seriously studied, and the Indian Famine Code was formulated twenty years later than that. At least, after a climax of suffering and death had been reached, the survivors were given enough food to keep most of them just alive. Typhus claimed many thousands of victims and little was done to combat it; but we should not forget how ignorant and impotent doctors were in the 19th century and how recent is our triumphant conquest of epidemic disease. These and other things can be said in extenuation of those who participated in the calamity. But when all is said, the Irish famine remains one of the most painful and distressing episodes in European history.

Chapter 5

Famine in India

A HISTORY of Indian famine was written just before the first world war by Loveday,[1] then a postgraduate scholar in Cambridge and subsequently a distinguished member of the Secretariat of the League of Nations. Loveday never visited India and obtained most of the material for his book in the India Office Library in London. His lack of direct knowledge of the country is evident in a few mis-statements, and in his detachment from the human realities of famine. Nevertheless his book is a scholarly and valuable work, which brings together much scattered historical data and analyses the reports of the Famine Inquiry Commissions published by the Government of India.[2] These reports are the chief source of information about Indian famine in the 19th century.

Loveday lists sixty-nine severe famines of which records exist between A.D. 297 and 1907, but the earliest of these are legends rather than attested historical events. The ancient Hindu scriptures do not mention famine, but they tell of great droughts and are full of prayers for rain like this one from the Vedas:

> "O Lord of the field, we will cultivate the land with thee! Bestow on us pure and copious rain even as cows give us milk."

No doubt famines regularly occurred in India in the first millennium B.C. The remarkable Indus valley civilisation, of the third millennium B.C., may have avoided famine because of its location beside a great river and extensive provision for grain storage. Excavators in Mohenjodaro have been struck by the large size of the municipal granaries in which early forms of "bread wheat" were stored. This civilisation ultimately perished not from famine but by the sword.[3]

Apart from areas watered by large rivers and irrigation systems associated with these, agriculture in India depends on monsoon rains. The monsoon sweeps over the peninsula from the south-west in June and July, and retreats in September, the main crops being reaped in December. There are also secondary monsoon rains,

48

arriving in November and December, which sustain smaller harvests
in March and April. It is the south-west monsoon which really
matters in most parts of the country; its arrival is awaited anxiously
by governments, central and provincial, and with deep personal
apprehension and anxiety by the cultivator. Even a few weeks'
delay will mean poor crops. The monsoon has indeed never failed
in one year over the whole of India, and meteorologists believe that
this is impossible. But it has failed over areas inhabited by 50
million people or more, declining to 20 per cent or less of normal
expectation. Years of drought are, of course, interspersed with more
frequent years of good and sometimes bumper crops. There is a
belief that drought is more frequent and severe in the second than
in the first half of the century, and this seems to hold good for the
17th, 18th and 19th centuries. A cosmic meteorological cycle, or
mere chance, may be responsible. It is noteworthy that in the first
half of the 20th century monsoons on the whole behaved well (the
Bengal famine of 1943 was not due to drought), but severe drought
has occurred in 1967 and 1972–73 (Chapters 8 and 20).

Woodruff[4] quotes a moslem saying that the devil holds an
umbrella over Delhi (the Hindus do not have a Satan). He adds,
however, that there are other parts of the country over which he
holds it no less diligently.

Theoretically, the people could store food against the danger of
crop failure, and save some money to buy food from outside an area
of shortage. But in India poor cultivators, living from hand to mouth,
can do little storing or saving. Their scanty resources are soon
exhausted. Equally, physical reserves are small. At the best they
have scarcely enough to eat, and no accumulation of body fat which
could be used in a period of dearth as a source of calories. Not only
are their diets often inadequate in quantity; they are also deficient
in protein and vitamins, so that ill-health and disease associated
with malnutrition are common, particularly among children, even in
so-called normal times.

These are among the factors which have brought about the
catastrophe of famine in India since early times. The extreme
poverty of the mass of the population allows no margin of safety,
economic or physical. The source of food is agriculture of a simple
kind dependent on uncertain rainfall. Until recently the great size
of the country and lack of communications have hindered transport
of grain from one area to another. The obtaining of food for famine

relief obviously does not depend on the mere distance between the famine area and areas where food is available; it depends on the communications between these areas. An abundant harvest in Madras would be of no use in a famine in Rajputana when the only means of transportation was by bullock cart. Until about a century and a quarter ago, before the coming of the railways, communities whose crops failed usually starved in isolation.

Apart from natural causes, a most potent factor has been the disruption of life by civil wars. Throughout most of history India has suffered from unending strife between emperors, rajahs and invaders. Wars have often converted mere scarcity into famine. Armies may not directly destroy crops and livestock, but their mere presence is a heavy burden on the peasant, since soldiers have to be fed and have to be paid, and unless they are fed and paid will ravage the countryside. Further, war may not only cause famine but prevent efforts to relieve it.

Against this background brief mention will be made of some great Indian famines. Two early famines, in Kashmir in 445 and 917 respectively, caused huge mortality; in the second of these, the chronicler relates, the land became covered with bones until it resembled a vast burial ground, while the king and his ministers, far from attempting to relieve suffering, amassed riches by selling rice at a high price. A famine in Bombay in the 12th century is said to have lasted twelve years, an obviously impossible duration. In the next century no rain fell for seven years, and a terrible famine, said to be the worst in Indian history and accompanied by cannibalism, ensued. This was in the reign of the bloody tyrant, Sultan Mahommed Talak, who did, however, make some attempt to feed the inhabitants of his capital, Delhi. His empire was so exhausted by drought and famine, together with excessive taxation, that it soon withered and vanished. In the three centuries which followed, wars between the various dynasties, Moslem and Hindu, ruling different parts of the country, were almost continuous and famine frequent. In 1540 no less than two-thirds of the population of the warlike Hindu kingdom of Vijaynagar are said to have perished from want. At about the same period the Moslem ruler Humayan put into operation a scorched earth policy, forbidding the sowing of grain and prohibiting its export, in order to deprive of food supplies an army which was threatening invasion. Somewhat later the great Mogul emperors were often faced with famine in their wide dominions and were pioneers in famine relief. Shah Jehan could indeed do little to mitigate a severe famine in the Deccan in 1630 caused by drought and war. The drought dried up the rivers and the crops; parents sold their children for a few pence. Of this calamity it was written:

> "Life was offered for a loaf, but none would buy; rank was to be sold for a cake, but none cared for it; the ever-bounteous hand was stretched out to beg for food; and the feet which had always trodden the way of contentment walked about in search of sustenance."

During this drought the destruction of livestock was exceptionally high. In parts of the country not a single male buffalo survived, and new stock had to be imported.

Later in his reign Shah Jehan more successfully alleviated famine, particularly in areas adjacent to Delhi. He distributed money regularly to the poor, established kitchens which provided cooked food, and remitted taxes. During a famine in 1660 his successor Aurangzeb bought grain from provinces unaffected by drought and sold it in famine areas at a low price. The emperor's praiseworthy efforts were hampered by the corruption and cruelty of his officials, but contemporary chroniclers credit him with the saving of millions of lives.

The Famine Commission of 1880 wrote as follows about Aurangzeb and a famine in 1661:

> "The Emperor opened his treasury and granted money without stint. He gave every encouragement to the importation of corn and either sold it at reduced prices, or distributed it gratuitously amongst those who were too poor to pay. He also promptly acknowledged the necessity of remitting the rents of the cultivators and relieved them for the time being of other taxes. The vernacular chronicles of the period attribute the salvation of millions of lives and the preservation of many provinces to his strenuous exertions. Even when a margin has been left for manifest exaggeration, there can be little doubt that Aurangzeb's foresight and administrative ability caused the area of this famine to be much less extensive than was the tract of that which had devastated the country thirty years previously."

It has been said that all the great famines of the past were "class famines" in which the main victims were the poor. The passage quoted above about the famine in the Deccan in 1630 show that all classes could sometimes suffer from hunger. There was indeed a famine in 1344 in which one of the earlier Mogul emperors could not obtain enough food for his own household. But it is more usual to be told, in accounts of famine in India, that the ruler and his ministers lived luxuriously in their palaces, while the people starved.

In the 17th and 18th centuries Europeans arrived in India, at first as traders. They left some accounts of famine, such as that of a Dutch merchant who reported that only a few families in Swally near Bombay survived the disastrous famine of 1630, and that the road from Swally to Surat was choked with corpses, with no one to bury them. After the death of Aurangzeb in 1707 and the subsequent break-up of the Mogul Empire, a perid of internecine wars, social disruption and frequent famines followed. Later in the century the English, as their territories in India grew and they became rulers as well as traders, were faced with the problem of famine. One of the most terrible famines of all time took place in 1770, affecting a population of about 30 million people in West Bengal and Bihar. Of these about one-third, or 10 million, are said to have died of starvation and disease. Torrents of starving and diseased people from the countryside poured into the cities. There was a vast epidemic of smallpox. This famine followed two years of poor crops, with complete failure of the rains in a third year.

At this period the idea that governments were responsible for relieving famine was a new one, in spite of the earlier efforts of Mogul emperors. However, the East India Company took action in a widespread famine in 1783, affecting large areas outside Bengal, in particular what is now Uttar Pradesh, and in the Punjab and Madras. The export of grain from famished areas was prohibited, and hoarding, when detected, severely punished. The Governor-General, Warren Hastings, was concerned by this calamity. On his instructions a huge granary was built in Patna in Bihar in 1784, bearing the inscription: "For the perpetual prevention of famines in these provinces" (Plate 2a). But the granary was never filled, and the building up of stores of grain in good years for consumption in years of dearth—the method of Joseph—was never followed in India.

War in South India with Hyder Ali, Sultan of Mysore and father of Tipu Sultan, accentuated the effects of drought during this decade.

Hyder Ali was fond of burning crops in hostile territories. Here a passage from the Memoirs of William Hickey, a skilled raconteur, may be quoted. During most of his stay in India Hickey lived in Calcutta, but he also visited Madras from time to time. His "dearest Charlotte" was a pretty young women he had casually picked up in London before departure, who lived with him happily in India until she died prematurely of typhoid or some other prevalent disease.

"On the 2nd of April (1782) Mrs Hickey and I went to pass the day at Mrs Barclay's garden house a few miles from Madras . . . In going to their house a truly melancholy spectacle met our sight, at which my dearest Charlotte was beyond measure affected, the whole road being strewed with the skulls and bones of the innumerable poor creatures who had there laid themselves down and miserably perished from want of food, being on their way from different parts of Madras in the hope of obtaining relief there, a relief it was not, alas! in the power of the British in-inhabitants to afford, from the thousands and ten thousands that daily flocked towards the Presidency".[5]

A famine which affected Madras and other parts of India a few years later became known as the "Dogi Bara", or Skull Famine, because it littered the countryide with skulls.

Adam Smith's book, *The Wealth of Nations*, influenced famine relief in India as in Ireland. In 1812 the Government of Bombay, faced with an episode of food shortage partly due to locusts, refused to interfere in any way with private trade. The Governor recorded in a special minute his adherence to the principles of political economy as expressed in *The Wealth of Nations*, and his conviction that unassisted trade could do more to relieve such distress as existed and to effect an equable distribution of supplies than the government could do with all its resources.[6] This dogma discouraged the control of prices, the prohibition of the export of food from famine areas, and its procurement and import into these areas by government action—methods of famine prevention and relief which seemed commonsense in earlier and later times. Another dogma which affected governmental action against famine was that giving anything away for nothing—even giving food to the starving—demoralised the recipients and led to "pauperism". Such convictions sometimes proved as disastrous in India as in the Irish famine of the 1840s.

The East India Company was abolished in 1858, a year after the Mutiny, and responsibility for governing India was taken over by the Crown. The first serious Indian famine after the dissolution of the Company occurred in 1860, mainly in the "North-West Provinces" and the Punjab. In handling this famine the government adhered to free trade principles and, as far as possible, to the canon "no work, no assistance". The newly-built railways brought grain into the deficit areas. The famine victims capable of work were employed in making roads and digging canals, in gangs of about 500, housed in temporary sheds, and given enough money to buy food. Others, incapable of ordinary work, were put into poorhouses and paid for light tasks provided they could establish a claim to such a privilege. Finally, a few were given direct assistance gratuitously in their homes by agents supervised by British officials. A point of importance was the proximity, in this part of India, of irrigated land to drought-desiccated land bearing no crops.

This was a textbook famine, with relatively small mortality. But, alas! it was followed a few years later by a calamity which was exaggerated by the teachings of Adam Smith. In 1865–66 there was drought in Orissa and along much of the east coast of India. In the previous year large quantities of rice had been exported from Orissa to meet the demand of cotton-growers in Bombay. When the rains failed in 1865, local officials proposed that rice should be imported immediately into Orissa by the government, but the Governor-General prohibited any such action. He was supported by members of the Board of Revenue who, says Philip Woodruff,[4] "held by the most rigid rules of direct political economy and rejected, almost with horror, the idea of importing grain". They would not even allow the authorities in Orissa to take the grain from a ship which ran ashore on their coast in March. It was bound for Calcutta and to Calcutta the grain must go. In fact the grain rotted in the holds while plans were being made to move it.

Rice refused to "flow in" to Orissa in accordance with the laws of supply and demand. Most of the remaining stocks were hoarded by merchants hoping to take advantage of rapidly rising prices. When at last—in the middle of 1867—the government began to move rice into the province, they found that access was obstructed by the torrential rains of the 1867 monsoon.

As a result of this sequence of events, the poor starved. It was estimated that one-third of the population, perhaps 10 million people, died of starvation and disease—human suffering on a tremendous scale. We shall see that there were objections to an official estimate of 1·5 million deaths in the Bengal famine of 1943, some maintaining that 3 to 4 million would be nearer the mark. But even the larger figure is small in comparison with estimates of mortality in earlier famines.

A few years later, another great drought occurred, affecting British territories and Indian states in much of Central India. Huge mortality again resulted, especially in the Indian states in Rajputana. In Rajputana nine-tenths of the cattle died and many of the surviving human inhabitants fled towards less distressed areas in the south. The Governor-General issued an order imposing on district officers responsibility for all deaths occurring in their districts, a gesture as futile as an official statement that it was the public's duty to support the sick and aged in famine times.

This was the nearest point to defeat reached by the British in the struggle to master famine in India in the 19th century. The next episode was the "Panic Famine" in Bihar in 1873–74, so-called because the government, disturbed by the grim holocausts of the 1860s, determined that people must be saved from dying of starvation at all costs. Large sums of money and large quantities of grain were poured into districts in Bihar where famine was reported to be acute, though indeed subsequent enquiry threw doubt on the existence of dangerous scarcity in these or other districts in the province. Seven thousand subordinate personnel were employed on famine relief. Later it was found that the government had lacked clear information about social and economic conditions in the threatened area, and about the extent of crop failure. They did not even know what crops were cultivated in different areas. When the famine, illusory or otherwise, was over, 100,000 tons of imported rice remained unconsumed. No excess mortality was evident. Curiously, Sir Charles Trevelyan, who returned to India in 1853, sent the Viceroy a pamphlet he had written on the Irish famine to help him deal with the Indian famine of 1873.[7] It seems probable from the liberal nature of the relief supplied that his advice was not followed.

Administratively speaking, the Panic Famine proved valuable, however embarrassing to the authorities at the time. During the rest of the century there were a number of extensive droughts, and in 1899–1900 a population of 59 million was threatened. Suffering and starvation were not eliminated, but their scale was reduced, and the government retained control of the successive emergencies. These advances were due to better communications, particularly the construction of railways, more efficient government services, and growing experience of relief measures. Between 1870 and 1911 the mileage of railways in India increased from 4252 to 32,839. The *Imperial Gazetteer* of India declared in 1907:[8]

"The greatest administrative achievement of the last twenty years has been the extension of communications. Railways have revolutionised relief. The final horror of famine, an absolute dearth of food, is now unknown."

The extension of irrigation was a valuable preventive measure. Sir Arthur Cotton constructed great irrigation works in various places in East and South India, and in the famine of 1877–78 the irrigated areas produced plenty of food for their own populations and were able to export enough to feed 3 million people elsewhere. Some authorities pressed for a huge increase in irrigation works, but the Government of India characteristically declared this to be financially impossible. The enthusiasts for irrigation works received strong support from Florence Nightingale. Writing from her bed in South Street in London, she accused the Government of India of faking estimates of the number of deaths from famine in order to minimise the need for the expensive development of irrigation. She asked for the real figures and was snubbed, but continued to write articles on the subject which her opponents described as "shrieks".

Progress was hastened by the bulky reports written after famines had subsided, dealing both with their causes and the success or otherwise with which they had been handled by the governments concerned. At first the reports were papers written by individual officials, and copies of official correspondence exchanged during the famine, but later it became the custom to appoint special commissions to collect evidence and prepare lengthy reports. One of the most impressive of these was the Report of the Famine Inquiry Commission of 1880, headed by General Richard Strachey, F.R.S., of the Royal Engineers, a distinguished member of a distinguished family, and a master of clear and precise English.* (It may be significant that an engineer and a scientist was chosen for the job, rather than a classically-educated "civilian", but actually the

* Richard Strachey had five daughters and five sons. One of his sons was Lytton Strachey, scarcely a chip of the old block.

1a Drought in India, 1973. Dead cow and watching vultures.

1b A little water from the bed of a dried-up river, Maharastra 1973.

2a Granary built in 1786 in Patna, Bihar at the order of Warren Hastings, and inscribed: 'For the perpetual prevention of famine in these provinces'. Water colour by Colonel Robert Smith, 1833.

2b Feeding children on goats' milk during famine. Woodcut by Lockwood Kipling.

Indian Civil Service, expected to take on any responsibility anywhere at any time, did not flinch from the practical problems of
famine.) The Strachey report dealt with famine throughout India
and became the basis of the Indian Famine Code which emerged in
the 1890s. Actually each province had its own code and there were
some differences from province to province. The underlying principles were, however, much the same everywhere. In addition to
giving broad instructions for action, the codes provided useful
practical ideas and tips about relief operations, drawn from the
experience of local officials. Foreign relief workers in Bihar in 1967
found to their surprise that battered Famine Code volumes written
by long-since dead and forgotten members of the Indian services
contained much good sense.

The following account of the Code is taken mainly from the
Madras version, and the singular is used because one version can
speak for all. The present tense is used because the Code remains
part of the administrative procedures of independent India; in
1967, for example, famine was "Declared" in Bihar in accordance
with the old system.

The Code emphasises the great importance of what are called
"standing preparations". Governments must keep themselves well
informed, through district officials and village headmen, about rainfall, the state of the crops and pasture-land, harvests and stocks of
grain and fodder. The country is mapped out into relief areas, and
public works projects for these are planned and kept on file. Reserves of tools and equipment are held in each area.

Should the signs be unpropitious—if harvests are obviously failing
and the price of grain is beginning to rise—the next step is to
establish "test works", at which people are offered wages in return
for work. At the same time poor houses or kitchens are set up to
provide for the hungry and destitute. The numbers applying for
work or food are watched, and if they increase rapidly the imminence
of famine is assumed. At this point the district concerned is classed
as suffering from food scarcity or famine and the Code is put into
operation. In official language, "Famine is declared". If the famine
is localised and not too serious, local district officers will be put in
charge of relief operations; if it becomes extensive and severe, a
Famine Commissioner with wide powers may be appointed.

Employment on relief works is offered to men and women. The
works to be undertaken, chosen and supervised by the Public Works

E

Department, are located so as to be accessible to several villages. Camps are established in the neighbourhood of relief works, and arrangements are made regarding water-supply, sanitation, medical care and the isolation of people with infectious diseases. The camps provide shelters for administrative staff, including a doctor, together with a dispensary and beds for a few patients. Accommodation for labourers is rarely provided, and these have to walk daily to the relief works to and from their villages. The task expected of them is defined as three-quarters of the task commonly performed by labourers in normal times. For this they are paid wages which enable them to buy food brought into the famine area and sold by private traders. The Code lays down that the wages should be the lowest sufficient to maintain healthy persons in health. The amount of money given is based on a "grain equivalent", i.e. on the cost of ordinary grain available in the district. If the workers are employed on digging or some similar kind of manual labour, they receive as daily wages for six days a week the cost of 36 oz (1020 g), which would yield about 3100 calories daily. It is assumed, however, that the food bought includes, in addition to cereal grains, some legumes, ghee or oil, condiments and salts, which would mean a diet providing about 2700 calories.

If food does not reach the famine area through private enterprise, the government is responsible for procuring and selling it at a controlled price. Those who cannot work, for example, children and old people, are given for nothing food cooked in camp kitchens, in amounts based on appropriate ration scales. If they will not accept cooked food because of caste interdictions, they can be given cash allowances to buy food. Food may also be provided directly in the villages to support people who cannot come to the camps, for example women in purdah. Sometimes pride may prevent families from seeking relief in the form of wages or cooked food; they prefer to starve at home.

Less direct but important relief measures are also envisaged by the Code. The collection of land revenue is temporarily suspended in areas suffering severely from famine. Small numbers of cattle may be preserved in special camps, by throwing open forest reserves for grazing, and by grants for fodder. Advances for land improvement, and the purchase of seed and equipment, may be made after the famine is over.

From the 1880s until 1943 India was free from great famines with high mortality. There were indeed extensive droughts, particularly in 1887 and 1899. The Code operated, no doubt in a rather lumbering fashion, and was modified in various ways as further experience was gained. Relief works were the subject of continuing controversy, some officials favouring large undertakings employing numerous people, and others smaller works close to affected villages. The finding of suitable relief works proved to be difficult, as the following quotation from an article written in 1951 by R. Passmore[9] shows:

"The quality of the work done by destitute labourers is so poor that the public works resulting are of necessity most expensive and usually quite outside normal economy. . . . Roads sufficient for local traffic exist in most districts; tanks (ponds) suitable for water storage have already been dug in places where they are likely to be of value. Railways are no longer being extended. In consequence labourers . . . are often given tasks which are for practical purposes as useless as digging a hole and filling it up again. Roads are thrown across the arid countryside to remote villages; these facilitate the visits of high officials to famine camps but perform no other purpose. Such roads usually do not survive the outbreak of the rains and the villagers soon resume the winding tracks which are adequate for pedestrians and bullock carts. On visits to famine camps I have always been depressed by the futility of the work undertaken; the psychological effect on the labourers of this type of work cannot be anything but bad."

The Famine Code was indeed far from perfect. It was based on an old-fashioned *laissez-faire* theory of economics and the conviction that gratuitous relief was degrading to the recipient. It placed too much reliance on public works. But it contained more than general principles. An American "Relief co-ordinator"[10] who witnessed the averted Bihar famine of 1966–67 has commented that:

"A manual of relief operations can save much time in the early organisation of a (relief) program. India's *Famine Code*, a thoughtful and detailed guide to local officials, was useful and surprisingly relevant, considering it had been written decades earlier."

Certainly the Code must have saved many lives in the great droughts which occurred in the last quarter of the 19th century. The British were firmly in control and Pax Britannica reigned from Kashmir to Cape Cormarin. Strong, disciplined subordinate services, manned by Indians, were available to carry out the orders of the authorities. The people trusted the government to save them from starvation. But, as we shall see, the Bengal famine of 1943 was a different story.

Chapter 6

Kipling and Famine

RUDYARD KIPLING wrote one story about famine in India, namely "William the Conqueror", which appears in the volume of short stories called *The Day's Work*, first published in England in 1900.[1] The story itself was probably written in 1895 or 1896, when Kipling was living in Vermont, a few years after he had left India for good. It happens that the years of his service with the Civil and Military Gazette in Lahore in the Punjab—1882 to 1889 —were relatively free from famine. But there had been severe famines in the 1870s, and a series of important official reports which had led to the establishment of the Famine Code. Kipling must have heard much about famine during his years as a journalist.

His story opens in Lahore, in the offices of the local newspaper. It is evident from the first pages that famine was hot news to the newspaper, while its editor, with access to cablegrams, was a source of up-to-date information to fellow-members of the Club. But the famine was located far away, in Madras in South India, which Kipling had seen briefly only once when he travelled by train from the deep south to Lahore, spending "four days and four nights in the belly of the train . . . unable to understand the speech around me".[2] This was in 1891, when he was returning to India from a tour in Australia and New Zealand.

As news of the famine, and its "Declaration" in terms of the Famine Code, comes in, a Punjabi official remarks: "What unholy names these Madras districts rejoice in—all *ungas* or *rungas* or *pillays* or *polliums*." It was reported that Madras "has owned that she can't manage it alone". This meant recruitment from elsewhere in India, particularly in the Punjab where, it is implied, all the best officials were to be found. The cast of the story is made up of Punjabis, including William the Conqueror herself, the sister of an Acting District Superintendent of Police. The Famine Commissioner, Jimmy Hawkins, a Jubilee Knight, had started his career in the Punjab; he was known to be a good chap, "even though he went to the Benighted (Madras) Presidency".

61

In the 1930s, when I was living in the Nilgiris Hills in the Madras Presidency, I had interesting talks about famine with Sir Frederick Nicholson, a distinguished I.C.S. official who had retired in Coonoor. He must have been about eighty-five when I knew him. As a District Collector he had been in the middle of the very serious famine of 1896–97, which affected northern Madras as well as large areas elsewhere in India. Later he had been a member of the Inquiry Commission which reported on the famine of 1899–1900. When I mentioned Kipling's story he could hardly contain himself. "The impudence of the man!" he said. "To suggest that Madrassis couldn't run their own famine!" Local officials, indeed, appear only once in "William the Conqueror", as "hollow-eyed weary white men, who spoke another argot". The reader gains the impression that the handful of people especially summoned by Jimmy Hawkins from the north are doing all the work.

When the party from the Punjab—Martyn and his sister, and Scott, an engineer in the Irrigation Department—arrived at the Famine Commissioner's headquarters in a famine camp, they were immediately assigned different jobs. Martyn was told to "live on trains" until further notice, moving about the famine area loading grain-cars and distributing grain, and picking up people and dropping them in famine camps. Kipling understood the importance of railways in preventing and relieving famine. In "William the Conqueror" the picture is that of abundant supplies of food—not always, unfortunately, the right sort of food—pouring by rail into the afflicted territories. But some famine-stricken areas were remote from the railway. Scott was ordered to take charge of a convoy of bullock carts and to go south, feeding as he went. Carts were immediately loaded with bags of millet and wheat from railway trucks, and he set out. The third number of the group, William, affectionately greeted by lady Hawkins, was retained at headquarters to help in the work of the camp. As Scott moved off with his carts, she called to him: "I want fifty rupees, please. Can you lend it to me? It's for condensed milk for the babies." Scott handed the money over.

At this point in the story a difficulty which has sometimes hampered famine relief in India arises. The people to be fed by Scott were rice-eaters, and though starving turned away from wheat and millet. "What was the use of these strange hard grains that choked their throats?" They did not know how to prepare or cook them and anyhow did not possess the household utensils needed for this purpose. Most left the open sacks untouched. Some of the disappointed women laid their emaciated children at Scott's feet. Then Scott's Mahomedan bearer, Faiz Ullah, full of contempt for the Hindu South, made his contribution. He had collected a few lean goats and added them to the procession to provide some milk for the Sahib's meals. These goats were being fed on the grains the people rejected. Scott hit on the idea of catching more goats, feeding them up, and giving their milk to the abandoned children. Though Faiz Ullah was reluctant—he held that there was no Government order as to babies and added that to become a goatherd was against his *izzat*—milking the goats and feeding the babies became part of the daily routine. The babies were fed three times a day.

When Scott reached the end of his outward journey, he found that a rice-ship had come in from Burma, so that his carts could be loaded with rice for the return journey. It was not very clever of Jimmy Hawkins to organise the distribution of foods that the famine victims would not eat. But the same mistake was made again and again. In a minor famine in rice-eating Orissa in 1888–89, when Kipling was still in India, the people would not eat wheat from North-West India. During the Bengal famine of 1943, I was shown large heaps of millet in the botanical gardens in Calcutta, rotting in the rain. The millet had proved quite useless for famine relief in Bengal. In the threatened Bihar famine in 1967 people on the verge of starvation resolutely refused to eat millet. Within recent decades rice-eaters in India have learned to accept wheat (but not millet) prepared for consumption in various ways. In Madras at the time of Kipling's famine the people had not the knowledge or means needed for converting wheat grains into eatable forms. Preparing the whole wheat chappatis of North India is a skilled operation and an iron grid is required.

The feeding of the children with goats' milk continued and Scott noted that some of them were putting on flesh nicely. When the rice in the bullock carts was exhausted, he headed for the headquarters camp on the railway. William saw him arrive.

"An accident of the sunset ordered it that, when he had taken off his helmet to get the evening breeze, the low light should fall across his forehead, and he could not see what was before him; while one waiting at the tent door beheld, with new eyes, a young man, beautiful as Paris, a god in a halo of golden dust, walking slowly at the head of his flocks, while at his knee ran small naked cupids."

This is really the climax of the story. The scene appealed to the American artist, W. L. Taylor, whose picture appeared in the *Ladies' Home Journal* of January 1896, with the sub-title "Walking slowly at the head of his flocks". Taylor accentuated the god-like bearing of Scott, as seen through the eyes of William, sitting at the entrance to her tent. The black cupids are there and a few capering goats in the foreground, while behind a cloud of dust suggests a large flock. There is no indication that Taylor had ever seen India, and the same can be said of a later artist who contributed a rather similar, but less dramatic, illustration to *The Kipling Reader*. Very different is a wood-cut by Rudyard Kipling's father, John Lockwood Kipling, in the 1899 Scribner's Edition of *The Day's Work*. Lockwood depicts the routine daily feeding of milk rather than the entry into the head-quarters camp. A row of real Indian bullock carts is shown as a background, and in front is a mother attempting to feed an emaci-ated child on the milk provided by an obstreperous goat. The process of transferring milk from the udder of a goat into a child's mouth is largely ignored by Rudyard; one gets the impression that he had no idea how it was done. Neither, perhaps, had Lockwood, but Lockwood's woodcut suggests that at least he was aware of difficulties (Plate 2b).

Scott had much more work to do before the famine ended. He was sent to a new district and continued to distribute rice until he was able to report to Hawkins that the district was safe. Then the rains arrived and he had a severe bout of fever, drastically treated by Faiz Ullah. Love between the convalescent Scott and William blossomed in the headquarters camp, to the sentimental delight of Lady Hawkins. They were able to leave for the north a few weeks before Christmas. Here the story becomes a sort of travelogue, no doubt reflecting Kipling's own return to the north in 1891.

"Morning brought the penetrating chill of the Northern December, the layers of wood-smoke, the dusty grey blue of the tamarisks, the domes of ruined tombs, and above all the smell of the white Northern plains, as the mail-train ran on to the mile-long Sutlej Bridge . . . The South of pagodas and palm-trees, the over-populated Hindu South, was done with."

We leave Scott and William singing carols together at the Christmas ball.

Kipling had a remarkable gift for mastering the technical aspects of subjects he wrote about, or rather for mastering these sufficiently to satisfy readers without specialised knowledge. Among such subjects are marine engineering, bridge building, the life of the jungle and frontier warfare. Talks with the technically-initiated gave him what he wanted. Famine can be included in the list. In Lahore he must have met officials eager to describe famine in their own districts. A single train journey through the Madras Presidency, and a look at some place names on a map of India, provided the scenario for a story about famine. But he should not have allowed Scott to pick up even broken Tamil in a few weeks, Tamil being among the most difficult of human languages for a European to learn.

As one would expect, the broad tableau of Indian famine is convincingly sketched—the land dried up in the baking heat, the dead cattle, the wailing mothers and emaciated children, the burning of corpses. On the other hand, Kipling did not know how the Famine Code worked, though he mentions it several times with an air of familiarity. One of its main features, as we have seen, is the establishment of public works where people can earn enough money to enable them to buy "the amount of food sufficient to keep healthy persons in health". These are first established on a "test" basis and the numbers applying for employment provide an index of the extent of hunger and indicate the need or otherwise for an official "Declaration of Famine". In "William the Conqueror" there is no mention of famine relief works until Scott sent in a report recommending the repair of a broken-down reservoir. Useful works on which famine victims can be employed are usually hard to find. Jimmy Hawkins would have been better advised to use a skilled engineer from the Punjab Irrigation Department on this aspect of famine relief, instead of sending him off to distribute wheat and millet to rice-eaters. The direct distribution of food to certain groups in the population was indeed part of famine relief, but according to the Code only a small part. The story suggests that it was the major operation.

Other technical errors in "William the Conqueror" could be mentioned. One omission is, however, striking. We are told that "the Rains fell at last, late, but heavily; and the dry, gashed earth was red mud". The coming of the rains after the two or more years drought which caused famine was usually more spectacular than that. In the Bible, Elijah, after a long period of drought and famine, heard "a sound of abundance of rain" (1 Kings, 18). He was at the top of Carmel. Six times he sent his servant to look towards the sea, and the servant reported, "There is nothing". But the seventh time there was something. "Behold," the man said, "there ariseth a little cloud out of the sea, like a man's hand". And within a short time "the heavens were black with clouds and wind and there was a great rain".

Old Nicholson told me that he and some members of his famine relief staff were sitting one day in front of his tent looking at the brazen and cloudless sky. It had not rained for nearly two years. Suddenly one of them saw something: a cloud like a man's hand. "Just like the Bible," Nicholson said; like many members of the Indian Civil Service in its prime, he was well read in the classics and the Bible. Very soon the sky became black and the rains came pouring down. He ended the story by saying that he and his staff broke down and cried.

Here is a recent account of the same event in Bihar:

"On the 16th June, 1967, the first shower of the monsoon came to this part of India. Our patients still recovering in the hospital jumped out of their beds, went back to their homes and started to plough the fields. In the face of the gravest situation, they never gave up hope."[3]

The eagerness of the famine victims to get back to their fields as soon as any prospect of cultivation appeared is at variance with the fear of some officials that they would be "pauperised" by relief and reluctant to start work again. The photograph "Clouds of Hope", from *The Times*, shows what really happens (Plate 6b).

Kipling, though himself soaked in the Old Testament, missed the dramatic coming of the rains. But against any errors and omissions must be set the fact that the story makes an original contribution in the field of applied nutrition. Infants and young children have exacting dietary needs, imposed by the speed of growth in early life; in particular, they need abundant protein. When the food supply of a community is drastically reduced, as in famine, this age group suffers most; together with the old, it has a large share in the increased mortality which the emergency imposes. Travellers in Ireland during the terrible Irish famine noted that few children were

to be seen out of doors; the children were dead or dying and any
still surviving were skeletons. But it is only recently that the vulnerability of the very young in times of food shortage and famine,
and the need to supply them with specially nutritious foods, have
been fully realised. No particular attention was therefore given to
children in famine relief operations; this applies to Joseph's famine
in Ancient Egypt and to the Indian Famine Code. Faiz Ullah was
right in saying that there was no Government order as to babies.

During the last thirty years, however, the provision of foods for
children has become one of the most prominent aspects of famine
relief, and also of many undertakings to improve nutrition in poor
countries in normal times. Milk in the form of skim milk powder has
been distributed in large quantities by United Nations organisations
and non-official agencies such as Oxfam and Catholic Relief
services. Usually, for purposes of child feeding, the skim milk
powder is mixed with other foods such as wheat flour, soya flour and
groundnuts. The value of the supplementary food or food mixture
depends mainly on its content of protein. To the best of my knowledge, the earliest reference to giving milk to children in a famine is
so be found in "William the Conqueror". Two kinds of milk were
given: goats' milk and "condensed" milk. Goats' milk contains 3·7
per cent of protein and 4·8 per cent of fat, and would be an excellent
food for starving children—provided, of course, that they get more
than a few drops of it. There is no indication in the story of any
shortage of supply. On the other hand, William's condensed milk
could not have gone very far. The Nestlé Company informs me that
in 1890 a large tin of condensed milk cost sixpence, which means
150 tins for 50 rupees. Calculations show that this quantity of condensed milk, diluted with water, would be about enough for 20
infants for 25 days.

Scott and William exchange their experience with goats' and condensed milk. Both confess to losses, but William admits that Scott's
babies are fatter than hers. The impression given by the conversation
is that goats' milk was preferable to condensed milk in the circumstances. At all events William takes over Scott's goats and children
and it appears that the condensed milk is replaced by goats' milk
from that point onwards.

Where did Kipling get the idea of "milk for children" in famine?
It is unlikely that anything of the sort should have been suggested in
an official document, or even in the correspondence columns of the

Civil and Military Gazette. Mr C. E. Carrington, author of the admirable biography *Rudyard Kipling: His Life and Work* has suggested to me that he might have got it from his father, as well as much else about famine in "William the Conqueror". Lockwood was in Vermont when *The Day's Work* was conceived and he inspired its title. He has nothing to say about famine in his own book, *Beast and Man in India*, but must have heard much about it during his years of service. He was a well-informed and sympathetic observer of the Indian scene. It may be significant that he chose the milking of a goat and the feeding of a child as the subject of an illustration in *The Kipling Reader*.

Whatever its merits and demerits, "William the Conqueror" is a highly readable story. The manly heroine, said to have been drawn from a lady well-known in North India, is a consistent character. But the reader is left to speculate why she was called "William the Conqueror" and why a story about famine in Madras was named after her. She was obviously dearly loved by Kipling— no doubt platonically, since his wife did not disapprove of the story. Kipling specially admired the hard-bitten district officer, struggling to carry on against great odds. He could not make his lady-love a district officer because of her sex, but he could give her a man's job in a famine emergency. He probably wrote his story about famine to give her a part, picking up enough information on the subject to make the story plausible.

Chapter 7

The Bengal Famine of 1943

IN this chapter Bengal means the Province of Bengal in British India, with a population of over 60 million, which after Partition in 1947-48 became the Indian State of West Bengal, and East Pakistan. East Pakistan, consisting largely of the deltas of the Ganges and the Bramaputra, comprised most of the area stricken by famine in 1943. It became Bangladesh in 1971, and later in this book there will be occasion to tell of the threat of famine in that year, arising out of very different circumstances from those of 1943, and how famine was averted. Calcutta, very much at the centre of events in 1943, is in West Bengal. Once the capital city of India, it is now merely the capital of one of the smaller Indian States, larger than ever as far as mere numbers are concerned, but having lost the dignity of its imperial past. Before Independence, it was sometimes called "the Empire's Second City".

On 22 August 1943, the principal newspaper of Bengal, the *Statesman*, published a pageful of photographs of emaciated and almost naked people—mainly women and children—lying on pavements in the middle of Calcutta. One of the most striking of these photographs is reproduced as Plate 3a. This was the first time that most of the world, inside and outside India, learned that Bengal was suffering from a great calamity. A week later a second pageful of photographs appeared, and the *Statesman* soon supplied grim information to go with the photographs, including an editorial on 23 September which baldly stated: "this sickening catastrophe is man made".* Calcutta was full of starving and destitute people from rural Bengal; it was reckoned that about 100,000 had reached the city. They begged for food and sought for scraps in dumps and bins, flocking round hotels and military kitchens in the hope of picking up edible refuse. Many soon gave up and died on the pavement.

* In his book *Monsoon Morning* (1966)[1] Ian Stephens, then editor of the *Statesman*, has described his qualms in publishing information about the famine, at a period of the war when government censorship was strict. I am indebted to *Monsoon Morning* for some facts and comments contained in this chapter.

Corpses became a familiar sight and at night tended to trip up the pedestrian, in the blackout. Complaints of delay and inefficiency were made against the municipal authorities responsible for the removal and disposal of corpses.

How had this terrible situation arisen? What events preceded and followed it? In this chapter I shall try to outline the miserable story. It happens that I was a member of the Inquiry Commission, appointed in July 1944 by the Government of India, to report on the causes of the famine[2]* and the prevention of famine in the future. The account given here is based largely on our report which was not published until the middle of 1945 when the famine was over. To begin by describing the make-up of the Commission and its work may therefore seem to be putting the cart before the horse. It is justified by the fact that the Commission's report is almost the only authoritative source of information available about the sequence of events. Further, since Famine Inquiry Commissions were an important part of the administration of British India from 1860 onwards, it is worth while saying something about the last of them.

The Chairman of the Commission was Sir John Woodhead, a retired member of the I.C.S. whose service had been spent entirely in Bengal, ending with a short spell as Acting-Governor in 1940. He was a Yorkshireman from Bradford. His obvious honesty and integrity, combined with native shrewdness and affection for India, appealed to witnesses, both European and Indian, of all professions and grades. Among all the officials I met during my service in India, he stands out in my memories as exemplifying the fine I.C.S. administrator of the old school.†

Then there were two Indian members: S. V. Ramamurthy, a senior I.C.S. official from Madras, with the remarkable mental qualities of the Madrassi Brahmin, often said to be the cleverest community in India; and Sir Manilal Nanavati from Bombay, a "secular" Indian with a modern mind. In 1943 it was necessary to include a Moslem in a body such as this; our Moslem member was

---

* Actually our terms of reference enjoined us to "investigate and report to the Central Government upon the causes of the food shortage and subsequent epidemics in India". Famine was a bad word, and officially famine had been vanquished in the 19th century. In the Irish famine, one hundred years earlier, the word 'famine' was not used in official correspondence from Whitehall, 'distress' being preferred.

† Sir John Woodhead died in January 1973, at the age of 91.

Afjal Husain, professor of animal husbandry in an agricultural college. Finally there was myself, Director of the Nutrition Research Laboratories in Coonoor in South India. I was specially concerned with the medical aspects of the famine, but took part with my colleagues in the investigation of economic and administrative matters. We had a very able secretary, R. A. Gopalswami, a young I.C.S. officer and also a Madrassi Brahmin, who subsequently had a distinguished career in independent India.

The Commission sat in a municipal building protected from Japanese air-raids by a newly-built surrounding wall. No fresh air entered the improvised court-room and the fans merely stirred the hot stagnant air within. There we sat, day after day, listening to one witness after another, and trying to keep alert in the sultry afternoon. Under Sir John's gentle but persistent questioning, followed by questions from other members of the group, the story gradually unfolded itself; an ugly story—sometimes it seemed as if abyss beneath abyss of bungling and greed was being opened up. There were, of course, many documents besides transcripts of evidence to be studied. All this was in due course woven into the Commission's report, though not very neatly. As a printed document our report reflects the time at which it was issued, when a desperate fighting conclusion to the war with Japan seemed imminent, and the food situation in some other parts of India was highly precarious. It was necessary to get the facts together quickly to prevent anything similar happening in India outside Bengal. The report is printed on wretched paper, which Sir Richard Strachey would not have tolerated in 1880. It lacks an index, for which the Commission itself must take the blame. Because of the war, a minimum number of copies was printed and only a few libraries in the United Kingdom seem to possess one. It was said that the Government of India did not like our report and tried to limit its circulation by printing only a small number of copies. This is, however, unlikely; the war-time shortage of paper was enough to account for restricted printing.

We praised the action of the *Statesman* in printing photographs of famine victims in August 1943. The editor of the *Statesman*, Ian Stephens, was no doubt grateful, but this would scarcely prompt a responsible journalist to say, in his book *Monsoon Morning*, that "the Famine Commission's report is as complete, painstaking and balanced an account of what happened, and why, as will ever be achievable".

Critics have objected to some statements in the report, but there could be no disagreement with its opening sentence:

"The Bengal famine of 1943 stands out as a great calamity even in an age all too familiar with human suffering and death on a tragic scale."

The Japanese came into the war on 8 December 1941, and on 15 January 1942 captured Singapore. Burma was soon over-run; the first air-raid on Rangoon took place on 23 January, and early in March Rangoon was evacuated. The total capture of Burma followed within two months. Refugees from Burma poured into Bengal through Assam and Chittagong, bringing with them a virulent form of malaria and frightening stories of atrocities. The invasion of Bengal itself by the triumphant Japanese was expected daily. This invasion never took place, but the Japanese remained, a disturbing and menacing presence, on the borders of North-East India until the war ended in the holocaust of Hiroshima in August 1945. Early in 1942 the authorities in Bengal enforced two measures, as part of a so-called "denial policy", which had some influence on the subsequent famine. They removed stocks of paddy and rice in excess of local requirements from coastal areas in the delta vulnerable to invasion; these were used later to feed Calcutta. They also removed all boats capable of carrying ten passengers or more. In this part of Bengal boats are the normal means of transport for people and goods. One result was that fishermen suffered badly during the famine.

In the past, as we have seen (Chapter 7), severe and extensive famines caused by drought have occurred in North-East India, including under this term the territories which today form the States of Bihar and Orissa. But the Famine Commission of 1880 commented that "the eastern districts of the province of Bengal enjoy so ample and regular a rainfall and such abundant river inundation as to ensure the safety of the crops in the driest years". These were the districts which suffered worst in the famine of 1943. Given the relative immunity to famine referred to by the earlier Commission, and the freedom of India from severe famine during the first four decades of the present century, it is clear that the calamity of 1943 must have been associated with unusual circumstances. The Japanese war was one of these, but there were others of great or greater importance.

3a Dead or dying children in a Calcutta street. Photograph published by the *Statesman*, Calcutta, on August 22nd, 1943.

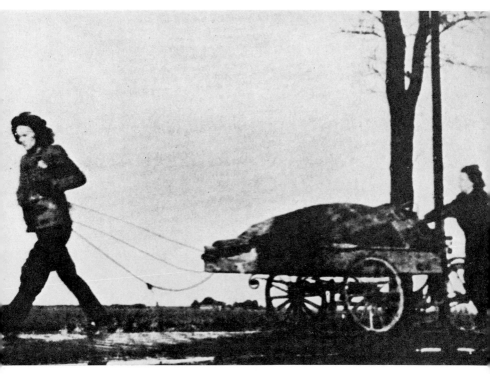

3b Dutch famine, 1945. Bringing home some food and fuel.

4a and b UNWRA camps for Arab refugees, East Jordan. *Left*: a solid meal in wet weather. *Right*: prefabricated shelters.

The principal food of the inhabitants of the Bengal delta was and is rice, and the majority obtain from rice some 80 per cent of their total calorie supply. Some wheat is eaten today, more than in the 1940s, when bread and other preparations made from wheat scarcely figured in the diet of most families. In this watery area, fish is the main and indeed almost the sole source of animal protein, but it is available only in small amounts and should be thought of as a supplement to rice rather than as a staple food. This basic dependence on rice rather than on several foods simplifies the task of tracing the course of events before, during and after the famine. In the circumstances the supply, stocks, distribution and rationing of *rice*, and those of *food*, meant much the same thing.

In the 19th century, Bengal was sometimes called the granary of India. It produced about one-third of the rice supply of undivided India. There are three crops a year, of which the *aman* crop, harvested in December, is much the most important. A smaller autumn crop, known as the *aus*, is harvested in August and September, and a minor crop—the *boro*—in March, between the two major ones. In normal times the complicated processes by which harvested rice reached consumers worked automatically. The rice grown by millions of cultivators was partially retained by these for their own use, and partially collected in small lots and sold to be stored, dehusked, transported and stored again, and finally distributed through tens of thousands of retail shops to millions of householders. For some years previous to the famine, rice supplies, consisting of harvested rice and any rice carried over from earlier years, had been sufficient in quantity to feed the masses at their customary low level of consumption, and its retail price had not risen beyond their means. The position had indeed been highly precarious. There had been poor harvests, due to natural causes, with specially poor harvests in 1941. But no starvation had occurred. At the beginning of 1943, however, the food situation was causing keen anxiety. During 1942 there had been a heavy drain on stocks, with increased exports and decreased imports. The December aman crop was 25 per cent below average, largely because of the damage done by a cyclone in Midnapore in October. On the morning of 11 October 1942, a typhoon or cyclone of great intensity, accompanied by torrential rains and followed later in the day by three tidal waves, struck the western districts in the delta. The waves swept over an area of about 3200 square miles, causing much loss of life, and the destruction of standing crops and

F

stocks of rice. In areas more distant from the coast the water level of rivers was pushed up, causing the flooding of about another 400 square miles. This was a bad cyclone, as cyclones go in the Bay of Bengal. But it was not among the major causes of the famine.

The Commission, allowing for all the circumstances including the cyclone, calculated that the total supply of rice in Bengal in 1943 was "probably sufficient for about 49 weeks which meant an absolute deficiency of about three weeks requirements". This calculation was made after the events and of course at the time no one knew what the real position was. The apparently small percentage deficiency suggests that sheer lack of rice was a less important cause of starvation and death than its enormous price.

In January 1941, the minimum price of rice per maund (82 lb: 37 kg) was about Rs 5/8: in January 1942, it was about the same. But in January 1943, it reached Rs 12/8 per maund, and in April of that year it was on the average twice this figure in markets throughout Bengal. In May and June it rose, in many places, to Rs 35/- to 40/- per maund. This meant starvation for poor people who found such prices fantastically beyond their reach. The small rice producer was not immune. He had often sold his stock eagerly early in the ascent of the market, feeling that prices had reached a zenith and could not possibly rise further. But when, a month or so later, he sought to buy back rice to feed himself and his family, he had not enough money to pay for it and he and his family starved. Landless labourers and non-producers of food—potters, carpenters, basket makers, weavers and others—were the first to suffer. Lacking rice and the money to buy it, the poorer villagers sold their domestic utensils, ornaments, tools, clothes, parts of their dwellings such as doors and windows and indeed anything that could be sold, to more fortunate neighbours at cut-throat prices. They reduced their food intake by degrees to make their dwindling reserves of food and money last as long as possible. But they could not hold out for long. Those on the right side of the economic fence, i.e. those in a position to sell, buy and store rice as a speculative commodity, and with enough to eat at the same time, did well out of the emergency. It was later reckoned that the amount of unusual profits made in the buying and selling of rice in 1943 was about Rs 150 crores (£11·5 million).

The death rate began to rise in May in six districts in the delta, the most striking rise being in Chittagong. In June it was double the quinquennial average and three to four times that average in July.

This ominous phenomenon escaped notice at the headquarters of the public health department in Calcutta, because it normally took several months for mortality returns from rural districts to be sorted out, officially recorded, and examined. The Surgeon-General of Bengal told the Commission that he was not aware that anything unusual was happening until August. But some weeks before that the terrible wandering in search of food began, with hordes of people moving in the general direction of Calcutta because of vague rumours that food was to be had there. While many of the victims died of starvation in their villages or by the roadside, thousands reached Calcutta to become part of the war news.

The victims made little attempt to loot food shops, and stores cornered by prosperous traders; sometimes they died in the street, just outside well-filled and locked storehouses. There was no organised rioting. Coming from different villages, the people lacked any corporate spirit which might have prompted efforts to obtain food by violent means. They belonged to the poorer sections of the population and were accustomed to accept misfortune passively. Moreover, they soon became physically incapable of such purposive action. During the famine, indeed, thefts of rice from stores or in transport became very common. But this was largely the work of ordinary thieves, stealing rice because it had become well worth stealing.

In August I was travelling by rail from Madras to Calcutta, on some business not connected with the famine. It was customary for the Madras–Calcutta mail to pick up a dining car at Khargpur Junction, some thirty miles outside Calcutta, to provide first and second-class passengers with breakfast. I stepped cheerfully down from my compartment en route for a hearty meal. The whole platform was thronged with emaciated and ragged people, of all ages and sexes, many half-dead, hoping to board a train for Calcutta. What I particularly remember is a loud, bleating, wailing noise which the starving crowd made, a combination of begging and misery. When some years later I read accounts of the Irish famine at its height, by visitors to stricken areas in West Cork, I was reminded of the platform at Khargpur Junction.

I could not eat breakfast in the dining car and went back to my compartment.

What was the Government of Bengal, with the Government of India in the background, doing while the clouds darkened? The answer is: many things, some good and some bad, none of which postponed or averted the disaster. A "Food Grain Control Order" was followed by policies of "de-control" and "unrestricted free trade" which were particularly disastrous. At one point the Government of Bengal, with the tacit approval of the Government of India, sent agents to neighbouring provinces to buy rice at very high prices; these provinces, in trouble themselves, obstructed the agents in every possible way and in effect they were chased back to Bengal. Throughout, the government was preoccupied with maintaining food supplies for Calcutta and its industrial suburbs. With the Japanese on the borders, to keep the factory workers adequately fed and capable of producing materials and equipment for the army was regarded as the first priority. Here success was achieved, with the collaboration of European and Indian employers of labour. The government encouraged and helped employers, through Chambers of Commerce, to set up grain shops, where rations of subsidised food could be bought by their own work people. In spite of numerous troubles and difficulties, which included a large-scale exodus from Calcutta after Japanese air raids in December 1942, the labouring classes in the city and its suburbs obtained enough food throughout the emergency. Later the Government was accused of having unjustly favoured Calcutta because of pressure from big business. It was pointed out that of 206,000 tons of rice which was procured by the Government during 1943, 140,000 tons were used to feed Calcutta while only 65,000 tons were sent to rural Bengal. Certainly, the contrast between starvation in the villages and sufficiency of food in the city was a striking feature of the famine.

The occurrence of widespread starvation in the middle of 1943 called for immediate and vigorous relief measures. The machinery of the Famine Code, involving the establishment of relief works and the payment of wages to labourers employed on these works, was inoperable in the circumstances. Equally futile were small payments of money as "agricultural loans"; with the price of rice at unheard of levels, and people already starving, the only thing to do was to provide food directly at special centres, in the form of cooked meals. But orders to initiate such relief were not issued until the end of August, and an official called a "Famine Relief Commissioner" was not appointed until the end of September. Arrangements to provide hospital accommodation and treatment for sufferers acutely ill from starvation and disease were equally dilatory. The medical and public health services of Bengal, badly paid, short-handed and thoroughly inefficient, were simply incapable of dealing with the emergency.

The death rate reached a peak in December 1943 and remained high (though falling steadily) during the first half of 1944. In the early days of the famine most deaths were due to sheer starvation, but later hundreds of thousands of deaths were ascribed to smallpox, cholera and malaria, all rampant in a disorganised and unresistant population.

Towards the end of our sessions the Chairman asked me, as the medical member of the Commission, to make an estimate, however rough, of the number of deaths caused by the famine. Realising the difficulties and fallacies involved, I set to work with whatever figures were available. The only possible approach was to calculate the number of recorded deaths, in the different districts, between June 1943 and June 1944, in excess of the annual average during the preceding five years. One knew, of course, that a percentage of deaths went unrecorded in normal times and that in famine this percentage increased, but the effect of this on the total figure could only be guessed. I covered sheets of paper, making allowances this way and that, and came out with the result that the number of deaths in 1943, in excess of the average, was of the order of one million and in 1944 about half a million. Such rounded figures are suspicious in themselves, but may have helped to indicate the uncertainty of the estimate. We were not as aware then as we are now that a large part of famine mortality occurs in infants and young children, and deaths in those age groups are likely to go unrecorded in a disrupted population. At all events, the figure of 1·5 million deaths is in the history books, and whenever I come across it I remember the process by which it was reached. I now think it was an underestimate, especially in that it took too little account of roadside deaths, but not as gross an underestimate as some critics of the Commission's report, who preferred 3 to 4 million, declared it to be. The lower figure is tragic enough.

Lord Wavell took up the post of Viceroy in the last week of October, in succession to Lord Linlithgow, who saw nothing of the famine before he left. Within a few days Wavell was in Bengal, dealing with the famine as his first duty on taking office. The army was brought in to help the exhausted and almost despairing civil authorities and to rescue Bengal. Substantial supplies of rice and

wheat were already being sent to Bengal by the Government of
India, but these could not be distributed because of a breakdown
in transport, due both to physical causes and administrative disorganisation. Convoys of army lorries, in the charge of brisk young
British officers to whom India was a strange and incomprehensible
country, brought supplies to rural Bengal. Broken-down roads and
bridges were quickly repaired. Centres for distributing cooked food
were set up, and also temporary but serviceable hospitals.
Hunger was alleviated, but it was too late to do much about the
epidemic diseases which continued to kill during much of 1944.

The change in the atmosphere and the situation brought about
by the army take-over was immediate and striking, with firm direction replacing drift. People said, "If only this had happened six
months ago."

Not much of note has subsequently been written about the Bengal
famine, from which recovery was inevitably slow. It was a dreary
disaster, reflecting discredit on British and Indians alike. The British
thought they had conquered famine, or at least found ways of preventing starvation when famine threatened. There had been no
serious famine in India for forty years and famine control was regarded as one of the triumphs of the Raj. There was failure in
Whitehall, New Delhi and Bengal. For some months the India
Office, under Mr L. S. Amery, refused to admit the existence of
famine, preferring the euphemism "food shortage". The Government
of India did not appoint an official to take charge of food administration until a year after the war with Japan had broken out. Then, in
1943, this post was held by five different people in succession; the
Commission commented acidly that "during the various critical
stages of the famine, heavy responsibility fell on individuals who were
new to their posts". The Government of India, indeed, gave little
useful guidance or help as the situation deteriorated.

In Bengal itself there was an administrative breakdown which was
only partly excused by the obligations of the war and the presence
of the Japanese on the frontier. The Government of Bengal tried
various expedients in a half-hearted way but failed to master the
appalling difficulties. Here a passage in the Commission's report may
be quoted:

"It lay in the power of the Government of Bengal, by bold,
resolute and well-conceived measures at the right time to have

largely prevented the tragedy of the famine as it actually took place. While other Governments in India were admittedly faced with a much less serious situation than the Government of Bengal, their generally successful handling of the food problem, and the spirit in which those problems were approached and the extent to which public co-operation was secured, stand in contrast to the failure in Bengal."

The Madras Presidency normally imported more Burmese rice than Bengal, but by forceful measures survived the cutting off of supplies without disaster.

At the beginning of the war in 1939, the leave of I.C.S. and other senior officials in Bengal was severely restricted. Home leave was, of course, impossible for the British, and even short breaks in Darjeeling were frowned on. Given the climate of Bengal, this cannot have made for vigour and efficiency when a formidable emergency arose three years later. Sir John Herbert, the Governor of the Province, was dying of cancer throughout 1943; he did his best to keep in touch with the course of events until the later stages of the disease. In the circumstances a strong and active governor, taking advantage of the emergency powers at his disposal, might have given the necessary leadership. The Viceroy, Lord Linlithgow, was more interested in political issues than in famine and left the task of handling the famine to his successor, Lord Wavell. How far personal factors contributed to the administrative breakdown it is impossible to say. At times it seemed as if the gods themselves had taken a hand in exacerbating the disaster.

On the other side, there was unquestionably what the Commission called "a moral breakdown". Many of the witnesses we interviewed expressed great indignation against "profiteers, speculators and hoarders", who forced the price of rice up to unheard of levels. They were blamed for causing mass suffering and death, while at the same time the government was blamed for not dealing drastically with such enemies of society. Profits were high. The Commission itself made what it called the "gruesome calculation" that for every death in the famine roughly a thousand rupees (£88) of excess profits were made. Some business organisations, both Hindu and Moslem, made fantastic gains out of speculating in rice; the Commission learnt of one of these which had profited to the extent of at least 4 million pounds. Such things became well known. Indian political critics of the British in their penultimate days in India, who would have liked to lay the entire blame for the Bengal famine on their shoulders, could not ignore the selfish greed of their fellow countrymen. Except for Lord Wavell, who had the advantage of plenary powers and an army to command, no one emerged with credit from the débâcle.

Chapter 8

China: Land of Famine

THE two great civilisations of east Asia, those of India and China, differ from each other almost as much as either differs from European civilisation and its offshoots. They differ in history, methods of government, administration, social structure, religion, philosophy, art and other aspects of life. But they have had one thing in common over the centuries, namely vulnerability to famine. In comparison with India, literature on famine in China is scanty. W. H. Mallory has, however, tried to get it together in his book *China, Land of Famine* published in 1926. His excellent work has been most valuable in writing this chapter.[1]

We may begin by giving an account of a fairly recent Chinese famine. The first part of the 19th century was a bad period for famine in China; it was reckoned that about 45 million people died from famine during this period.[2] In the 1870s, drought, lasting three years, affected an area of about 300,000 square miles in five provinces in northern China, where the principal crops were wheat, millet and sorghum. According to contemporary appraisals, between 9 and 13 million people died of starvation, disease and violence. Attempts to relieve the famine proved fruitless because of lack of communications. Some comments of the Chairman of a Foreign Relief Committee set up in the coastal city of Tientsin may be quoted:

'In November, 1877, the aspect of affairs was simply terrible. The autumn crops over the whole of Shanzi and the greater part of Chihli and Honan had failed . . . Tientsin was inundated with supplies from every available port. The Bund was piled mountains high with grain, the Government storehouses were full, all the boats were impressed for the conveyance of supplies towards Shansi and the Hochien districts of Chihli. Carts and wagons were all taken up and the cumbersome machinery of the Chinese Government was strained to the utmost to meet the enormous peril which stared it in the face. During the winter and spring of 1877–78, the most frightful disorder reigned supreme along the route to Shansi. Hwailu-hsien, the starting point, was filled with officials and traders all intent on getting their convoys over the pass. Fugitives, beggars and thieves swarmed. The officials were powerless to create any sort of order among the mountains. The track was completely worn out and until a new one was made a dead block ensued. Camels, oxen, mules and donkeys were hurried along in the wildest confusion, and so many perished or were killed by the desperate people in the hills, for the sake of their flesh, that transport could only be carried on by the banded vigilance of the interested owners of the grain, assisted by the train bands, or militia, which had been hastily got together, some of whom were armed with breech-loaders. Night travelling was out of the question. The way was marked by the carcases or skeletons of men and beasts, and the wolves, dogs and foxes soon put an end to the sufferings of any wretch who lay down to recover from or die of his sickness in these terrible defiles. . . . Broken carts, scattered grain bags, dying men and animals so frequently stopped the way, that it was often necessary to prevent for days together the entry of convoys from the one side, in order to let the convoys from the other come over. No idea of employing the starving people in making a new, or improving the old, road, ever presented itself to the authorities."

This famine was of the same dimensions as some of the great Indian famines. Transport of food to the afflicted population was obstructed by lack of communications. In China, as in India, the construction of railways helped in organising famine relief, but only 6000 miles were built between 1870 and 1911, as compared with about 30,000 miles during the same period in India. In 1926 five of the twenty-six Chinese provinces were entirely without railways and in several others there were only a few miles of line.

In the early 1920s a drought of about the same duration and intensity occurred in much the same area. Suffering and death ensued, but on a much smaller scale than forty-five years previously; it was claimed that deaths were kept down to under half a million. Some effective relief was organised, with assistance from the foreign powers who occupied parts of China at that time.

According to a study made in the University of Nanking, 1828 famines occurred in China between 108 B.C. and A.D., 1911, which means a famine nearly every year in one or other of the provinces. This figure is quoted without comment in the FAO publication *Lives in Peril*.[3] Such estimates cannot be taken seriously, but at least they indicate that famine has been a frequent calamity in China. Some references to cannibalism are to be found in the early records of the provinces most subject to drought and starvation. Yao Shan Yu[4,5] studied Chinese official records of floods and droughts from 206 B.C. to A.D. 1911, but found these difficult to interpret. The mere existence of such records is, of course, remarkable. Floods and droughts seemed to occur more often during certain centuries, for example the 14th century. Records declined during periods of political instability, but increased with the invention of printing in the 15th century. Yao Shan Yu, who found the study tedious, felt it might be possible to elicit a series of meteorological cycles from the data, but did not himself undertake this job.

Droughts are most frequent in the northern and central provinces largely dependent for their water supply on the monsoon of June, July and August. Apart from the monsoon, the total annual rainfall is small—21 inches has been given as an annual average. To pray for rain on behalf of his people was among the principal duties of the Emperors, one of whom addressed heaven in the following moving terms.'[1]

"This year the drought is most unusual. Summer is past and no rain has fallen. Not only the crops and human beings feel the dire calamity, but beasts and insects, herbs and trees almost cease to live. I, the Minister of Heaven, am placed over mankind and am responsible for keeping order and peace in the world. I am scorched with grief and tremble with anxiety, but no genial and copious showers have been obtained.

"Some days ago I fasted, and offered rich sacrifices on the altars of the gods, and had to be thankful for gathering clouds and slight showers, but not enough to cause gladness. Summer is past and autumn has arrived; to wait longer will really be impossible. Knocking head, I pray Imperial Heaven to hasten and confer gracious deliverance—speedy and divinely beneficial rain, to save the people's lives and in some degree redeem my iniquities. Alas! Oh Imperial Heaven, observe these things. Alas! Oh Imperial Heaven, be gracious to them. I am inexpressibly grieved, alarmed and frightened."

One is reminded of the sacred texts of the Hindus and their prayers for rain. Supernatural significance was attached to catastrophes such as drought and flood; they were ascribed to behaviour which upset the balance between nature and mankind. Transgressions on the part of the emperors were particularly likely to affect the well-being of the people, for which he was personally responsible. At one period he had to rise from his bed before dawn to ensure that the sun would appear at its appointed time.

Floods loom large in Chinese history, though perhaps they have not produced famine to the same extent as drought. Fed by torrential rains, rivers, large and small, have often burst their banks and inundated vast areas of arable land. The great Yellow River, known as "China's Sorrow", flowing westward across the central plains to end in the Yellow Sea, has changed its course completely three times during recorded Chinese history, and on other occasions has returned to its old bed after a period of wandering. Incalculable destruction was the result. In 1889 2 million people were drowned in Yellow River floods and starved in the famine that followed. Nearly a whole province was inundated. Drainage after floods was slow and it was often several years before the drowned land could be replanted with crops. Exceptionally heavy rainfall may also wash away cultivated terraces on the hillsides, built with prodigious labour. Flood control was among the important duties of the emperor and his officers. Many dykes built hundreds of years ago to hold rivers in their courses are still standing. It is stated that during the Suong Dynasty, contemporary with the Norman Conquest in England, some 500 public works projects concerned with waterways and flood control were undertaken.

Typhoons or cyclones are of common occurrence in China south of Shanghai. They are often followed, as in India, by tidal waves which break down sea walls and cover the land along the shore with seawater for miles inland. But typhoons have not been a major cause of famine. Another persistent scourge of a different kind has been the locust; the first recorded major invasion was in 125 B.C. Destructive swarms were most frequent in the central and northern provinces.

The great bulk of the population has been engaged, since the dawn of history, in food production based on human and animal muscle, mainly the former. Farmers were not entirely without beasts of burden, but possessed few wheeled vehicles. The cheapest means of transport was the human carrier; a man could carry a load of 60 kilograms for a distance of 26 kilometres daily. Intensive farming by time-honoured methods has been the rule. A classical book on Chinese agriculture was called *Farmers of Forty Centuries*.[6] Soil fertility has been maintained, in spite of intensive cultivation and without chemical fertilisers, by the use as manure of treated human excreta and fuel waste. Great use has been made of river irrigation channels which carry not only water but also fertile soil. Soil erosion has been countered by ingenious methods of field construction and terracing.

The principal crops grown have been well adapted to the environment—wheat, millet and sorghum in the northern and central provinces, and rice in the south. Between the 13th and 17th centuries China acquired maize, the sweet potato and the groundnut, and, more recently, the Irish potato. The sweet potato was grown everywhere, thriving on poor soil; it is said that its introduction in the 14th century substantially increased the rate of population growth. Sugar was cultivated in early times, having reached China from India in the 1st century B.C. But sugar production did not flourish until some centuries later, after a Chinese technical mission had visited the Ganges valley to study Indian methods. In the 13th century Marco Polo was greatly impressed by the extent of sugar cultivation in an area near the mouth of the Yangtze.

Chinese agriculture has been in fact remarkably efficient and even progressive at the technological level prevailing in the world until two hundred years ago—probably a good deal more efficient than Indian agriculture. Since the country was oppressed by the density of its population, use was made of every patch of cultivable land. In 1917, E. A. Ross wrote as follows:

"In parts of China the earth is utilised as it has never been utilised before. Little land lies waste in highways. Throughout the rice zone the roads are mere footpaths, one to three feet wide, yet the greedy farmers nibble away at the road from both sides until the undermined paving stones tilt and sink dismally into the paddy fields. Pasture or meadow there is none, for land is too precious to be used for growing food for animals. Even on the boulder-strewn steeps, there is no grazing save for goats, for where a cow can crop herbage a man can grow a hill of corn. The cows and the water-buffaloes never taste grass except when they are taken out by an old Nanny and allowed to browse by the roadside and the ditches, or along the terraces of the rice fields.

"The traveller who, in dismay at stories of the dirt, vermin and stenches of the native inns, plans to camp in the open, is incredulous when he is told that there is no room to pitch a tent. Yet such is the case in two thirds of China. He will find no roadside, no common, no waste land, no pasture, no groves or orchards, not even a dooryard or a cow-pen. Save the threshing floor, every outdoor spot fit to spread a blanket on is growing something."[7]

Such a picture of extreme lack of land for growing food probably applied only to limited areas, mainly in the south. It does, however, illustrate the precarious balance between food supplies and the needs of the people. There was no margin of safety, except perhaps that provided by the granaries to which reference will shortly be made. If drought or some other calamity hampered production, food shortage was bound to follow with little delay.

The series of dynasties which governed China began with the Sheng Dynasty dating from the middle of the first millennium B.C., and ended with the Manchu Dynasty which was replaced by a Republic in 1911. Between the major dynasties, six in number, each of which lasted from two to three hundred years, there were periods of disorder and bloodshed, with bandits ravishing the countryside and a breakdown of civil administration. Famines were most frequent and severe during these interludes. From early times governments constructed granaries and filled them in years of relative plenty, as Joseph did in Ancient Egypt. The granaries were located in towns and cities, but no doubt the country people had access to them when famine threatened. Moreover, the authorities were anxious to prevent the wandering in search of food to which starving populations are prone and which often proved so terrible an accompaniment of famine in India. It is likely, therefore, that food was transported from civic centres to the countryside for famine relief. The canals connecting north and south and east and west, built by millions of impressed workers, facilitated the transport of grain. The first large canal, from Peking to Hangchow, was begun in 540 B.C. Much later, there was a great outburst of canal building in the Sui Dynasty in the 6th century at which, it is said, over 3 million workers were employed.

Through much of Chinese history the civil administration has depended on officials (mandarins) who were selected by an examination in the Chinese classics and reported directly to the Emperor. Famine relief was among their most unenviable responsibilities.

Some speculation whether China or India has suffered more from famine down to recent times may be permissible. Both countries seem to have been equally susceptible to drought, and both have relied on staple crops highly vulnerable to shortage of water. The Chinese unquestionably led in the construction of canals which provided a means of transport and protective irrigation; the praiseworthy efforts of Mogul emperors to build canals in northern India should not, however, be overlooked. China, with its tremendous rivers, has suffered more than India from floods, even though the Ganges could at times burst its banks like the Yellow River. Both countries depended on agricultural techniques which supplied nearly enough to eat in normal times, but Chinese agriculture seems to have been more capable of admitting new crops, and Chinese methods of conserving waste material to provide fertiliser were of unsurpassed efficiency. The Indian practice of using cattle droppings as fuel rather than as manure would be sacrilege to a Chinese farmer.

There was no equivalent in India to the granaries in towns set up in China to store reserves of grain. Warren Hastings's huge granary in Bihar was never used. For the local transport of grain in famine areas, India had the bullock cart as long as the animals could be fed, while China relied more on human carriers.

The relief of famine depends on administrative vigour and efficiency. China had its mandarin officials, selected by proficiency in the Chinese classics and steeped in the wisdom of Confucius. Their main job was to collect taxes and their training did not cover the realities of Chinese agriculture. However, since a high death roll from famine would mean the Emperor's displeasure, leading to loss of face and even to loss of head, the mandarins no doubt tried hard to prevent and relieve starvation. In India there was no equivalent to the Chinese mandarins until the British established their civil service late in the 18th century. Many of the British administrators, like their Chinese counterparts, were steeped in the classics, but in different classics—in Plato, Vergil and Livy. They seemed none the worse for it.

The passage quoted from Ross's book *Standing Room Only* suggests that China—especially south China—has suffered acutely from over-population. Malthus had a good deal to say about famine and population in China. He refers to the writings of two of the Jesuit savants whose presence was tolerated in China for several centuries and who made many useful contributions to their host country. Both mention the frequency of famines in the 17th and 18th centuries, an era when other aspects of Chinese civilisation were much admired in Europe. Malthus commented that there must have been periods when the population "increased permanently without an increase in the means of subsistance . . . if the accounts we have of it (in China) are to be trusted, the lower classes of people are in the habit of living almost upon the smallest possible quantity of food . . . A nation in this state must necessarily be subject to famine. Where a country is so populous in proportion to the means of subsistence that the average produce of it is but barely sufficient to support the lives of the inhabitants, any deficiency from the badness of seasons must be fatal." This was written in the 1790s.[8]

In 1911 the last of the Dynasties ended and China became a Republic. There were promising developments in education, agri-culture and medicine, generously supported by the Americans through the provision of money and first class personnel. But the people suffered terribly at the hands of ambitious war-lords. In the 1930s Generalissimo Chiang Kai-shek and the so-called Kuomintang imposed some order, and considerable progress ensued until the Japanese invaded China in 1939. Resistance to Japan was led by the Generalissimo, but the state of the country deteriorated. In 1949 Chiang Kai-shek was thrown out of China by the Communists and with his Methodist wife took over the island of Taiwan or Formosa. Taiwan, with a present population of over 14 million, has become one of the best-governed, best-fed and most prosperous countries in Asia. Until 1971 it was "China" in the United Nations, which did not recognise Communist of "Mainland" China. In that year Communist China was admitted, becoming a member of the Security Council, and Formosa was thrust into the outer darkness.

Something will be said later about happenings in Communist China. There is already much to show that China, under her latest over-lords, will no longer be a Land of Famine.

Chapter 9

Famine in Russia
and elsewhere in Europe

RUSSIA is a land of uncertain harvests. As recently as 1972–73, the Russian wheat crop was about 10 million tons short because of bad weather and other causes. The U.S.S.R. had to ask her great rival, the United States, to sell her 6 million tons of grain. Without these supplies, the Russian authorities felt, it would be necessary to ration bread.

In this book a history of Russian famine will not be attempted, but an account will be given of two famines, one in 1891 and 1892 in which Tolstoy played a part, and the other the famine which followed the first world war and was the most terrible famine in Europe in the last 100 years.

The association of Tolstoy with famine relief has some affinities with relief in the Irish famine, and the efforts of the gentry to help the victims. Famine was widespread in central and south Russia in 1891 and 1892. In his biography of the great man, Henri Troyat[1] tells how Tolstoy went with members of his family to the famine-stricken province of Ryazan, some 200 miles south-east of Moscow, where a friend of his, a doctor called Rayensky, owned property. He made his friend's house the centre of relief operations in neighbouring villages. At first he was without the help of his wife Sonya, who was staying in Moscow with the four youngest of their numerous children. At this time Leo and Sonya were in the middle of one of their bitterest quarrels.

Many of the peasants had died of starvation and the survivors were so weak that they could scarcely move. Children in rags lay huddled together for warmth in unheated huts. In the doctor's house and in other centres in the district, food was distributed to the sufferers on a liberal scale. There were hunks of rye bread, cabbage soup, potato mash or barley porridge, and beet greens. Meals were provided twice a day and some clothes were given to the children. The cost of relief feeding was borne by public subscriptions, elicited by a letter written by Sonya in Moscow and published in every newspaper in Russia and also in some European and American papers. In this letter she chided the well-to-do for living in well-fed comfort while peasants were starving and dying. In two weeks 13,000 roubles were subscribed. Sonya joined her husband for a few weeks in the famine area and cleared up some of the administrative confusion only to be expected in relief operations with a Slavonic genius in charge. Later, food poured in from countries in Western Europe and even from America; seven boatloads of maize were despatched from America, together with wheat flour from millers in Minnesota. Tolstoy himself wrote an article called "Help for the Hungry" in which he said that the misery of the peasants was due to their being exploited and robbed by the landowners; this was so heavily censored in Russia as to become almost meaningless, but was published abroad in unexpurgated French, German and English translations.

The government and the Church were furious. "There is no famine in Russia," the authorities declared. "Some localities have had a poor harvest. That is the whole truth." Pobyedonostcev, Minister to the Holy Synod, who had been the Czar's tutor and had great influence over him, submitted a report accusing Tolstoy of seeking to foment a peasant revolution. Informers were sent to Ryazan to watch his every move. The local clergy were instructed to tell the peasants that Tolstoy and his family were heathen people who did not eat meat and did not say grace when they sat down to table. The peasants were ordered not to accept relief under pain of damnation. It was rumoured in Moscow and St Petersburg that Tolstoy would be exiled or imprisoned in a monastery.

The Czar Alexander III had more sense. He knew that Tolstoy was a great figure not only in Russia but throughout the civilised world. *War and Peace* had been published in 1865 and *Anna Karenina* in 1877. He did indeed express annoyance with himself for having graciously received Sonya, a remark which frightened Sonya so that she wrote to Leo saying that his provocative behaviour would ruin all the family. But when the idea of punishing Tolstoy was put before him, the Czar enquired acidly whether Tolstoy was plotting an attempt on his life. A little later he said to his Minister of the Interior: "I will ask you not to touch Tolstoy. I have no desire to make a martyr of him and provoke a general uprising."

There was a good harvest in 1893 and the famine came to an end.

The peasants were restored to their customary level of privation. Tolstoy, dissatisfied with the whole undertaking, went home to pursue further the ideal of universal love. Sonya complained to her diary that his vegetarian diet meant preparing two menus daily, making twice as much work for the household.

The great Russian famine of 1921–22, in which up to 3 million people perished of starvation and disease, was centred in the Volga basin in an area about the size of Belgium, normally one of the best grain-producing areas in Russia. Both war and drought were responsible. Granaries were depleted by the European war, during which most able-bodied men were conscripted into the army. Disintegration was continued and intensified by the Civil War and nearly half the arable land in Russia went out of cultivation. Russia was subject to blockade until 1921, and unable to obtain credits to make purchases abroad. On top of all this there was partial failure of the rains in 1920, succeeded in 1921 by complete drought which turned some of the most productive cornlands of Europe into a parched and blackened waste. By August 1921 hunger was almost universal, and in the middle of 1922 an area of a million square miles, and some 30 million people, were affected. This was famine on the scale of 18th century India.

Unlike the Czarist government in 1892, the newly-established Bolshevik government admitted widespread famine and in August 1921 appointed a commission consisting of a group of Russian doctors and four foreign newspaper correspondents to report on the situation. A member of the Society of Friends, Anna Haines, was allowed to accompany the commission. It was impossible to visit much of the whole afflicted area, and the commission confined its attention to the Province of Samara, traversed by the Volga. They reported that over the greater part of this Province, with a population of about 3 million, 70 per cent of the cornfields had failed completely and that without help the majority of the peasants could not survive the winter. By September, 1·2 million were already starving.

This was clearly a hopeless situation, and Samara was only one of seven stricken provinces. The relief which could be immediately provided by the government and foreign organisations was only a drop in the ocean. Among the foreign organisations was the Society of Friends, which put English and American Units into the field. After negotiations in Geneva, Dr Nansen, the famous Arctic explorer, was appointed High Commissioner for Relief, in charge of

the International Russian Relief Commission which was recognised
by the Soviet authorities.

The work of the English Quaker Unit, with headquarters in the
town of Buzuluk in Samara, was realistically described by a member
of the unit, Michael Asquith, and his account will be drawn on here
to give a picture of this terrible famine.[2] An advance Quaker party,
arriving in September 1921, found that most of the grass had been
eaten, while acorns were a luxury. A member of the party wrote:

"I saw in practically every home benches covered with birch
or lime leaves. These are dried, pounded, mixed with acorns, some
dirt and water, and then baked into a substance which they call
bread, but which looks and smells like baked manure. The
children cannot digest this food and they die. There are practically no babies and those that survive look ghastly. The mothers
have no milk and pray that death may come quickly. Slow
starvation is too painful. All the children have distended stomachs,
many are rachitic and have enlarged heads . . . According to
Government figures, ninety per cent of the children between the
ages of one and three have already died from the famine."

During the first few months the Quakers saw many people die
before their eyes. "The first snowfall took heavy toll," wrote one,
"and I remember noting that forty were dead in a single morning
at the beginning of November." The Russian authorities tried to
set up homes for children which they hopefully called Receiving
Homes, Distributing Homes and Permanent Homes, but all were
swamped by famished children, most of whom soon died. The record
of one Home was: Admitted, 1300; Died, 731. A Quaker worker
wrote about a "Receiving Home" in Buzuluk:

"As a home it was intended for 50 children, but yesterday 654
children were crammed within its walls. On such days as many
as 80 are brought in. The stench inside was indescribable,
although a little band of women bravely tried to grapple with a
terrible problem and could point to newly scrubbed floors. . . .
as we entered we became aware of the continual wailing sound
that goes on day and night. In each room . . . there were at least
a hundred children packed like sardines in canvas beds—six on a
bed intended for one, and underneath the beds as well. The
typhus cases, some of them completely naked, lay on straw in a

separate room. They had neither bedding, medicines nor disinfectants, though we had been able to give them a little soap and clothing. They had no doctor.

"Each morning the attendants picked out the dead from the living and put them in a shed to await the dead cart which every day makes its round of the Children's Homes."

At this stage of the relief programme, one of the painful difficulties of the relief workers was to decide whom to feed and whom not to feed. Not giving food was tantamount to sentence of death. Strict discipline within the group was needed to keep to feeding priorities once these were established. It was also essential for the relief workers to feed themselves properly so as to remain strong and active; on no account must they give away even the smallest part of their own meals. "You must be prepared", wrote a member of the Unit, "to have people crying for food on your own doorstep while you eat your evening meal, and to find them lying there dead in the morning. You must pass them lying on the road and appealing to you for help, or even collapsing at your feet. You have simply got to steel your heart and realise that it is worse than useless to give any food to any individual who is not on the feeding list." In the early months, the Friends were seriously under-fed.

Cannibalism occurred, as it does in many major famines, but it was apparently confined to a few people driven mad by suffering. The Friends had to give up buying cheap sausages when some were found to contain human flesh.

Slowly the International Russian Relief Commission began its rescue work. Dr Nansen concluded an agreement with the Soviet authorities by which they guaranteed the passage of foodstuffs and other goods across Russia and gave the Commission, which came eventually to include all European organisations working in the famine area, complete freedom in the handling and distribution of supplies. In due course—by the middle of 1922—the Commission was feeding about 2 million people: at this stage of the famine the burden of relief was somewhat lightened by the fact that so many of the victims were dead. The Friends were affiliated to the Commission and included in the Nansen Agreement. After the appalling initial stages, and as more volunteers arrived to strengthen the group, they turned their attention to "soup kitchens" in the villages, possibly prompted by old memories of famine in Ireland. They fed some

19,000 people through "soup kitchens", as compared with 6,000 through "Homes". The Soviet government thought highly of their efforts. There is a story, probably without foundation, that a decree was issued threatening officials who failed to attend to the Quaker relief affairs within twenty-four hours with the death penalty.

Relief feeding continued until the autumn of 1923, when a good Russian harvest was reaped. The relief agencies turned their attention to other needs, in particular clothing, farm equipment and harness; most of the harness had been boiled to make soup. Horses were imported, mainly from Siberia. Some 13,000 abandoned children needed care. The surviving population was still weak and many needed further hospital treatment with good food to restore them to health and strength.

The U.S.S.R. remained precariously free from hunger until 1929, when the country suffered from the serious food shortage verging on famine, referred to by Malcolm Muggeridge in *Winter in Moscow*.[3] After the second world war, UNRRA supplies were available to prevent famine in much of Europe (see Chapter 11). But as recently as 1971, as was noted at the beginning of this chapter, the U.S.S.R. was once more in trouble and forced to import large amounts of wheat from the United States.

*   *   *

The Friends were concerned with two other famines during the inter-war period—in Austria and in Spain respectively.[4] These could perhaps be better described as malnutrition on a large scale rather than as famine due to sheer lack of food. During the Kaiser's war, Austria ceased to be the centre of the Austro-Hungarian Empire, and its capital, the great city of Vienna, became thronged with people from the lost territories. At the same time Vienna was largely deprived of the food supplies which the old empire provided. By 1918, before the war was over, it was known that at least 2 million people in Vienna were hungry and that many were suffering from disease due to insufficient and unsatisfactory food. Large numbers of previously prosperous people turned to begging. Family valuables were offered to neighbouring farmers in exchange for food, not always successfully; farmers' wives were known to refuse gold watches, saying they had several already.

The victorious Allies were aware of the straits to which Austria and other parts of Central Europe had been reduced. Early in 1919 they sent General Smuts to Vienna to report. A rich pre-war meal was somehow prepared for the General, to welcome an important envoy, but he indignantly refused it and retired to his cold hotel bedroom to eat army rations. No doubt the meal was avidly consumed by others. Among the results of his visit was a request to the Society of Friends for help, and a representative of the Society, Dr Hilda Clark, immediately went to Austria to survey the situation and assess needs. The "Save the Children" organisation was also asked to assist. It was at this time that the devastating post-war epidemic of influenza struck Europe, but in Vienna itself tuberculosis caused more deaths in 1919 and 1920 than influenza.

The Society of Friends launched an appeal for funds in England and America, which was highly successful. Large stocks of processed milk, flour, sugar, cocoa, fats and soap were bought, mainly for children below school age. Older school children were given the job of packing these commodities in parcels representing two weeks supply for individual children; this task they performed admirably, sustained by a morning meal to prevent them fainting. The parcels were distributed through the welfare centres for consumption at home—many of the recipient children were in a miserable state, and it was felt that they would benefit more from eating extra foods in familiar surroundings. This system of distribution, later somewhat modified, leaving to parents the responsibility of feeding the children with the imported foods, did not bolster the black market in hungry Vienna. There was of course one check: children given milk and other foods put on weight without fail, provided they were not suffering from infective disease. In just one instance, at one centre, it was found that the children were not putting on weight as they should; the nurse threatened to withdraw the rations and at subsequent sessions weighings were satisfactory.

Later the distribution of rations was taken over by depots each in the charge of an Austrian woman, with mission members supervising the running of several depots. The Austrian workers gave their services free, but from time to time they were allowed food parcels, a most desirable recompense. The depots were linked with child welfare centres at which children were graded by doctors according to their degree of malnutrition. Those in the lower grades were given extra care and extra milk and other foods.

An extensive relief programme was developed along such lines, by the Friends, the Government and other organisations. Depots were opened in some towns, as well as in Vienna. Cod liver oil was distributed liberally, when the need for it was realised. Relief in the form of food and clothing was given to poor students, living in the extreme of misery. People were supplied with shoes as well as clothing; sound footwear is a paramount need in such circumstances. Establishemts were specially equipped for the rehabilitation of badly nourished children, and for the care of cases of tuberculosis. Groups were sent abroad—to Holland, Switzerland, England and the Scandinavian countries—but the long train journeys proved very exhausting and the sudden change to a richer diet tended to upset the children, who also became homesick for dismal Vienna. In due course it was realised that it was preferable to look after the children in their own country.

In famines in the temperate zone the deficiency disease rickets, due to lack of vitamin D, is usually common among children. Its analogue in adults, osteomalacia, is also common—giving rise to a painful and crippling condition in middle-aged and elderly women. Vitamin D can be provided to the body by the action of sunshine (ultra-violet light) on a precursor of vitamin D in the skin, converting it into vitamin D. This is readily possible in the tropics, but not in cooler regions where sunshine is weak and intermittent. In the latter vitamin D must be obtained via the mouth, through animal fats which contain it, such as butter, eggs, and fish liver oil, or in pure or concentrated form out of a bottle. In post-war Vienna cod liver oil was the principal anti-rachitic agent. It happened that laboratory research on vitamin D in England and America had reached a stage at which the answer to a rather intricate scientific puzzle seemed in sight. The British Medical Research Council sent a team of experienced research workers to Vienna, under Dame Harriette Chick, to note the effects of cod liver oil on children with rickets and women with osteomalacia and to make other observations. The result was further clarification of the problem of vitamin D deficiency in man, particularly in its practical aspects.[5] The subsequent highly successful campaign to eliminate vitamin D deficiency in Europe and America and elsewhere in the world, one of the great triumphs of modern medicine and public health, owed a good deal to the sufferings of Austrian women and children. It is not often that famine brings benefit to humanity.

The food shortages and famines arising out of the first world war—in Russia, Poland, Serbia, Austria and Germany itself—slowly disappeared. For a few years Europe did not lack food, though in the 1930s there was much undernutrition and malnutrition due to unemployment. Later in the decade a serious famine occurred in Spain as the outcome of civil war. This began in 1937 when refugees from Franco's armies moved into the government's capital city, Barcelona, in search of food. Spain is an unfertile country at the best of times, with low rainfall and unproductive soil, and unable to stand the strain of a bitter fratricidal campaign. The story in Spain was the typical story of famine, with all age-groups, but particularly children, suffering severely. The Society of Friends, "Save the Children" and other charitable organisations, as well as the Government itself, strove valiantly to provide relief. But by 1938 food shortage was merging into famine and an experienced relief worker wrote, with reference to children: "The time of pallor, dead eyes, listless bodies, shocking thinness and distended stomachs has come." Memories of the Civil War and the misery it caused are not fading quickly in Spain.

War, civil or between nations, leads to famine. This sequence has never been more tragically demonstrated than in Europe between the two world wars. Those who start wars do not usually remember the lurking spectre of famine which in due course will probably cause more suffering, and kill more people, than war itself.

Chapter 10

Famine in the Netherlands

THE Dutch do not like the Germans. Their dislike, which has temperamental and historical roots, was exacerbated by the tyrannical German occupation during the second world war and especially by the famine in western Holland in 1944–45, which was directly caused by German action. This famine, which led to the death of perhaps 10,000 people, was not on the same scale as the great famines of the world; at about the same time, between 1 and 2 million people died of famine in Bengal. But the Dutch famine was remarkable in that it took place in Western Europe in a previously well-fed community, which recorded precisely the phases of the disaster that struck them.[1,2,3 and 4]

Before the war the Dutch had an excellent diet containing an abundance of animal products, with wheat and rye as the staple cereals. A surprisingly large proportion of food supplies was, however, imported, and dependence on imports extended to fodder for livestock and to fertilisers. Approximately half the butter, cheese and eggs produced in the country was exported. When war broke out in September 1939, the Dutch realised that their food situation was highly precarious and tried to build up stocks, but little stockpiling was possible. The rationing of fodder was initiated immediately. Then came the German invasion in May 1940, when Queen Wilhelmina and her government fled to England. The Germans were delighted with the acquisition of the rich agricultural resources of Holland, which they used for the liberal feeding of an army of occupation and to increase the food supplies of Germany; from May 1940 to September 1944, the output of about 60 per cent of cultivated land in Holland was commandeered by the Germans. The Dutch had to make do with what was left; this was not much, but they made do very skilfully.

They cut down drastically the production of pigs and poultry and diverted the cereals thus made available to human use. They broke up grass land to grow more rye and other foods, especially potatoes; by 1943 the acreage of land under potatoes was increased by two-thirds. Synthetic fertilisers could no longer be imported, and supplies of farmyard manure were carefully husbanded. A system of rationing, with ration books and coupons, was instituted by which the population was divided into age-groups and work categories, those performing heavy work being entitled to larger rations. Special regulations covered the needs of sick people and expectant and nursing mothers. Communal kitchens were established which provided about 450,000 workers with an extra meal daily; children in schools also received extra food, with milk as long as this was possible. A Food Council, with appropriate sub-committees, assumed charge of the emergency measures and of the arrangements for producing and distributing food.

All this meant considerable changes in the Dutch national diet. The quantity of carbohydrate consumed increased, while that of protein and fat decreased. Milk, cheese, meat and eggs became rare foods, milk being to a large extent reserved for children. There was a fall in the average weight of children of all ages, and a definite rise in the death rate from tuberculosis. But the calories available, mainly from rye and potatoes, were just sufficient to prevent hunger and to allow ordinary work to be done. Actually the Dutch diet during the first four years of the war was in many respects like the British wartime diet (but not as good), and their food control system was like the British one. There may well have been consultations between Dutch authorities and experts and the highly efficient advisors of Lord Woolton, the British Minister of Food, both before and during the German occupation.

In the Netherlands most of the big cities and the main industries are located in the west, the traditional "low country" adjacent to the sea. The remainder of the country is largely agricultural. The west was dependent for food on import through Rotterdam and other ports, and on supplies from the agricultural area. During the war import by sea ceased. In September 1944 Montgomery launched his airborne attack on Arnhem in eastern Holland, near the German border, as a preliminary to an advance into the Ruhr. The attack was a bloody failure, with high casualties on both sides, though Montgomery claimed it was a 90 per cent success. At the same time, the exiled Dutch government in London ordered Dutch railwaymen to go on strike, with the object of hampering the German forces in Holland. This order was accepted by the authorities in the Hague and immediately obeyed by the railwaymen. In retaliation

Seyes-Inquart, the Nazi Reichskommissar, prohibited all movement of food from the north and east into western Holland. The people of western Holland heard of these happenings over the radio, for almost every home had its hidden wireless receiver, tuned into the B.B.C.

Seyes-Inquart himself told the Dutch that if the strike were not called off there would be famine. He was right; famine came quickly. Rations were drastically cut in October and people began to lose weight progressively. Signs characteristic of hunger were soon evident: fatigue, apathy, a feeling of cold, obsession with the thought of food. Owing to shortage of fuel, it became more and more difficult to keep warm; actually an abnormally low body temperature is often found in the starving. Diarrhoea became common. Famine oedema, which appeared in January 1945, was not as marked as in the Irish famine; swelling of the ankles and feet in the evening usually disappeared by morning, to be replaced by puffiness of the face. Among unpleasant symptoms were pains in the limbs and back and dull burning sensations in the hands and feet. Lice and skin infections, including scabies, were troublesome, because of lack of soap and disinfectants.

Any stocks of food in the towns were soon exhausted and people— at least those who were strong ehough—went out into the country to forage for food, on bicycles or with handcarts (Plate 3b). There was not much to be picked up, but a few potatoes or sugar beets, or indeed anything remotely edible, made an exhausting expedition worthwhile. Elderly and old people stayed at home in bed and many of them, particularly those living alone, starved to death. Even if they had friends and relations they might be neglected because of that distressing phenomenon characteristic of famine—indifference to the sufferings of others. Hospitals did what they could; in some towns "starvation hospitals" were established where patients could be given some food for a short time and then discharged so that others could be admitted. There was no indifference to suffering on the part of doctors and nurses, who worked day and night on the following diet:

Breakfast: one slice of bread and a cup of tea.
Midday meal: two potatoes, a small portion of "vegetables", some watery sauce.
Evening meal: one or two slices of bread and a plate of soup, with a cup of "coffee substitute".

As things got worse, the Dutch doctors sent an open letter to the Reichskommissar, Seyes-Inquart. Parts of this letter will be quoted:

"We hold your Administration responsible for the dire shortage of even the most necessary foodstuffs. The want and distress of the Dutch people living in the most densely populated parts of the occupied territory increase day by day. The ration allotted to adults has a nutritive value of only 600 to 800 calories. That is even less than half what is needed for an adult to survive, even when resting; it is less than a third of what is required for work. The small stocks of food which many families had been able to put aside are disappearing or are already exhausted. The amount of milk available for young children is seriously insufficient and, except in some cases, extra rations for the sick and aged have been withdrawn altogether.

"As a result of serious malnutrition, insufficient clothing and the great shortage of fuel, endurance has been seriously undermined, so that there is an increase of grave illness. These evil consequences are made even more serious by the shortage of means for carrying on medical work, cleansing and disinfection. Tuberculosis, dysentery, enteric fever and infantile paralysis are rapidly increasing in severity, while epidemics of diphtheria and scarlet fever have already reached proportions formerly unknown in Holland. The danger of typhus must be seriously faced.

"The Occupying Authorities are to blame for these conditions. In the first place, because they broke International Law by transporting to Germany the large reserve supplies available in 1940, and, in the years following 1940, by carrying off a considerable portion of the livestock and food produced in our country. Secondly because, now, in 1944, they are, by confiscation and abduction of nearly all transport material, preventing the Dutch people from distributing the remaining food satisfactorily over the whole country. The occupiers attempt to blame the Dutch organisations, but this charge must be rejected, as every measure taken by these organisations to improve the food situation has been opposed. Ships that were to be used for conveying supplies were prevented from sailing, many of the cargoes were seized, and supplies stored in factories, warehouses and in cold storage, were carried off after famine conditions had already been established. It was a false argument to allege that the railway-strike was the cause of this state of affairs; even under normal conditions only a very small proportion of our food was transported by rail.

"The writers of this letter fear that humanitarian arguments will be disregarded and considered by you as unbusinesslike. Yet, we are impelled to ask whether you have forgotten the hospitality that once was given to starving German and Austrian children by the very same country that is now being plundered by your fellow countrymen, and so subjected to a famine.

"There was a time when Germany herself suffered from the terrible effects of a hunger blockade. Then, she condemned the action as being criminal; now, without necessity, she is starving an unarmed people."

The Reichskommissar did not answer this letter. In January the Swedish Red Cross and the Swiss and International Red Cross were allowed to supply small consignments of food which helped very little.

Meanwhile the British and Americans were making plans for famine relief. Stores of food were accumulated and mobile teams of doctors were organised, together with trained personnel to handle the treatment of those suffering from severe starvation. Here a mistake was made. It was thought that starving people could not swallow and digest even liquid foods such as milk and that they should be given "pre-digested" foods either by the mouth or by intra-venous injection. Accordingly, large quantities of pre-digested protein foods were prepared, together with glucose solution containing vitamins.

By March as many as fifty-one trained feeding teams (Dutch, American and British) with foods and other supplies were standing by, eager to move into the occupied zone. Three "nutrition survey teams", led by experienced American and British nutrition workers, were ready to collect detailed information about the situation and provide guidance for action. Arrangements were made to set up laboratories in suitable places.

As things turned out, famine relief personnel moved into western Holland in advance of the allied armies. Strong pressure was brought on Seyes-Inquart, who was not happy about the famine and had received orders from the Fuhrer's increasingly hysterical headquarters in Berlin to break down the sea-dykes and flood western Holland in the event of Allied attack. Clearly, the end was near for Nazi Reichskomissars. A meeting between Allied and German officers was arranged on 28 April and a second meeting, attended by Seyes-

Inquart and, on the Allied side, by Prince Bernhard, was held two days later. The Germans were forced to allow a non-military medical mission, under a flag of truce, to pass through the lines to confer with the Dutch public health authorities about immediate measures for dealing with starvation. Among the members of the mission was Sir Jack Drummond, the Chief Scientific Advisor to the Ministry of Food, who did as much as any man to win the war. They entered western Holland on 5 May and were received with ecstasy by the people. Curiously, these first liberators and the armies which followed a few days later were surprised because the Dutch looked so well and happy; the people in the streets, though thin, were flushed with excitement and waving flags. A correspondent of the London *Times* declared that "we had expected to find the most horrible conditions, but we did not need the special teams which stood by ready for action. There were some cases of advanced malnutrition, but no cases of actual starvation". The special teams soon found, however, that the starving were in the emergency hospitals or at home unable to leave their beds. They found that famine oedema was rife in the big cities.

From this point relief proceeded satisfactorily. It was soon found that the pre-digested protein foods were useless and unnecessary, but these were readily replaced by ordinary foods. There was some friction between exhausted and under-fed Dutch doctors and their foreign colleagues; it should always be remembered that liberated people are in a highly irritable state and inclined to quarrel with their liberators. But in spite of difficulties great improvement in the condition of the people was visible in one month, and by the middle of June the situation was well under control.

The official report comments that the Dutch famine came near to being a "very terrible catastrophe. Had the German occupying forces held out another two or three weeks against the Allied attack, nothing could have saved hundreds of thousands in the towns of the western Netherlands from death from starvation."

Seyes-Inquart, born in the Sudetenland in 1892, became a friend of von Schussnigg (whom he later betrayed) during the first world war. In 1938 he took office in Austria under von Schussnigg and in 1940 Hitler appointed him Reichscommissar in the Netherlands. Capured by the Canadians in May 1945, he was tried at Nuremberg and hanged on 16 October 1946, with the group of important Nazi leaders which included Ribbentrop, Rosenberg and Streicher.

Chapter 11

The United Nations and International Action

A TURNING point in the history of famine was reached in the year 1944, when it became evident that the defeat of the Axis could not be long delayed. The crucial event was the establishment of the United Nations Relief and Rehabilitation Administration (UNRRA). It was obvious in 1944 that much of the world would be in a sorry state when the war was over; the food shortages and famines which had afflicted humanity after the first world war were a recent memory. Accordingly President Roosevelt called to the White House the representatives of forty-four nations, and gave them the mandate to set up an organisation to help in relieving post-war suffering and want. This they did, and the new organisation moved quickly, though it was not easy, at this stage in the war, to find people to man its staff, and to acquire the things needed for relief. But generous funds were forthcoming: £675 million from the U.S.A., £155 million from the United Kingdom and £35 million from Canada. An armada of American ships was gathered to carry the supplies, which included locomotives and other railway rolling-stock, farm animals, tractors, ploughs, seed grains, blankets and medical equipment. Most important of all, they included large quantities of foods of various kinds, especially Canadian and American wheat and cheese. The recipient countries were mostly war-devastated countries in Europe. UNRRA helped many millions of people to survive and to pick up normal life again. The *Encyclopædia Britannica*[1] comments that it prevented at least three famines, a vivid if perhaps inexact way of assessing the results of the great undertaking.

Ten years later I was having dinner with some colleagues in Warsaw—a good dinner because the Poles are hospitable and like good food. My host recalled how, when living somehow in their unheated and ruined city in the winter of 1945–46, they would say sardonically to each other, "Pass the UNRRA, please," this being usually bread and cheese and perhaps a can of baked beans. The world has rather forgotten what UNRRA did during the few years of its existence. But the Poles, a gallant and generous people, have not forgotten.

This was not the first time that food and other necessities were donated to hasten recovery from war. After the first world war, Hoover, later to be President of the United States, led a generously supplied and well-equipped mission to Belgium to feed the population, and particularly children, and help the country in other ways. On the other side of Europe, as we have seen, war, national and internal, was followed in Russia by a famine of tragic dimensions, and other neighbouring countries were almost as seriously affected. Famine conditions and social disruption were associated, as in Ireland seventy-five years earlier, with epidemics of typhus and other diseases, which raged in east and South-East Europe. An international "Epidemic Commission" was set up, under the auspices of the newly-established League of Nations, to deal with the epidemics, and to prevent, by *cordons sanitaires*, their spread westward. In 1922 the Epidemic Commission was merged into the Health Organisation of the League of Nations which in turn gave place, after the second world war, to the World Health Organisation.

UNRRA finished its emergency operations in 1947. The worst was over. The devastated countries were producing food and essential commodities again, and life was slowly returning to normal. But in many countries which had benefited from UNRRA assistance the health of children remained unsatisfactory. They had not fully recovered from wartime privation and were still thin and stunted. Child health and welfare services were still restricted. It happened that UNRRA had not fully spent the large sums donated at its foundation, notably by the United States. Dr Ludwig Rajchman, then a representative of Poland at the United Nations in New York, and previously Director of the Health Section of the League of Nations, proposed to the UN Assembly in 1947 the formation of a new United Nations organisation, to be called the United Nations Children's Emergency Fund, with special responsibility for child welfare. The proposal was accepted and UNICEF was launched on the solid foundation of "residual" UNRRA funds, together with large subscriptions from governments. People respond readily to appeals on behalf of children. The first thing UNICEF* did was to

* In 1960 the word "emergency" was dropped from the title, and the organisation

H

supply milk to children in Europe. Whole milk containing milk fat and vitamins A and D (in evaporated or powdered form) was reserved for infants under one year, and most of the milk available was skim milk—called "milk solids non-fat" in America. Skim milk though lacking vitamins A and D, retains the protein present in whole milk; in fact it has a somewhat higher protein content than whole milk because of the removal of the milk fat. At that time (1947) there were still doubts about the nutritional value of skim milk, which was regarded by some as a waste product perhaps suitable for calves and pigs. The newly-established Food and Agriculture Organisation of the United Nations (FAO), had to convene an expert committee in Washington to vouch for its value as human food. After this, UNICEF went ahead with its child-feeding operations which, beginning in Europe, were subsequently extended to many other parts of the world. Countries were helped to set up modern milk processing plants and dairies to increase their own output of safe milk of good quality; in this field, FAO has provided the technical expertise. Apart from milk, UNICEF has supplied many things which children in poor countries need: foods of various kinds other than milk, vitamin tablets, medicines, footwear and child welfare centres. But this is not the place to describe UNICEF's total programme, which has included the support of successful campaigns, led by WHO, to combat malaria, tuberculosis and yaws. Theoretically any UNICEF contribution to a country must be "matched" by a contribution of equal value made by the country itself, but this stipulation has not always been taken too seriously by the UNICEF officials holding the purse strings.

The main point here is that UNICEF has provided milk and other foods to children in areas of food shortage and famine, and also to children in schools and other institutions in countries where undernutrition and malnutrition are prevalent. Between 1947 and 1961, UNICEF distributed about 500,000 metric tons of skim milk powder, which is a lot; since 1961 distribution has somewhat declined, more attention being given to helping countries to improve and increase their own milk supplies. Again, as we shall see later (Chapter 17), remarkable progress has recently been made in developing what may be called "milk substitutes", composed mainly of vegetable foods.

---

became the "United Nations Children's Fund". The familiar initials were, however, not changed.

Another United Nations organisation must be mentioned in this context, namely the "United Nations Relief and Works Agency for Palestine Refugees in the Near East", rather unfortunately called "UNRWA", which leads to confusion with the great pioneer relief agency "UNRRA". In May 1948, the British mandate in Palestine expired and the State of Israel was proclaimed. The Arabs in Palestine took fright at a rumour that they were about to be massacred, and most of them fled to neighbouring countries, especially to Jordan, Syria and Lebanon. With nothing except the clothes on their backs, they sheltered in deserted buildings and even in caves. Voluntary organisations, whose activities were co-ordinated by Count Bernadotte, soon to be assassinated, helped to keep them alive. Towards the end of 1948 responsibility for relief was taken over by the United Nations, and in the following year the United Nations General Assembly formally established UNRWA, which has been looking after the refugees ever since. The number of refugees was estimated in 1950 as nearly 1 million and in 1966 as over 1,300,000, the difference being due to natural increase. At least half are under 18 years of age. The refugees are mostly housed in the countries bordering on Israel, in great camps which over the years have acquired the appearance of dingy and dreary permanence. Rations are not liberal but adequate, and sanitary conditions in the camps are reasonably satisfactory (Plates 4a and 4b).

In 1967 there was a second displacement, after the Seven Days War between Israel and neighbouring countries. The new refugees came mainly from the West Bank of the Jordan, Jordanian territory until annexed by Israel as a result of the war, and from the Gaza strip which had belonged to Egypt. There were some 400,000 newly "displaced persons", of whom about 150,000 had been wards of UNRWA between 1950 and 1967. By gallant improvisation, UNRWA, though desperately short of funds, managed to cope with the situation. New camps were set up and "family kits" issued, consisting of a cooking stove, pots and pans and other eating utensils. Much the same rations as those which had sustained the refugees for nearly twenty years were supplied. The rations, issued monthly to families, include flour, rice, lentils, oil or fat, and sometimes tinned fish. Children under 2 years of age are given a mixture of whole milk and skim milk, and reconstituted skim milk is provided in schools, and also to pregnant and nursing women through special distribution centres. Cod liver oil is given to infants and young children during the winter months. From the start, feeding arrangements have been guided by scientific advice. UNRWA employs trained nutritionists on its staff and from time to time well-known doctors from outside have visited the camps to report on the diet and health of the refugees. In the early days many of the children were in a poor condition, and some cases of famine oedema, and also of scurvy, were seen. Epidemics of diarrhoea have continued to be troublesome during the hot months, as they are throughout the Middle East. But on the whole health has been good. Examinations made in the early 1960s showed that children in the camps were healthier and better grown than children in poverty-stricken neighbouring Arab villages not cared for by the United Nations. Apart from their good diet, the refugee children benefit from well-run maternity and child welfare centres and also from "rehydration" centres for treating cases of severe infective diarrhoea.

Education is an important part of UNRWA aid. Children are offered six years of elementary education, followed by three years of further schooling for those who complete satisfactorily the elementary cycle. A limited number of carefully selected pupils receive higher secondary education. UNRWA has also organised vocational education programmes, including teacher-training, on which it rightly places great stress. Through these some of the brightest boys and girls have the opportunity of escaping from the dreary circumscribed world of the refugees. Vocational training courses for boys equip them to work in the building, mechanical and electrical trades and also in some semi-professional and commercial occupations. For girls there are clerical and secretarial courses, and also courses in dressmaking, hair-dressing, and technical work in medical laboratories, as well as vocational training in other fields. An UNRWA brochure (1969) comments hopefully:

"In a normal year some 1600 students and trainees now graduate from UNRWA's training centres, each equipped with a skill needed in the developing Arab world. Over 10,000 have graduated since the training programme was launched in 1953. Most of them work in the Middle East, both in the host countries and further afield. Many are in the oil industry."

But some of the educated refugees are causing a lot of trouble.

The World Food Program

The World Food Program (WFP) is a relatively young UN agency; its establishment was proposed in 1961 and it did not get going until 1963. The principles on which it operates are simple. On the one hand, a few countries, such as the United States and Canada, usually have surpluses of food and other commodities which are difficult to dispose of commercially on the world market; on the other, there are numerous poor countries which are short of food and can benefit from more food to accelerate their development. A pamphlet describing WFP comments:

> "The idea of food aid has been evolving since the 1930's when people first became seriously aware of the cruel paradox that in a few countries there were huge agricultural surpluses that could not be sold, while in very many more there was widespread hunger."

Donating countries pledge contributions to the WFP in the form of food or fodder, cash, or services such as shipping; food, mainly cereals, is the most important contribution. By 1967 more than eighty countries had pledged assistance. Countries wishing to benefit from the resources of the WFP put in requests to WFP headquarters in Rome asking for supplies of foods (and other things) for various purposes, for example to feed labourers building a dam, a highway or a railway, or engaged in clearing waste land for crop production. The requests are drawn up in consultations between WFP field staff and officials of the government concerned. These are scrutinised in Rome or Geneva by representatives of WFP and other UN Agencies, and, if approval is forthcoming, the food and other goods are despatched as soon as possible. According to recent figures,[2] by September 1971 WFP was helping to feed 11·1 million people in sixty-three countries, under projects "approved for economic and social development". It need scarcely be said that the whole procedure is subject to hitches and delays and is liable to abuse at the receiving end. The surprising thing is that it has worked as well as it has. Its first Director was the Dutchman, A. H. Boerma, later Director-General of FAO.

WFP also provides food in emergencies due to natural disasters including floods and drought, and also to hungry refugees. In 1965, when harvests were poor in many parts of the world, it contributed to supplementary feeding in twenty-two countries. Assistance was given in the feeding of the new batch of Arab refugees in the Near East after the war of 1967. But such emergency distribution accounts, in terms of total cost, for only one-fifth of its total activities. A difficulty about emergency feeding is that the most suitable kinds of food cannot always be supplied immediately by donor countries. Delays are inevitable. Hence such assistance has tended to be most valuable when the stage of rehabilitation has been reached.

UNRRA, UNICEF, UNRWA and WFP all show what a world authority can do, in different ways, to combat hunger and malnutrition. We are concerned here with this aspect of their operations, not forgetting that they do many other things to help their beneficiaries. Large quantities of surplus food have been transported across the world, which can only be done, of course, if surplus food is available. UNRRA, as has been said, prevented three famines; UNICEF has improved the state of nutrition and health of millions of infants and children. These are happy results. WFP has not been in action long enough to enable its usefulness to be fully assessed, but it seems to be proceeding along sound lines.

UNWRA has kept alive perhaps a million and a half Arab refugees and that is also a happy result, in the sense that it is better to be alive than dead. But it is hard for anyone who has visited Arab refugee camps in Jordan and elsewhere to use the word "happy" (Plates 4a and b). In winter heavy rains are likely to turn the camps into quagmires, and in summer hot sandy desert winds obscure the sky and fill everything with sand. The refugees have few prospects of a different life; little attempt has been made by their host countries to absorb them, since these countries insist that their real home is in Israel and that they must return to Israel. The Jew–Arab feud is kept on the boil by their mere presence. Understandably, bitter discontent among young refugees without prospects, both men and women, makes them a danger to Israel and to their host countries. The terrorists who specialise in skyjacking and assassination and were responsible for the murders and counter-murders at the Olympic Games in 1972, were kept alive in the refugee camps. In taking reprisals, the Israelis attacked ten camps in Syria and Lebanon, and later have made such camps special targets after further outrages on the part of the refugees.

FAO

The UN body with primary responsibility for the food and nutrition of the world's peoples—FAO, the Food and Agriculture Organisation of the United Nations—is not itself directly concerned with famine relief operations, except through its connection with the World Food Program. Nevertheless, it has the duty of keeping watch, through its field officers, for threatened famine anywhere. In 1951 it was charged by the UN Economic and Social Council (ECOSOC) "to keep existing and emerging food shortages in individual countries under continuous surveillance". In response it has established an "Early Warning System" through which monthly reports on crop conditions in drought-prone countries are received. In 1973 the Director-General of FAO issued a series of warnings on the imminent danger of world food shortage and the FAO *The State of Food and Agriculture*, 1973 summarised the situation in realistic terms (see Chapter 20).

FAO has produced a careful brochure called *Food and Nutrition Procedures in Times of Disaster*, which can almost be described as a world Famine Code.[3] This deals lucidly with major famine problems such as early detection, food hoarding, price control, rationing systems, communal feeding arrangements and the care of refugees. It considers in some detail the dietary requirements of famine victims according to age and sex, and a chapter is devoted to "medical problems in a famine". It gives special attention to the care of livestock in famine; we have seen how farm animals failed to survive in some of the great famines of history. Apart from broad principles, the FAO brochure contains numerous practical tips likely to help people concerned with famine prevention and relief.

In May 1971 the Economic and Social Council set up the "United Nations Disaster Relief Organisation", with headquarters in Geneva, under the command of an official called the Disaster Relief Co-ordinator. The Co-ordinator was given the job of entering into working relations with UN bodies and organisations concerned in one way or another with disaster relief. At that date there were twelve of these, including the organisations mentioned in this chapter. Outside the United Nations, the Co-ordinator was instructed to establish contacts with the International Committee of the Red

Cross and the League of Red Cross Societies as well as with "numerous other non-governmental organisations", which presumably means some of the larger bodies which will be referred to in the next chapter.

In October 1972, the Co-ordinator made his first report to the UN General Assembly, through the Secretary-General. In this he emphasised the importance of "preparedness", which means having plans for relief ready, and information on tap about the location and availability of supplies and trained personnel. Since the Co-ordinator was appointed there have been cyclones and floods in Mauritius and Madagascar, floods and landslides in Peru, and unprecedented rains and floods in the Philippines. But these minor disasters have been overshadowed by the terrible earthquake in Nicaragua in December 1972, which directly struck the capital, Managua, destroyed the city, killed thousands of people and caused many thousands more to flee into the surrounding countryside. UN bodies, non-governmental organisations and countries in various continents were eager to provide relief and there was danger of overlapping and waste of effort. It was sensible to distribute blankets and bandages available nearby and not blankets and bandages expensively flown from 3000 miles away. The new organisation was faced with a formidable emergency in the early stages of its existence. It succeeded in imposing order on the Managua relief operations in a short time.

The disaster of famine falls within the new co-ordination agency's sphere of responsibility. But it will be more concerned with sudden emergencies such as those caused by earthquakes. Supplies of food are usually needed in these emergencies, but only for a short period. Famine, on the other hand, tightens its grip slowly and may last for a year or more, leaving time for co-ordinating programmes of relief.

In Chapter 19, reference will be made to the United Nations and the growth of population. We shall see how the United Nations and its Agencies have become involved, step by step, in this vast problem, the solution or otherwise of which will determine the world's prospects of conquering famine in times to come. Meanwhile immediate world food shortage due to drought has needed international attention (Chapter 20).

Chapter 12

The Voluntary Agencies

A NUMBER of non-governmental or "voluntary" agencies make a useful contribution to famine relief. Their principal aim is to improve conditions in the poor countries, often with special emphasis on health and state of nutrition, and they stand ready to give help in times of food shortage and famine. Most have their headquarters in affluent countries and are dependent on charitable funds. Some have religious affiliations, but do not restrict assistance within denominational limits. Among the better known, in the United Kingdom, are Oxfam (Oxford Committee for Famine Relief); Save the Children Fund; War on Want; Christian Aid; the League of Red Cross Societies: CARE (Co-operation for American Relief Everywhere) and Catholic Relief Services, are prominent in the United States. Most voluntary bodies of this kind are of quite recent date; like the United Nations and its Agencies, they did not come into existence until after the second world war, though one or two of them, like the "Save the Children Fund", have a longer history.

A short account of the aims and activities of a few of these bodies will illustrate this aspect of the subject.

CARE

CARE was established in 1946, with the beneficent function of arranging for the despatch of food parcels from America to Europe. Some British readers will have happy recollections of the receipt of ham, butter, chocolate and other delicacies, which enlivened the cheerless post-war years. At that time CARE was called "Co-operative for American Remittances to Europe". Later it extended its geographical range to under-developed countries throughout the world, and broadened its interests. Among its main activities has been the feeding of children in primary and secondary schools, as well as children of "pre-school" age; it claims that in 1971 alone it provided food for 23·5 million children. CARE had the great advantage of having access to American surplus supplies, furnished under what is called Public Law 480.* In 1969 it received from the U.S. government (at no cost except for distribution) "Agricultural Commodities", which presumably means principally food, worth 7 million dollars.

As well as feeding children, CARE contributes to the building of schools and encourages the education of mothers in better child-feeding practices. It has agricultural interests, concerned with wells, tools, seeds, fertilisers and livestock. In 1962 it became affiliated with a medical relief body, known as "Medico", and as a result organises programmes through which medical and surgical special-ists are assigned to hospitals in the less advanced countries, to help in the training of local personnel, for example nurses. Most im-portant of all, in the present context, it provides what is called "Disaster Assistance"; that is, it is ready to help when some calamity renders people destitute and in need of food. In some threatened famines of recent years, for example in Bihar in 1967, CARE carried out most valuable relief work.

In 1971 supporters in America and Canada contributed 15·6 million dollars to CARE's programme and upkeep. With an ex-perienced staff of about 250 men and women, CARE operates in some 36 countries. In a recent brochure it made this claim:

> "The phrase 'Send a CARE package' has become part of the language of nations, but today's 'package' is apt to be bulk in-gredients for school lunches, lumber to build fishing boats, tools to build roads, seeds and livestock and tractors, water pipes and sewing machines, drugs and medical services."

Oxfam

Oxfam (the Oxford Committee for Famine Relief) was founded on 5 October 1942, at a meeting of five people in the Old Library of St Mary-the-Virgin in Oxford.[1] Dr Gilbert Murray, then aged seventy-six, was a member of the group. The Committee wished to find ways of mitigating hunger in Europe, especially hunger among

---

* Under PL 480 foods are supplied to countries in return for payment in local currencies, the funds thus accruing being largely used to support the development of agriculture and food technology within the country concerned, as well as other developmental purposes.

children. Britain was then entirely cut off from Europe; she was just about keeping alive and unbeaten; her ally Russia seemed on the point of defeat; destructive air raids were still to come. It was therefore a brave but unpropitious moment for founding a body concerned with anything beyond mere national survival. The Committee collected a few thousand pounds and was reluctantly allowed by the government to send some food and clothing to women and children in Greece. It was natural for a group which included the great Greek scholar, Gilbert Murray, and was located in Oxford, to take a special interest in Greece. But it was not until the war ended in 1945, with much of Europe in ruins and many of its people underfed and almost in rags, that unimpeded relief became possible.

At first the Committee remained essentially an Oxford committee and confined its appeals and attention to Europe. It gradually became known throughout Great Britain, mainly as an organisation looking for old clothes to send to the needy. The extension of its interests outside Europe began in 1949, when the world had to deal with hundreds of thousands of displaced Palestine Arab Refugees in Jordan and other countries. Oxfam helped the United Nations in its efforts to mitigate the calamity (Chapter 11). Some members of the Committee, however, felt that since the war was over, and Europe was on the road to recovery, the Committee could now be disbanded. This proposal was rejected and a broader objective was adopted, namely "the relief of suffering arising out of war or any other cause in any part of the world". The abbreviated title "Oxfam" came into general use, and Leslie Kirkley took charge, at first as Executive Secretary and then as Director. Kirkley is a Quaker, and Oxfam, as it grew, benefited from the hard-headed Quaker approach to good works.

It grew rapidly. To house its considerable but not over-paid staff, it acquired a building at 274 Banbury Road, Oxford, serviceable though by no means beautiful. By 1961 it was handling some 400 projects in 50 countries, and collecting, by various means, about 2 million pounds annually from the British public. Many of the projects were concerned with relief in emergencies due to hurricanes, floods, earthquakes and droughts. Some were carried out in collaboration with other organisations, including the FAO Freedom from Hunger Campaign. But most were supported directly by Oxfam in response to requests for help from missionary and other bodies in the developing countries. They were, and are, especially concerned with public health, food production and the training of subordinate workers. In organising and superintending such a wide programme it was found necessary to appoint a number of Field Directors, of whom there were ten in 1971, in the different regions. Major disasters still occur regularly, but as far as Oxfam is concerned there has been somewhat decreasing emphasis on disaster relief and more on long-term activities to prevent hunger and malnutrition and raise living standards. In 1968 Oxfam decided to include "family-planning" in its programme; while it can operate in this field only in a very small way, this gesture, well received by the great majority of its supporters, was felt to be worth while.

Annual income rose to a peak of £3,253,076 in 1967–68, then fell a little, to exceed the 3 million mark again in 1971. These are large sums for a charitable organisation to collect, mainly through small individual subscriptions and sale of articles in Oxfam "gift-shops", of which there are now nearly 300 in Great Britain, producing about £530,000 annually. The mere size of Oxfam's income shows that it has gained a firm hold on the British public; "Oxfam" has indeed become a household word, familiar to the man in the street. In pubs people can be heard saying: "Prove me wrong and I'll give a pound to Oxfam." But an organisation dependent on charity is in a precarious position. Subscribers may lose interest and decide to support something more fashionable and exciting. The public did indeed become rather bored with the miserable starving child whose picture usually accompanied Oxfam appeals, and some of the poor countries benefiting from Oxfam help did not like the picture because it suggested that their children were not properly looked after. Recently, Oxfam and its publicity advisers have been trying to change Oxfam's public image—away from "disasters"—of which there are always plenty—in the direction of what is called "development aid" which renders poor countries more capable of dealing with disasters themselves. This trend is illustrated by some of the chapter headings in a recent paper-back on Oxfam:[2] "Following the famine"; "planning families"; "forgotten people"; "disaster in Peru"; "national effort"; "missionaries in development"; "escape and refuge".

In 1968 Oxfam decided, with considerable hesitation, to include "family planning" among its activities, which meant encouraging the practice of birth control in countries seeking technical help in this particular field. It was felt that its supporters, who include many

Roman Catholics, might object to this departure. These fears proved groundless, no fall in subscriptions being evident. Today family planning occupies a modest position in the Oxfam programme, and in that of certain other voluntary agencies. The work of one powerful agency, the "International Planned Parenthood Federation", which deals exclusively with family planning and does not give aid in other fields, will be described later.

Save the Children Fund

Save the Children Fund (SCF), sometimes called simply "Save the Children", was founded in 1920. Its patron is Her Majesty the Queen, its President Princess Anne, and its Chairman Lord Gore-Booth. Its headquarters are in Queen Anne's Gate, a socially superior address. The Fund's annual income (1973), derived from investments and public donations, is about £2·5 million, a very substantial sum, though somewhat less than Oxfam's income at the present time. Probably SCF's chief supporters are to be found in the Establishment, while Oxfam looks to the man in the street.

The founder of SCF was Miss Eglantyne Jebb, who was born in 1876 and came of a family of landed gentry in Shropshire.[3] After studying in Oxford in the 1890s, she took a teacher's training course and became a teacher at a large church school in a provincial town. As an earnest young woman she became obsessed by the miserable condition of poor children in England and elsewhere, and this obsession dominated the rest of her life. In a minor way she resembled the great Florence Nightingale. She went to live in Cambridge in 1894 and became a member of the Cambridge Education Committee. She carried out a social survey at a time when such surveys were uncommon; the results were in due course published as a book called *Cambridge: A Brief Study of Social Questions*, which was widely read.

In 1912 war broke out in the Balkans, with the not-surprising result that in 1913 there were thousands of starving and homeless Balkan peasants, with many children separated from their parents— a situation with which the world was to become all too familiar later in the century. Miss Jebb went to the worst areas and helped to organise and run travelling canteens and soup kitchens; she was specially shocked by the effect of privation on the behaviour of the children. When this little war was over, arrangements had to be made for the care of a few thousand orphans. But this task was nothing in comparison with the task to be faced in a few years time at the end of the first world war, when perhaps 17 million starving and stunted children in central and eastern Europe were in need of food and care.

During the war Miss Jebb and a number of associates formed a body called the "Fight the Famine Council". In 1919 the Save the Children Fund was established, after a meeting in the Albert Hall in London. The first financial target, which was soon subscribed, was £1000 for the children of Vienna. The support of the churches was forthcoming. Pope Benedict XV received Miss Jebb in the Vatican and made a generous donation, subsequently issuing an Encyclical Letter about SCF, the first time that a Pope had boosted a non-Catholic body in this way. Miss Jebb died in 1928, at the early age of 52, leaving behind a flourishing organisation and a draft "Declaration of the Rights of the Child".

SCF has subsequently followed the aim of its founder, i.e. the protection of children from disease and death. It differs from Oxfam in that it works mainly through its own teams, employing over 1000 people in the field. To give a few examples: it has run a school in Simla for the children of Tibetan refugees who followed the Dalai Lama into exile—children who were found to be easy to manage and indeed altogether charming; in Basutoland it has distributed foods for the prevention of protein-calorie malnutrition; in Greece, where it has been active since 1945, SCF has supported a medical care, nursery and child welfare centre; in Agadir in Morocco it runs a Blind Boys Home and feeds 1000 school children. In comparison, Oxfam is less "operational", preferring to help other organisations, often missionary organisations, to carry out projects in public health, agriculture, irrigation, technical education and numerous other fields, while retaining, of course, the rôle of periodic inspection. Oxfam employs a considerable field staff, but, in relation to its total income, fewer people in this capacity than SCF.

War on Want

"War on Want" (Campaign against world poverty) has the unpretentious address of 2b The Grove, Ealing, London, W.5. It was established in 1951 by Victor Gollancz, Harold Wilson, Sir Richard Acland and William Clark "as a pressure group to make world poverty into a social issue", an objective not altogether clear at first sight. Like other non-governmental organisations referred to in this chapter, it relies principally on public subscriptions for its funds. During the period 1 January 1971 to 31 March 1972, its income amounted to about three quarters of a million pounds. War on Want thus operates on a considerably smaller scale than Oxfam or SCF. Like Oxfam, it obtains money from its own shops, of which there are about sixty in England and Scotland.

The field projects assisted by War on Want resemble those of Oxfam and include family planning on a small scale. In 1971 it published a brochure listing some forty-eight of these in four continents. The subscriber is invited to express preference for supporting a Girls Training Centre in Tanzania, an irrigation scheme in Orissa, a clinic in Korea and a health centre in Peru. While this system may appeal to subscribers it must increase the burden of the staff; actually it is extremely difficult to assess progress from year to year in projects in a remote country.

In 1971 War on Want gave substantial assistance to the emerging country of Bangladesh. It provided a mobile hospital and sent medical teams to work in four of the refugee camps (see Chapter 16). Somewhat later it made a loan of £100,000 to the Bangladesh government for the purchase of rice and other cereals, taking repayment from the government in the form of local currency to be spent on agricultural development projects. But this support led to trouble, as the following passage from the latest "Income and Expenditure Account" shows:

"At the beginning of March, 1972, the offices of the organisation at Ealing were entered and many records of the organisation were removed, including books of account. A note was left by the thieves, which implied that the reasons for the theft were political and were motivated by what was considered to be the biased involvement of the organisation in the events which led to the creation of Bangladesh. The thieves indicated in their note that the records would be returned. However, this has not happened."

The police failed to catch the culprits.

Unquestionably the contributions of these and other agencies do not together amount to more than drops in the ocean. To lift the threat of famine, and relieve famine should it appear, are tremendous tasks for governments and the United Nations and its powerful specialised agencies. But the voluntary agencies do possess certain valuable attributes. Being non-official, they can move quickly, usually more quickly than governments and United Nations organisations. They can be on the spot with offers of help or even a cargo of blankets and food while the governments concerned are considering political implications, and information is being exchanged between the disaster area and Rome, Geneva and New York. They provide earnest young people with work that seems worthwhile in a world where little seems worthwhile. They remind members of affluent societies of their responsibilities towards the less fortunate. In earlier days the charitable public subscribed to missions for saving souls; now they prefer to support missions with non-religious objectives.

Most of the non-governmental agencies enjoy "consultative status" with the principal UN bodies. This does not normally mean much more than the right to sit as observers at certain UN meetings, and to receive copies of numerous and voluminous UN reports. An "International Council of Voluntary Agencies" was set up, which organised a conference in November 1971, in New York, with the theme of "International Voluntary Action for Human Needs". The Director of Oxfam was President of the Conference, which was attended by representatives of 124 non-governmenal organisations (N.G.O.s). Encouraging messages were transmitted by the President of the United States and the Secretary-General of the United Nations. The prestige of the N.G.O.s has been enhanced by the concrete contributions which some of them have made during recent years to famine and disaster relief.

Chapter 13

Kwashiorkor

I N the 1930s a discovery of great importance was made in the field
of nutrition, which has helped in reducing mortality in times of
famine. It was found that lack of enough protein of good quality in
the diet makes people dangerously ill and may kill them as readily
as lack of calories. Infants and young children are particularly
susceptible, because of the exacting demands for protein imposed by
rapid growth. This now seems almost self-evident, but it was not
self-evident forty years ago. Doctors and scientists in different parts
of the world contributed to the discovery, but doctors in Africa led
the way.

The first step—apart from earlier hints which are always found
when some important medical advance is made—was the description of a condition in young children in what was then the Gold
Coast, now Ghana, by Dr Cicely Williams, a doctor in the Colonial
Medical Service. Dr Williams, who comes of an old Jamaican family,
is one of the most remarkable women of our times. In the Annual
Report of the Medical Department of the Gold Coast for 1931–32,
she described a serious and often fatal disease in young children
characterised by oedema, under-weight, diarrhoea, skin changes, an
enlarged fatty liver, apathy and misery. She also insisted that the
disease was due to diet deficiency. The Annual Report of the Medical
Department of the Gold Coast was not an impressive or widely-read
publication, but Dr Williams's article, published as Appendix E
in the Report, attracted attention and started an avalanche.
Doctors in other parts of Africa found that they were confronted by a
similar disease, and previous accounts of something very like it in
Mexico, Haiti, Central and South America and Indo-China came
to light. A few years later Dr Williams made a further invaluable
contribution. She found that Africans in Ghana knew about the
disease and had given it a name—*kwashiorkor*. This attractive word
first appeared in the medical literature in an article she wrote for
the *Lancet* in 1935. In due course linguists told us that, in the Ga
language of West Africa, the word carried the significance of "what

happens to the first child after the second child is born"—an astute conjecture of causation on the part of the Ga's. But traditional names for the condition, some of which embody similar concepts, are to be found in other African languages.

Abundant proof that kwashiorkor is a disease of nutritional origin was soon forthcoming. It occurs mainly in children, usually aged from 9 to 30 months, after they have been partially or wholly weaned, i.e. deprived of the breast milk which provides essential protein. A common cause of deprivation is the arrival of the next child. The disease is not seen in countries in which plenty of cows' milk, in various forms, is available for child feeding at a reasonable cost. The most effective treatment is to give the sick child milk, and for this purpose reconstituted skim milk powder is commonly used. "Surplus" skim milk powder, produced mainly in the United States, has saved many hundreds of thousands of children suffering from kwashiorkor, or disease closely resembling it.

Kwashiorkor has come to be regarded as a manifestation of "protein-calorie malnutrition", an ugly and cumbrous term applied to a range of conditions due primarily to deficiency of protein and calories and occurring mainly in infants and young children. One of these is "marasmus" (extreme wasting) principally due to lack of calories, which is specially common up to the age of about 12 months. The highest incidence of kwashiorkor, in which the emphasis is on deficiency of protein, comes a little later—in the second and third years of life. Between marasmus and kwashiorkor there is a range of conditions with some of the features of both. Infection, especially infective diarrhoea, plays a most important part in the causation of protein-calorie malnutrition in its different manifestations. One refinement, which has a bearing on modern methods of dealing with the problem, is that it is not so much lack of protein which causes kwashiorkor, as lack of constituents of protein called amino acids. This means that certain proteins which are rich in essential amino acids, such as milk proteins, are particularly valuable in prevention and treatment, while others are less effective.

If you walk down a children's ward in a hospital in the tropics, you can immediately pick out the children with severe kwashiorkor by their appearance of extreme misery. These children are withdrawn into a dim wretched world of their own and take no interest in toys and people. After proper treatment for a few weeks, often by "drip feeding" with skim milk, they will suddenly and unexpectedly smile; the nurse and the doctor then know that all is well and that the child will recover. All this shows that lack of protein has a striking effect on the brain and mind of a small child, though the physiological and biochemical changes underlying these remarkable phenomena are not yet understood. But it is important to note that the child with kwashiorkor who recovers has suffered not only from deficiency of protein; it has also passed through a period, perhaps several months in duration, when it was almost unaware of external stimuli. Such a period of withdrawal, at a receptive time of life when the growing brain should be receiving daily a multitude of new impressions, may perhaps in itself result in subsequent retardation in mental development.

Much attention is now being given to the question whether dietary deficiency during the early stages of life may check the development of the brain and perhaps cause life-long mental impairments.[1,2] The behaviour of a child with kwashiorkor shows that there is a relation between protein deficiency and the mind. This question is eagerly discussed by nutritionists and others, but with reference to the widespread undernutrition and malnutrition prevalent in children in underdeveloped countries at the best of times, rather than to the effects of famine. The growth of millions of children in the world is retarded because they do not obtain the calories and nutrients they need, and many of them fail to make up later for their poor start. They remain stunted as adolescents and adults. It is plausible to suppose that the same "stunting" affects their heads.

In experimental animals a bad diet during the period of rapid growth, particularly a diet deficient in protein, leads to skulls and brains which are smaller than those of well-fed animals, and to a decrease in learning capacity. It results in a reduction in the number of brain cells, in comparison with the normal. Such changes have been demonstrated in several species, including pigs and rats. It seems that similar changes may take place in human beings; children severely malnourished during their first year were found to have a smaller head circumference than well-fed children ten years later, sufficient to produce an intercranial volume nearly 14 per cent below normal. When height and weight for age are markedly retarded, head circumference is also reduced. In Mexico a series of tests concerned with "motor performance", social behaviour, language skills and other things were applied to groups of children; it was found that the smaller children achieved lower test scores. In most poor countries underprivileged children with retarded growth are in the majority.

These ideas are highly provocative. They imply that a poor diet affects human intelligence in a direct physical way. But conclusive proof has not yet been obtained. Children who suffer from serious malnutrition in early life usually belong to a miserable environment; their families are badly housed and uneducated and proper maternal care is lacking. They do not have toys and picture books to stimulate their growing minds. It has long been recognised that children in institutions who are deprived of company and affection are likely to be mentally backward even though they are well-fed and free of obvious disease. The simple conclusion that slow wits are the result of poor feeding in infancy and early childhood is unjustified. But there is more than enough to show that the danger exists. Certainly an episode of famine will not increase the chances that the children who survive will turn out to be highly intelligent citizens.

Adults suffering from starvation in famine should if possible be given their familiar staple food—rice-eaters, rice, and wheat-eaters, wheat—to supply the calories they need. Some food which provides protein additional to that in the cereal should also if possible be supplied—for example, legumes or pulses in India and dried salt cod (stock-fish) in tropical Africa. While adults will benefit from such "extra" protein, children, with their exacting needs, will die for lack of it. They readily develop kwashiorkor or conditions very like it, which usually responds quickly to the ingestion of good protein.

Skim milk powder was first distributed on a big scale by UNICEF after the second world war to malnourished children in Europe. Subsequently it was supplied to children in many other parts of the world, both through UNICEF and directly by countries, particularly the U.S.A., with surpluses to give away. The principal aim of this distribution was the general improvement of the health and physique of children, as well as the treatment of protein-calorie malnutrition in hospitals. But as far as this book is concerned, the successful use of skim milk powder in famine emergencies is of special significance. It proved a life-saver in the distressing famine in the Congo in 1960, when many thousands of children developed kwashiorkor, and it was extensively distributed, with equally good results, in Nigeria during the Civil War in 1968–70 (see Chapter 14).

But supplies of skim milk powder are not inexhaustible; its abundance has depended on farm policies in the United States, making it a surplus product. These policies are liable to change. Expanding local dairy industries and increasing the production of meat, eggs and fish, are a slow business in poor countries. Hence scientists have turned their attention to producing what are sometimes called "milk substitutes", mixtures of foods which provide the proteins, or rather the amino acids, needed by young children. Another name is "weaning foods". Over twenty such mixtures have been devised in different parts of the world. A list of some of the more important of these, taken from a recent FAO publication[3] and other sources, is given below. They consist mainly of foods of vegetable origin—cereals, legumes, soybean, groundnut, chickpeas, and flour made from the residue of oil-seeds after the oil has been pressed out, for example cotton-seed flour. Many include soybean flour, which has a very high content of good protein. "Fish protein" is an ingredient in a few, for example in "Pronutro" from South Africa; this is refined "fish flour" derived from coarser fish meal used for the feeding of livestock and also as manure. Many of the mixtures contain skim milk powder, usually from 5 to 10 per cent, providing a little animal protein. The presence of some skim milk powder enhances their nutritive value for experimental animals and children.

The various protein-rich food mixtures now available do not differ very widely in their nutritional properties, though of course some are better than others. Their development has depended on increased understanding of human requirements for protein and amino acids; in particular it has arisen directly out of the discovery of kwashiorkor and its cause. Originally, these products were thought of primarily as nutritious foods for infants and young children in countries where there is little milk and malnutrition is prevalent; this is likely to prove their most important role. But, as we shall see, some of them have been found to be just the thing for the feeding of children during famine, and, like skim milk, have saved many lives in famine emergencies.

Much of the work on "protein foods" has been guided and encouraged by a United Nations body called the Protein Advisory Group which, following UN practice, has become the "PAG" for day-to-day purposes. The PAG is an organ of FAO, WHO and UNICEF with a full-time secretary and supporting staff, and offices at UNICEF headquarters in New York. Its membership consists of about twelve experts from different countries experienced in the

Examples of "Protein-rich Mixtures"

Product Name	Country	Composition	Protein content (per cent)
Incaparina	Guatemala	Maize, cottonseed flour, vitamin A, lysine, calcium carbonate	27·5
	Colombia	Same, plus defatted soybean flour	27·5
	Mexico	Same, plus defatted soybean flour but without cottonseed flour	27·5
Fortifex	Brazil	Maize, defatted soybean flour, vitamins, methionine, calcium carbonate	30·0
Pronutro	South Africa	Maize, skim milk powder, groundnut, soybean, fish protein concentrate, yeast, wheat germ, vitamins, iodised salt	22·0
Arlac	Nigeria	Groundnut flour, skim milk powder, salts and vitamins	42·0
Supro	East Africa	Maize or barley flour, yeast, skim milk powder, salt, condiments	24·0
Indian "multi-purpose food"	India	Groundnut flour, chick pea flour, calcium carbonate, vitamins	40·0
Superamine	Algeria	Wheat, chick peas, skim milk powder, vitamin D	20·0
CSM	United States	Maize (precooked), defatted soybean flour, skim milk powder, vitamins, calcium	20·0
Dried skim milk			35·0

fields in which it operates. The main committee meets at least once a year and special sub-committees more frequently. The PAG lays down standards of acceptability for "protein foods" in general, and recommends appropriate methods of testing new products. It is interested in problems of storage and deterioration. It promotes studies of how unfamiliar food mixtures can be introduced into countries and popularised. Among its pre-occupations is whether pure amino acids, manufactured on a large scale, can be used to supply the needs of children for more protein. On this point it has so far adopted a cautious attitude.

The PAG has been described as follows in an FAO publication:[3]

"PAG has come to stand as a marked success in co-operation among international agencies as well as among experts drawn from outside the United Nations family. Because it is small and can call on any adviser it needs, the Group can respond rapidly to technical and scientific innovations relevant to the protein problem and inform those agencies best able to exploit them. In this sense PAG represents a world council on protein matters. It also provides the multidisciplinary approach needed to tackle a problem with so many different facets. Nevertheless, no matter how successful its efforts within the United Nations family, PAG's effectiveness will still be judged largely by the improved prospects for future life of preschool children, the group which indirectly led to its creation."

Chapter 14

Africa

AFRICA has been less prone to famine than Asia. The territories east and west of the Sahara are indeed subject to much the same system of monsoon rains as India and hence liable to droughts. To the east, there were serious droughts in Tanzania and Kenya in 1961 and 1966 respectively, but in each case the resulting food shortage was effectively dealt with by the government concerned, with help from the United Nations and voluntary agencies. Little loss of life took place. In 1973 some countries to the west of the Sahara were struck by severe drought and needed famine relief.

The hot humid territories of West (coastal) and Central Africa, where the rain forests flourish, rarely suffer from drought. There are, of course, good seasons and bad seasons, and "hungry months" before the harvest, but famine, when it occurs, is usually man-made rather than due to natural causes. In other words, it is the result of civil war and civil disturbances, which means in effect inter-tribal conflicts. A short account of two recent emergencies, in the Congo and Nigeria respectively, will illustrate aspects of famine prevention and relief in tropical Africa.

In 1960 fighting broke out between the Luluas and the Balubas in the Kasai province in the former Belgian Congo, which the Belgians had just hurriedly left. The Balubas were beaten and many thousands fled from their homes in the north and west of Kasai, to arrive in south Kasai destitute and almost starving, having been on the road for several months. Almost the only food the refugees could obtain was cassava, which is practically pure starch and devoid of protein. The principal result was not starvation—though there was a good deal of ordinary starvation—but a tremendous epidemic of kwashiorkor affecting mainly children but also some adults. A WHO nutrition specialist reported:[1]

"The seriousness of the situation became more obvious when the woeful inadequacy of the most important item—namely

128

sufficient food of good quality and of a high protein content—became apparent . . . However, thanks to a most generous relief action organised through the United Nations Operation in the Congo, with help from some other international agencies, supplies of food—dried skim milk, dried and canned fish, maize flour and rice—began to arrive by airlift from Leopoldville together with some medical supplies."

For treatment skimmed milk, as always, proved invaluable. It was given to the sick children in generous amounts—a minimum of 60 grammes, in terms of powder, per day—usually reconstituted as liquid milk, and accompanied by a gruel made of cassava or maize. Sometimes it was given in powder form, mixed with cassava or rice. Mortality was immediately reduced by this dietary treatment, and the state of most of the children quickly improved. A number of UN organisations contributed to the relief programme, which included measures other than emergency feeding. For example UNICEF supplied not only foods but also vehicles for distributing them and carrying relief workers from place to place. It also provided funds for training workers belonging to the Congolese Red Cross.

This epidemic of protein deficiency was part of the débâcle which led to the death in an air crash of Dag Hammerskjöld, Secretary-General of the United Nations. The situation was handled almost entirely by the United Nations and its Agencies. The runaway colonial power had not trained any local people for senior posts in the administrative and technical services. There were some Congolese hospital orderlies, but no district officers, school-masters or doctors.

Famine in Nigeria in 1967–69 was also due to inter-tribal conflict. In the modern country of Nigeria, with a population of about 55 million, there are three main ethnic groups—the Hausa-Fulani in the north, the Yorubas in the west and the Ibos in the east. Apart from these broad groups there are numerous tribal sub-divisions. The Ibos are mainly Christian and belong to various different Christian denominations, with Roman Catholicism predominating. They had benefited more from education, provided by the mission-aries and schools of the denominations to which they owed their conversion, than other Nigerians. Previous to 1967 many were employed in good jobs, administrative, technical and commercial, throughout the country, and a high proportion of army officers were

Ibos. Their success did not make them popular with their fellow countrymen.

The Federal Government, and the Federal Assembly, established after independence in 1960 and located in Kano in the Northern Region, failed to dominate the country. Discontent became general and lawlessness grew. Early in 1966 a group of army officers, mainly Ibos, organised a coup in which the Federal Prime Minister, the Premiers of the Western and Northern Regions and many senior army officers, were murdered. One senior Ibo officer attempted to restore law and order. He failed, and was murdered in his turn as were many more Ibo officers, particularly in the Western Region. All this resulted in the precipitate flight of Ibos into their own homeland in the east; at least 3 million people, including members of other tribes besides the Ibos, sought refuge in this region of the country, the total population of which was reckoned, early in 1967, at about 15 million. Their leaders declared that Biafra, the name which they gave to this territory, was independent of the rest of the country. A war of secession started in July 1967, and lasted for thirty months. Other Nigerians refused to recognise the existence of the state of Biafra, and in fact called its inhabitants not Biafrans but rebels.

In the 1960s Nigeria as a whole was nearly self-sufficient in food supplies, though a few important foods, such as dried salt cod (stockfish), processed milk, and wheat for bread-making, were obtained from abroad. There was normally much interchange of food between the different regions; for example, the Northern Region was the main source of meat, beans and groundnuts. Supplies of these and other foods to the rebel territories were cut down by a blockade imposed by the Federal Military Government before the Civil War began. Biafra itself produced cassava, yams, plantains, and red palm oil, and also goats and poultry in small quantity. Throughout the war it was short of many foods, but especially of foods rich in protein. Because of this there was a lethal outbreak of protein-deficiency disease in the middle of 1968, affecting the population confined within the contracting Biafran borders. Some starchy foods were procurable, notably cassava eaten as a sort of porridge called *gari*, and not many deaths from sheer starvation took place. But thousands of children died of kwashiorkor, or of clinical conditions very like kwashiorkor. From the clinical standpoint the situation had affinities with that in the Congo a few years earlier. In normal times, kwashiorkor is not common in eastern Nigeria. No reliable figures of the numbers of deaths are available; according to some reports, the death toll reached 1·5 million. But it is difficult to accept rough estimates put forward by hard-pressed missionaries, doing magnificent work in almost intolerable circumstances.

As the Federal Nigerian army advanced, slowly tightening its grip on Biafra, the area of the seceding territories, and the numbers of people confined to them, shrank. By August 1968, numbers were estimated at about 8 million, of whom about a half were children. The only access to Biafra from the outside world was through a two mile air-strip at Uli in the west of the rebel territories. A slender and perilous "air bridge" was established between this strip and the Portuguese islands of Fernando Po and São Tomé in the Bight of Benin and, somewhat later, Cotonou in Dahomey. Across this bridge, supplies of essential materials were carried, night after night, by dare-devil and highly-paid expatriate pilots. The planes were chartered by relief agencies—by the International Red Cross, the World Council of Churches and "Caritas", a Roman Catholic agency. The most essential of the materials transported were protein-rich foods for the children and of these the most important were skim milk powder, CSM* and stockfish. On one occasion an American pilot, flying a Boeing "stratofreighter", made three runs on one night, delivering 42 tons of food.

A system was built up for distributing foods from the air-strip to feeding centres. The principal centre was the Queen Elizabeth Hospital in Umuahia, the largest town in Biafra and the seat of the rebel government. The hospital itself, planned for a daily complement of 200 patients, sheltered about 800 in 1968; in the children's ward, designed for 20 beds and cots, there were never fewer than 80 children and often 120. About 300 children attended the outpatient department daily; here they were given food and the most seriously ill referred to the doctors. Some blood transfusions were given by two

---

* See Chapter 15. CSM was developed through the U.S. "Food for Peace Program" and has been supplied to many countries. Its principal ingredient is precooked corn (maize) flour, 70 per cent, with 25 per cent defatted soya flour and 5 per cent skim milk powder. Vitamins and essential minerals are also included. For young children the dry CSM powder is mixed with water in suitable proportions (1 to 4 is usual) and some salt and sugar added to improve the taste. The mixture is boiled for about five minutes and fed, warm or cold, to the children. A serving of about 80 grammes (2 to 3 ounces) will fulfil the protein requirements of a child and provide 300 calories.

medical students, one African and one British—the latter on the Oxfam pay-roll. Refrigerated blood for transfusion was flown in on most nights from Fernando Po.

The bulk of the protein-rich supplementary foods were distributed through village schools. A picture of how this was done is given in an article by a London paediatrician, Dr Bruno Ganz, published in the *Lancet* on 29 March 1969:[2]

"Feeding sessions at schools are held once, twice or three times a week and at each session between 700 and 1000 children are fed. The usual routine is to line the children up outside the school building, make them drink their half-pint of skimmed dried milk, then herd them into the school. When all have had their milk, the process is reversed and on emerging from the building each child is given a helping of vegetable and stock-fish stew. Most feeding-centres are denominational—that is, they are run by Catholic, Methodist, Mennonite or other staff. There is considerable rivalry between the various feeding-centres, and a fair amount of proselytising takes place. Also, despite the 'security' arrangements, an energetic child can have an early-morning Seventh Day Adventist breakfast and arrive at another centre a few miles away in time to be given a late Baptist meal."

The foods conveyed by the air-lift, with their somewhat happy-go-lucky denominational distribution, sufficed to check the high mortality among children which had occurred in the middle of 1968. They took the edge off starvation and malnutrition. Dr Ganz was struck by the high rate of recovery in Queen Elizabeth Hospital itself. The condition of expectant and nursing mothers, who participated in the supplementary feeding, also improved. But while deaths were prevented, the state of nutrition of all sections of the population, young and old, remained poor. An American team which visited Biafra in February 1969 reported that they did not see a single well-nourished child.[3] When, at the end of the Civil War in January 1970, the victorious Federal army admitted an international group of journalists into Biafra, the journalists were shocked by the poor state of the children and blamed both sides impartially.

With the cessation of hostilities, surveillance of relief in Biafra was taken over by the Federal Government. As a co-ordinating agency, the International Committee of the Red Cross (ICRC) was replaced by the Nigerian Red Cross. American foods were available in plenty in Lagos and the nutritional status of the population returned slowly to normal. A National Rehabilitation Commission was set up. The work done by the churches and voluntary agencies, in circumstances which were not only intensely difficult but also perilous when the bombs began to fall, together with the remarkable if ramshackle air-lift, had prevented thousands of deaths. Nigerians and expatriates in Biafra had risen bravely to the occasion.

To mention some of the shortcomings of the relief programme does not detract from what was accomplished. But in famine relief it is necessary to learn from mistakes. Hence it is justifiable to quote certain criticisms put forward by two workers with responsibility for nutrition and relief on the Federal Nigerian side—one a Nigerian, Dr A. Omololu,[4] and the other a Norwegian, Dr Cato Aall.[5] Both based their comments on what they saw in parts of Biafra taken over by the advancing Federal army rather than the situation in Biafra itself in the last stages of the war, but most of what they said was intended to apply to relief throughout the rebel territories.

Among the points made by Dr Omololu was that the foreign relief workers were ignorant of Nigerian life and customs and often left the country after a stay of only 2 to 3 months. Some of the foreign medical teams, he said, had no idea of tropical medicine or malnutrition, and their reports of numbers of patients and their diseases were outrageously wrong. The relief workers from abroad were responsible to the headquarters of their agencies in London or New York rather than to any local authority. Sometimes one agency did not know what another was doing. "The ICRC (the International Committee of the Red Cross)," said Dr Omololu, "started its work in Nigeria backed and motivated by lots of overseas sentimental propaganda and no actual experience or facts to direct its activities. It seems, in retrospect, that the ICRC was convinced that no Nigerian nor the Federal Government could help or give advice on its relief work in Nigeria."

Educated Nigerians outside Biafra were angered by clever propaganda put out by the Government of Biafra with the help of a Swiss "News Feature Service". Films produced by this service, shown on British television, convinced many viewers of the righteousness of the Biafran cause and the iniquity of their opponents.

It seems that famine in tropical Africa tends to assume a pattern which differs from that of famine in Asia. It is usually precipitated by Civil War rather than drought. Starchy foods, such as cassava and yams, remain available to some extent and prevent sheer starvation. But children are killed by protein deficiency. The Biafran famine was a confused catastrophe, but it demonstrated again the value of protein-rich supplements in saving life. It also demonstrated the need for a co-ordinated relief programme and the disadvantages of relief based on sectarian charity.

In the future, famine emergencies in Africa will no doubt be dealt with by Africans rather than by helpers from abroad. The African relief workers will scarcely follow the approach recommended by an African leader, who said: "Give men and women the foods to keep them alive and well. Never mind the children. We can make plenty more when the famine is over."

Chapter 15

Bihar, 1967

BIHAR, an area about the size of France lying mainly in the Ganges valley west of Bengal, has long been subject to drought and famine. It has been a Hindu Kingdom, a Province in British India, and is now the second largest State in Independent India, with a population of some 54 million. The antiquity of Bihar is attested by the fact that in the 6th century B.C. Prince Siddharta attained enlightenment in Gaya, near the present capital Patna, and later became as Gautama Buddha the founder of one of the world's great religions, a tolerant and unexacting religion which in due course spread throughout South and East Asia, but died out in Hindustan. Bihar can also claim a place in history as the original home of the sugar cane.

A terrible famine took place in the 18th century (1769–70) in Bihar and neighbouring areas. A contemporary estimate of mortality was one-third of a population of 30 million. It was this famine which prompted Warren Hastings to have an enormous granary, never to be filled, built in Patna "for the perpetual prevention of famine in these provinces" (Plate 2a). During the 100 years after this calamity, Bihar suffered from a series of less severe but nevertheless formidable famines. No doubt its gloomy record was partly responsible for the so-called "Panic Famine" of 1873–74 when the Government of India poured grain, relief workers and money into the province on the strength of reports of crop failure which later proved to be exaggerated, and found itself, after the panic had subsided, with 100,000 tons of uneaten rice on its hands (page 55).

In 1965 there was extensive drought in Bihar and adjacent territories. Next year, when reserves of food were almost exhausted, the monsoon failed almost completely, South Bihar being the area worst affected. As 1966 proceeded, phenomena characteristic of imminent famine appeared. The price of food rose sharply, beggars increased in numbers, and male villagers began to migrate into the few towns in search of jobs, leaving their dependants behind. About 90 per cent of the population lived in villages. Cattle and land were sold

135

at prices ruinous to the seller, and the people became depressed and listless.

Physical signs of approaching famine were soon evident. A team of doctors from the All-India Institute of Medical Sciences, New Delhi,[1] making a rapid survey late in 1966, found that, as usual, people belonging to the lowest socio-economic groups, and, within these groups, infants, young children and the old, were most affected. It was estimated that at least 5 per cent of infants and young children were suffering from severe undernutrition and malnutrition. Famine oedema was common in adults. Many continued to work in the fields in spite of mild oedema; only when the oedema became more grossly manifest, the team reported, did the victims begin to think that something serious was the matter with them. The team was struck by the high prevalence of anaemia in people of all ages.

The drought had turned the land into a sunbaked desert; in Bihar in 1966 not more than 7 per cent of cultivated land was protected by irrigation. Desiccation went so far that there was a serious shortage of water for drinking and domestic use, a shortage which seems to have been more acute than that recorded in most Indian famines of the past. Domestic animals suffered, and also wild animals whose plight was described in moving language by Ramalingaswami and his colleagues, as follows:

"The splendid wild life of South Bihar faced extinction. As the hill streams dried up, tigers and panthers frequented the remaining water holes. The fast-vanishing Indian gazelle showed up at water points in full view of people. One could see as one drove through the vast expanse of South Bihar an unending stretch of parched and dry fields."[1]

In Kipling's story in *The Second Jungle Book*, "How Fear Came", the animals declared a truce when they met at dwindling waterholes during a drought.

Bihar was regarded as one of the most backward States in India. The civil service lacked energy and efficiency and was below the level of the services in most other States. Politicians were preoccupied by an election which was held in February 1967, resulting in an overwhelming defeat of the Congress Party, possibly not sorry to be relieved of power at that particular moment. The coalition government which followed faced the emergency with some energy and courage. The Prime Minister of India, Indira Gandhi, after

touring Bihar and other drought-stricken areas some months previously, reported as follows to the nation:

"Countless millions of our people, men, women and children
. . . have had the bread taken out of their mouths by an abnormal
failure of the rains . . . Green fields that promised an abundant
harvest have withered. The grain has died on the stalk. The toil
and sweat of months have been reduced to dust. There is hunger
and distress in millions of homes."

Everything seemed set for an Indian famine of the traditional kind
with widespread starvation and high mortality. Pessimists pointed
out that Bihar had the lowest income per caput in India and that
more than a quarter of its agriculturists were landless labourers, a
class highly vulnerable in times of famine. The American Ambassa-
dor, Mr Chester Bowles, reported that "although there is much
uncertainty and, in some quarters, much confusion, we are watching unfold what could be a tragedy of major proportions".

The tragedy never unfolded, to the surprise of some knowledge-
able people in responsible positions. It never unfolded because, as
Ramalingaswani and his colleagues[1] claimed, "the most massive
and stupendous relief operation ever known in history was mounted".
The flow of food came mainly from the United States—actually 9
million tons of wheat, equivalent to one-fifth of the U.S. annual
crop, were sent, to India. An armada of 600 ships, arriving in India
at the rate of three a day, was needed to transport food supplies for
Bihar and other drought-stricken areas. Food ships destined for other
parts of the world were diverted to India. The internal movement of
food, by rail and road from the ports, was successfully organised by
the Government of India and the State governments concerned.
Some of the food needed in the deficient areas was procured within
India. The principal cereal used in relief was necessarily wheat;
while many Biharis prefer rice, they have learnt to tolerate wheat
within recent decades.

With abundant imported food at their disposal, the central and
state governments followed the Famine Code, still enjoying high
status in Independent India. The principal measure was the establishment of a "fair price" ration shop in every fourth village throughout the State, some 150,000 being opened in threatened areas. At
these, men and women, in accordance with the principles of the
Code, could obtain just enough grain for their needs at controlled

K

prices in return for wages paid for work of different kinds. In 1967 the shops sold about 2 million tons of grain to 30 million people. After famine was formally "declared" in April 1967, the ration became 10 ounces (280 g) per adult daily. Aged and infirm people were given food for nothing.

Most of the famine works were designed to save existing crops and raise short-term emergency crops. The digging and boring of wells and the installation of pumps were of great importance. In large areas in Bihar, abundant water, even in the worst droughts, lies not far beneath the surface of the land. Muscular young men of the American Peace Corps—there were nearly 900 of these in India in 1966—gave vigorous help in the sinking of wells, and Oxfam also participated actively in this kind of relief. Until the efforts of the government and the voluntary agencies ensured that enough accessible water was available, some villagers had to walk two miles to obtain water to drink. It was reckoned that about half a million shallow wells were dug, and perhaps 10,000 old wells were improved. No one died of thirst.

The measures taken to feed children were a significant and novel feature of the relief programme. In most villages there was a village school, not indeed an impressive or well-equipped building, but still a building which could be used as a feeding centre—a place where grain could be stored, and meals for children and expectant and nursing mothers prepared and issued. There was also, in each village, an ill-paid school headmaster, sometimes with one or two worse-paid assistants. The State Education Department employed 50,000 men and women to teach in some 25,000 elementary schools throughout the state. These were made responsible for emergency feeding. Some of them did not relish the job, which interrupted the teaching of children belonging to the higher castes whose parents could find food for them in spite of the famine. Many of those fed were outcasts* still on the edge of the educational system. The meals given at the schools were not the same everywhere. But they usually consisted of about 4 ounces of wheat and 1 to 2 ounces of some protein-rich food or mixture, mixed together in a porridge. Children aged 1 to 14 received the daily ration, with emphasis on the younger children who are particularly susceptible to malnutrition. Some 5 million children were sustained by the programme. In-

* Called "Harijans" or "Children of God" by Mahatma Gandhi and (for some obscure reason) "Scheduled Castes" by the British.

fants were benefited by the feeding of expectant and nursing mothers, which meant more abundant supplies of breast milk.

Skim milk powder was widely used as the protein-rich food for "strengthening" the porridge. As always, it proved an admirable food for malnourished children. It had the slight disadvantage that it was saleable in Calcutta and hence was liable to disappear during transport or in storage. But such depredations were never extensive. Apart from skim milk powder, various food mixtures, including the admirable CSM from America (see page 126), were supplied. A preparation called in India "multi-purpose food", consisting of groundnut flour and chick pea* flour, and containing added calcium carbonate and vitamins, was found to be particularly good. It had been manufactured in India for some years, but only on a small scale, and it was necessary to organise much greater production during the Bihar emergency. Then there was "Balahar" (which simply means "child's food") consisting of defatted oil-seed flour and wheat flour, with added vitamins and calcium. This preparation, sometimes known as Indian CSM was successfully used during the famine and subsequently manufactured on a considerable scale in India.

CARE and Oxfam gave valuable help to the Government of Bihar in organising and running the feeding programme through the schools. CARE provided a considerable proportion of the various foods needed and Oxfam substantial quantities of skim milk powder, paid for by the British public. At its peak the programme was impressive. An Oxfam field officer reported:

"There is something very satisfactory in driving along roads any morning and passing hundreds of women and children, clutching plates, making their way to the nearest school; or to go miles into the jungle along really rough terrain and arrive unexpectedly at a school to find the preparation of food under way and beneficiaries beginning to arrive."

The most striking thing about the operation was the good it did the children. After perhaps ten weeks of regular feeding their behaviour and appearance changed. Misery was replaced by the good spirits of childhood. They put on some weight and the dull dry skin

---

* *Cicer arietinum*—a legume widely consumed in India and commonly called Bengal gram.

of hunger and malnutrition became less evident. Those in charge of the centres did not keep careful records of physical changes; they were not doctors and had plenty of other things to do. But they could use their eyes. All agreed that the condition of the children fed at the centres was better after the famine than it had been before the famine began. A daily meal providing 450 calories and 18 grammes of protein brought about this difference, making it clear that poor village children in Bihar (or for that matter everywhere in India) are wretchedly fed at the best of times. A Government of India publicity officer wrote, with perhaps some exaggeration:

"For the poorest sections of the society, 1967, the Year of the Famine, will long be remembered as a bonus year when millions of people, especially children, probably for the first time, were assured of a decent meal a day. In a 'normal year', these people hover on the bread line. They are beyond the pale, nobody's concern, they starve. In a famine year, they eat. Their health is better and the children are gaining weight. For them this is a year of great blessing. This was the deep irony, the grim tragedy of the situation."[2]

Workers in the feeding centres noted differences in the value of the various "protein supplements". These were all good, including of course the father and mother of them all, skim milk powder. But many observers gave top marks to "Indian multi-purpose food". This preparation, devised in the Central Food Technological Research Institute in Mysore as a modification of a preparation made in California, can readily be produced in large amounts for the benefit of malnourished children in India.

Famine in Bihar was kept at bay until the rains came in the middle of 1968 and new crops were planted, to be reaped some months later. No exceptional mortality was recorded. No one died of starvation. What were the factors underlying this achievement? The most important was, of course, the influx of food from America. In no previous famine in India had so much food for relief been available, and with modern communications its transport from the ports to the hungry countryside was easy. The Famine Code indicated methods of distribution to adults. Epidemic disease was not a serious menace: malaria has been largely eradicated in India, and outbreaks of smallpox and cholera are today easily controlled. The

feeding programme through the schools took care of the most
vulnerable sections of the population.

A remarkable feature of the emergency was the way in which the
Government of Bihar, after a slow start, rose to the occasion. With
some highly competent officials of the Government of India acting
as a spur, the slow moving administrative machinery of the State
was accelerated. A "Control Room" was set up in Patna, in which
data were collected and charted, on food stocks, food prices, disease,
deaths, water levels, numbers receiving relief and other essential
matters. Instructions by telegraph and telephone replaced the slow
postal circulation of government orders. Bulletins outlining the
current situation were broadcast over the radio. District officials
and their staffs were encouraged to show initiative. The voluntary
agencies unquestionably gave solid assistance and useful leadership,
and their representatives set a good example by the amount of work
they got through in twelve hours. But it was Biharis who saved Bihar.
It may be added that the State was fortunate in having, as Chairman
of the Bihar Relief Committee, a distinguished and trusted senior
statesman, Jayaprakash Narayan.

Some Indian publicists have drawn unfavourable comparisons
between the Bengal famine of 1943 and the averted Bihar famine of
1967—the first a British débâcle, the second an Indian triumph. But
this is not very fair. Bengal was short of rice in 1943 and so was the
rest of India, and rice was hard to come by. There was no American
ships unloading cargoes of food daily. The apparently invincible
Japanese were on the frontier and the government was burdened
with war-time anxieties. No system of food rationing in India had as
yet been worked out and applied. Trade in food was in the hands of
rapacious Bengali dealers who cared nothing for the hunger of other
Bengalis.

But the differences in the situations in Bengal in 1943 and in
Bihar twenty-four years later do not detract from the achievement in
1967, which was indeed another landmark in the history of famine.
This was not a small easily-managed local emergency; many
millions of people were in danger of death from malnutrition and
starvation. The scale of relief was immense and new measures for
feeding sections of the population were introduced. Nor does the
fact that much of the food needed came from across the ocean make
the achievement less creditable. Rather it underlines the responsibility of the world as a whole for relieving famine in one of its

nations. The same applies to the useful help given by foreigners in the relief operations.

In a book about the conquest of famine the Bihar emergency of 1967 deserves a prominent and honourable place.

Chapter 16

Bangladesh

WHEN Mahomed Ali Jinnah and his Moslem League made an independent federated Moslem/Hindu India impossible in the closing years of the British Indian Empire, it became necessary to partition the peninsula between the people of the two religions. There was no easy way of doing this and the solution reached in 1948, after much bloodshed, was clearly a shaky and impermanent compromise. The new Moslem country of Pakistan was divided into West Pakistan and East Pakistan, separated from each other by over 1000 miles of Indian territory. The two parts of the country differed from each other in almost everything except religion, and even with regard to religion the similarity was not clear cut, since East Pakistan, though mainly Moslem, retained millions of Hindus living near its borders with India. The presence of these Hindus was to prove a dangerous factor in the Civil War of 1971 which led up to the establishment of Bangladesh. West Pakistan had 50 million inhabitants as compared with 70 million in East Pakistan, but was five times larger in size. East Pakistan was, in fact, one of the most densely populated areas in the world. Two completely different languages (with different scripts) were spoken, Urdu in West, and Bengali in East, Pakistan. Their products had little in common: West Pakistan grew and consumed wheat and East Pakistan rice, while the most valuable export crop of the country as a whole—jute—was grown exclusively in the hot humid delta country of what for centuries had been Bengal.

In 1969 General Yahya Khan, who succeeded the dapper Ayub Khan as dictator, planned to set up an elected civilian government which would take over power from the military dictatorship. Accordingly he arranged an election in both sections of the country on the basis of one man, one vote. This had disconcerting results. The leader of what was known as the Awami League in East Pakistan, Sheikh Mujibur Rahman, gained 160 out of 162 seats in the Assembly of East Pakistan and thereby control of the 313 seat National (all-Pakistan) Assembly. He put forward Six Points which, for practical purposes, meant secession for East Pakistan. A meeting of the National Assembly, to be held in Dacca in March 1971, was boycotted by the elected leader of West Pakistan, Z. A. Bhutto, and President Yahya Khan postponed the Assembly indefinitely. But things had gone too far and what amounted to civil war between West and East Pakistan broke out, with murder, arson and loot on one side and cruel military occupation on the other. The West Pakistani soldiers, mostly Punjabi Moslems, were indeed far from home; they could reach Bengal only by a circuitous air journey via Ceylon so as to avoid flying over Indian territory. But they were tough and well-armed, and regarded themselves as the finest troops in the Indian peninsula, despising by old tradition all Bengalis, whether Moslem or Hindu. Burnings and massacres provoked thousands of villagers into flight in the direction of India. This movement, once started, gathered momentum, and soon millions of refugees were trudging along the roads of Bengal, taking with them some portable household belongings and sometimes a little food. Most were Hindus, since the West Pakistani army had displayed special brutality towards Hindus, and the Hindus felt they could not survive in a country dominated by Punjabi Moslems.

In 1943 starving Bengali villagers had walked along the same roads and paths towards Calcutta in search of food. The 1971 migration was of a different kind, prompted by fear and not by starvation. But it seems that the exodus from East Pakistan was on a scale never previously recorded in history. Attempting to convey its extent, a journalist said: "suppose the whole population of Scotland suddenly decided to walk into England, needing shelter and food when they had crossed the border". Over 9 million refugees from East Pakistan reached India between April and October 1971.

The Government of India set up some 1150 camps to accommodate—if that is the right word—from 2000 to 50,000 refugees each. These were located in Indian territory round the borders of East Pakistan, and many were spread along the routes from Pakistan to the urbanised part of West Bengal. It was essential to stop swarms of refugees from reaching the foetid crowded slums of Calcutta. There was, however, one very big camp, called Salt Lake Camp, housing some 160,000 people, on the northern edge of Calcutta, near the airport. Because of its proximity to the air-conditioned hotels of the capital, Salt Lake Camp was convenient for showing distinguished visitors how the emergency was being handled. They could be back in their hotels for a cold beer and lunch after a morning expedition.

In May and June there was an outbreak of cholera among the refugees, and a major epidemic was feared. But inoculations and elementary sanitation soon brought the disease under control, rather to the surprise of the western world. As has been said elsewhere, the effectiveness of modern medicine and public health in dealing with infectious disease is not yet generally realised.

The housing in the camps varied greatly. At first tarpaulins, slung over poles and pinned to the earth at the edges, were the main stand-by. But the supply of tarpaulins soon gave out. Then there were hovels of straw and palm thatch, or hovels with walls of coconut matting, and polyethylene sheets for roofs. Large drain pipes proved very serviceable as living quarters in some camps. Everything became more difficult when the rains broke in June, presaging a monsoon of exceptional ferocity, which, lasting as usual about three months, transformed East Pakistan into a flooded quagmire with some drier spots along the sides of roads and railways. Given the absence of sanitation in the earlier stages, ditches traversing the camps were turned into malodorous sewers.

Yet, somehow or other, the camps provided succour for millions of people. Drawing on what he saw in October 1971, an American observer wrote:

"Housing 'structures'—they can hardly be called buildings—are neatly aligned in streets. There are warehouses for the food rations, elementary hospitals, the beginnings of schools. Wells have been drilled and equipped with power pumps. Latrines are being built and the stench from the earlier absence of all sanitary facilities has been suppressed by a liberal spreading of chloride of lime. In all the camps, those who were in business in East Bengal have again set up shop, for wherever more than two people congregate in India, one opens a store. Often the total stock-in-trade is a few cents' worth of sticks for cooking fuel or a handful of greens. A couple of crude tables and some chairs make a tea shop. Presiding, not without authority, over each of these vast and sudden communities is the camp commandant, like many others concerned with the refugee effort usually a former Indian Army officer. Many people owe their survival to the availability of these men who are experienced in the best British Army tradition of camp sanitation, administration and discipline and accustomed (also like British officers) to exercising authority with more than a modicum of pleasure."[1]

But here our main concern is the feeding of the refugees. Many of those reaching the camps, particularly the children, were in a miserable condition after several weeks on the road. Dr Ramalingaswami, Director of the All India Institute of Medical Sciences in Delhi, reported in July 1971 that one-fifth of the children under five were critically malnourished. There were numerous deaths, but no accurate records were kept of their number.* Bravely the Government of India embarked on the tremendous task of feeding the millions of survivors, drawing on the experience gained a few years previously in Bihar.

Food was conveyed to the camps and stored in warehouses, and ration cards given to families as they arrived. These enabled them to obtain 14 ounces of rice or wheat and 3.5 ounces of legumes per head daily, together with vegetables and some salt and oil. About a pound of fuel for cooking was distributed. But the children also needed foods to satisfy their protein requirements. They were given supplements which had proved so efficacious in Bihar and elsewhere —skim milk powder, Indian multi-purpose food, CSM and "Balahar" (Chapter 15). UNICEF and various voluntary agencies helped in the care and feeding of the refugees, but the Government of India was primarily responsible for the operations. Dr Nevin Scrimshaw, a well-known American nutrition specialist and a member of a team which accompanied Senator Edward Kennedy to Bengal (see below) wrote:

"The organisational, administrative and humanitarian accomplishments of the Government of India in providing food and shelter for some 5 million refugees in the short period of 4½ months was a remarkable achievement without historical precedent. The number a month later was 6 million in camps and a total of 8.6 million refugees . . . This extraordinary achievement merits much greater recognition and appreciation by the world community."[2]

It is indeed necessary not to overlook the assistance given by the voluntary agencies; for example, Oxfam provided £230,000 for

* Wiser than the author, the Government made no attempt to estimate mortality (see page 77).

refugee relief, which was spent on vaccines, inoculations instruments, tarpaulins, roofing materials, tents, saline solution, powdered milk, medical equipment, vitamin tablets and drugs. But the contributions of all the voluntary agencies put together represented only a small fraction of the total cost and the total programme of relief.

A striking fact about this emergency was the conviction of the outside world that a major famine, leading to millions of deaths in India and East Pakistan itself, was imminent, and more or less unavoidable. It was felt that within East Pakistan, soon to become Bangladesh, civil disturbance and the breakdown of local administration and transport, would prevent the reaping and distribution of the harvest. Similar forebodings of extensive disaster had been voiced during the Bihar emergency of 1967. In October 1971, Oxfam published a document called *The Testimony of Sixty*[3] in which the impressions of sixty people who had recently visited Bengal were presented, beginning with those of Senator Edward Kennedy who had toured part of the area outside East Pakistan in August. The keynote was struck in an Introduction by the Director of Oxfam:

> "Let the facts speak. Perhaps it is that we just cannot comprehend the extent of the disaster. A population the size of Sweden and New Zealand together have already fled from their homeland. *Millions* more who remain face famine. It does not bear thinking about. But we must."

But once again the catastrophe of large-scale famine was averted The phenomena seen in Bihar were repeated. The people receiving regular rations for a few months began to flourish, particularly after the monsoon abated. The children, sustained by extra protein, became playful and boisterous, smiling at the world. Indian officials from other states, visiting the camps, asked foreign relief workers what all the fuss was about; the people in the camps, they said, were in a better physical condition than poor villagers in normal times. This improvement again showed that many of the inhabitants of rural Bengal—whether this is called East Pakistan or Bangladesh—live on an inadequate diet even when undisturbed by civil war or other calamities. The same applies to much of the rest of India. A little more good food, consumed regularly, and particularly additional food rich in protein for the children, would greatly improve the health and well-being of the population.

The Government of India spent about 450 million dollars in 1971 on the care and feeding of the refugees within India. Foreign countries and agencies contributed or pledged about 100 million dollars. It has been reckoned that the net cost for India was equivalent to about one-fifth of the present annual expenditure on economic and social development. Any check to development is much to be deplored, but the burden of looking after the refugees was not crippling. Nor was there any difficulty in finding the supplies of foods they needed.

In November 1971, no end to the emergency was in sight. Then, on 3 December, war broke out between India and Pakistan, the Indian army entered East Pakistan in force and on 16 December the Pakistan army capitulated. The remarkable Parsi General, Sam Maneckshaw, chief of staff of the Indian army,* with his magnificent moustache, took the surrender of the Pakistanis in Dacca, offering them the full protection of the Geneva Convention as prisoners of war. For a moment, graduates of the same military academies, trained in the traditions of the British army, met in honourable accord. Bangladesh was established as an independent country and was soon recognised by India. At the end of January it was recognised by the U.S.S.R., the first country outside India to do so.

Among the most formidable problems to be faced was that of getting 9 million refugees out of India and back into Bangladesh. The Indian authorities declared the intention of repatriating 80 per cent of the refugees by the end of February and the rest by the end of March. The camps were closed one by one and reception centres set up to handle the flood of migrants, this time moving in the opposite direction. They were somehow fed en route and given a little "journey money". They were also allowed to carry home some useful supplies from the camps—clothing, blankets, utensils and some rations. Some were transported by train or bus. Feeling and looking better for their incarceration in India, they reached their former homes, or what was left of them, and were well received by their stay-at-home neighbours. Help in rehousing was given by UN agencies and voluntary agencies, especially CARE. Contrary to expectations, there was no shortage of rice at that time in Bangladesh. The 1971 *aman* crop had been an excellent one, with fewer mouths than usual to eat it.

Within four months of the surrender all the reception centres

* In January 1973 he became the first Indian Field-Marshal.

had closed down and it was claimed that the repatriation exercise had been 100 per cent successful.

The new country of Bangladesh, though beset by appalling political, economic and social problems, seemed to make a fair start. An experienced newspaper correspondent, describing the first meeting between President Bhutto of Pakistan and Prime Minister Indira Gandhi of India to discuss the future of the country, could give his article the headline: "Bangladesh confounds the pessimists". Other commentators reported in the same strain. But subsequently the pessimists seemed more justified. The country was scarred by the Civil War, railways, roads and bridges were damaged or destroyed, and behind all this were black memories of arson, torture and execution. Fields were neglected, and fertilisers and pesticides were scarce. But starvation had so far been avoided. India has continued to supply grain, as she did during the exodus and return, up to the amount of 900,000 tons during the remainder of 1972. India could, however, provide little in 1973 because of formidable drought and her own heavy needs.

In March 1973, Sheik Mujibur Rahman was unanimously elected head of Bangladesh. The most urgent problem which he faces is the feeding of his 70 million people, who are likely to increase at the rate of 3 per cent per annum.

Chapter 17

More Food

WHETHER the world can provide enough food to feed its expanding population obviously depends on the quantity of food which can be produced and the numbers to be fed. Let us consider first the expansion of food production which is possible in the modern world. Many striking examples could be given of the increases which have taken place through the development of agriculture, especially in recent years. Two common foods, namely sugar and wheat, are convenient for purposes of illustration.

To choose sugar as one of these may seem strange, since sugar is not a staple food, like one of the cereals. Moreover, nutritionally speaking, it is an "incomplete" food, being pure carbohydrate and lacking protein, fat and vitamins. Early in the 19th century physiologists discovered that a dog could not live long on sugar and water alone. But in spite of its nutritional shortcomings, sugar is a most useful source of energy; one gramme provides four calories. In certain countries, for example, the United Kingdom, it contributes as much as 18 per cent of the total calories provided by the national diet, and in most of the world its contribution of calories, though smaller than this, is rising all the time. Sugar has thus come to occupy an important position in the world's larder. Because of its sweet taste it appeals strongly to children and adults, and those used to plenty of sugar are unhappy when deprived of it. A survivor of Wingate's disastrous campaign in Burma in 1942 told me that in his hunger in the jungle he craved for sweet things above all else; visions of well-stocked confectioners' shops kept floating before his eyes amongst the trees.

Nearly all the world's sugar comes from the sugar cane and the sugar beet. Sugar is a relatively recent ingredient in the human diet. For millennia after the birth of agriculture, cereals, supplemented by legumes, were the main source of calories for man, occasional sweetness being provided by honey, a rare and precious food. The cane was first cultivated in India in the second half of the first millennium B.C., small amounts of crude sugar being extracted from it and crystallised by primitive methods. It did not reach Western Asia and Europe until many centuries later, and was for practical purposes unknown in Ancient Greece and Rome. In the Middle Ages, there was a small trade in sugar between Egypt, North Africa and Southern, Central and Western Europe, making sugar available in limited amounts to the nobility at a fantastic price. It was also used to disguise the taste of the horrible medicines of the day.

The transatlantic slave trade—an odious episode in human history from which some of the troubles of the modern world have sprung—began in the 16th century and lasted for three centuries. Its primary motive was the cultivation in the tropics of the sugar cane, from which sugar was extracted and transported to Europe. The busy and highly lucrative sugar industry based on slaves and the sailing ship made sugar a most abundant and cheaper commodity in Europe and North America. In England, for example, per caput consumption rose from about 2 kg a year in 1700 to about 6 kg in 1780, the demand being stimulated by the growing popularity of two other tropical products, coffee and tea. But it remained an expensive luxury, largely beyond the means of the poor. The craving for sweetness of Europeans and North Americans was still far from satisfied.

Two new developments made sugar a cheap and abundant food. One was the spread of the cane throughout most of the tropics, leading to sugar production on a large scale in countries not dependent on slave labour. The other was the discovery of the sugar beet as a source of sucrose. Beet sugar is one of the few important human foods whose production and processing have been based almost entirely on science and technology, beginning with its extraction and crystallisation by Margraff in 1740. There is, of course, no difference in the refined white substance, for practical purposes sucrose, which emerges from the processing of the cane and the beet. The present proportion (1972), in terms of global production, is 60 cane sugar to 40 beet sugar.

The world now possesses resources for producing sugar, from both the cane and the beet, on a very large scale. The following chart shows the growth in world supplies since 1900. In 1970 world production of refined sugar was nine times larger than at the beginning of the century, involving huge expansion both in cultivation and factory capacity. FAO has forecasted that a figure of about 93 million tons will be reached in 1980, implying a continuing increase in output of 2 million tons a year. In a series of FAO "Commodity Studies", the curious picture of world sugar consumption, reflecting human craving for sweetness, has been presented. The United Kingdom, together with Australia, consumes between 50 and 60 kg of sugar per head annually, which supplies about 18 per cent of total calories. This seems to be the upper limit of consumption; apparently no country can, or wants to, swallow more sugar than that. In the U.K. consumption has remained almost stationary for

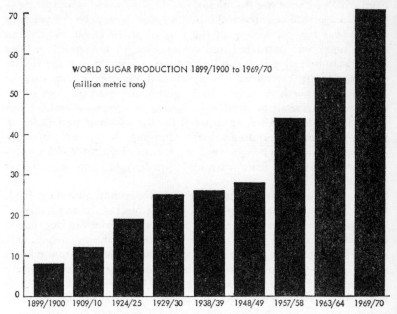

WORLD SUGAR PRODUCTION 1899/1900 to 1969/70
(million metric tons)

ten years and has even declined a little. In some countries with different dietary patterns—France, for example—the summit is a good deal lower, say 40 to 50 kg annually. There are plenty of countries well below the summit, but mounting the ladder all the time. In these, urbanisation is rapidly extending and sugar is a food highly favoured by town dwellers. It fits into their dietary practices. During recent decades, according to FAO, the greatest increase in consumption has been in Latin America, the Near East and Africa. At the outbreak of the second world war the ten high-consuming countries of North-West Europe, with the United States,

5 Water to drink, Maharastra 1973.

6a Norman Ernest Borlaug, Nobel Peace Prize winner, 1970. Originator of new high-yielding varieties of cereals, and hence of the Green Revolution.

6b 'Clouds of Hope'. The coming of the monsoon after long drought, India 1973.

Australia and New Zealand, accounted for 52 per cent of the world utilisation of refined sugar; in 1958 their share was only 39 per cent. During the same period consumption rose rapidly in southern and eastern Europe and in many parts of Asia. The rates of increase in some countries well down the consumption scale have been remarkable—from 100 to 200 per cent in ten years.

This was the picture in 1958; recent studies have shown that since that date similar trends have prevailed in accentuated form. Consumption continues to "falter" in a few affluent countries and to rise steeply in most developing countries. Trends are so clear-cut and universal that FAO can confidently predict a world output of 93 million tons in 1980. The rising curve of sugar production and consumption from 1900 to 1980 is much steeper than that of world population—from 8 to 93 million tons as compared with 2600 to 3500 million people, according to a "medium" United Nations estimate. It has followed human demand, with consumption expanding as more people can afford it. No "wonder canes" or "wonder beets" giving much greater yields have been evolved. Improvements in existing methods of cultivation and sugar technology have shown themselves capable of fulfilling the growing demand. The International Sugar Organisation, which sponsors international sugar agreements from time to time, is more concerned with the abundance than the scarcity of sugar, and seeks to ensure that producing countries find markets for their sugar at satisfactory prices.

Sugar, as has been said, lacks some essential nutrients; it compares unfavourably with familiar cereals in nutritive value. In certain forms it is bad for our teeth. Some people think that it causes other diseases. One of the most striking changes in the human diet during the last century has been the large increase in sugar intake and when some new, or apparently new, disease makes its appearance it is likely to be ascribed, without convincing evidence, to too much sugar.

Wheat is another story, and here what has been called "The Green Revolution" is of great importance. This term, originating in India, usually relates to the remarkable increase in wheat production resulting from the evolution of "dwarf" varieties of wheat which give yields per acre three or four times larger than those of earlier varieties grown in the same locality. These high-yielding varieties were first evolved in Mexico and were ready for distribution only a few years ago. Dwarf varieties of rice, developed mainly in Japan and the Philippines, are proving almost equally productive. The

L

quality of dwarfing is associated with larger yields because the dwarf plants have shorter, stiffer stems, half the length of those of ordinary strains of wheat, and can utilise large quantities of fertilisers without becoming top heavy through the weight of the ears and bending over—a process called "lodging". They have other qualities. Resistance to rust is built into their genetic constitution. They are relatively independent of season and the duration of daylight, which facilitates the cultivation of more than one crop on the same fields annually. On the other hand, they may be more susceptible to certain parasites to which the crops they replace have become immune, and, most importantly, they have high moisture needs. To flourish, they must be grown on land with an assured watersupply. Further, their very nature as high-yielders calls for fertilisers in abundance.

Wheat is the world's most widely-grown food plant, the seeds of which are eaten in various forms by more than 1000 million people. It has been cultivated for perhaps 10,000 years and was the staple food of the earliest civilisations in western Asia. In one form or another it is acceptable to most human beings. Bread, for example, is a most convenient food for city-dwellers, and even rice-eaters learn to consume it as a partial substitute for their own beloved grain. The evolution of the new varieties of wheat, and consequent spurt in production, are the latest chapter in its long history. They accelerate trends which have prevailed during the present century. Annual world wheat production rose from about 125 million metric tons in 1900–10 to almost 300 million tons in the early 1960s, i.e. it more than doubled during this period. Success was achieved in raising yields both by the genetic evolution of new strains and by improving conditions of cultivation; for the best results, both are needed. From start to finish, i.e. from the selection and sowing of the seed to consumption in the home, the wheat industry has become increasingly subject to the influence of science and technology.[1] But even allowing for this general progress, the contribution of the new dwarf varieties to world supplies during recent years is a remarkable one. They were evolved by the "Mexican International Maize and Wheat Improvement Centre", which has been supported since 1944 by the Rockefeller Foundation and later by the Ford Foundation—two offshoots of the capitalist system—working in collaboration with the Government of Mexico. The Centre, as its name shows, has been concerned with maize as well as wheat, but its main business has been with wheat. Originally intended to help Mexico itself—and it has enormously helped Mexico—it has become an institution of world-wide importance. Its achievements can be illustrated by a sentence from a recent review: "The dwarf varieties of wheat, Sonora 64 and Leima Rogo 64, commonly yield 4 tons per hectare and sometimes 5 to 8 tons, in conditions where the usual yield with standard varieties is 1·3 tons."

The Director of the Centre, Dr Norman E. Borlaug (Plate 6a), is an American of Scandinavian descent, a plant pathologist by training. He has not only directed the scientific side of the programme but has also done much to introduce the new varieties into countries in Asia and elsewhere. He has been supported by a carefully selected staff of high calibre. Scientific workers elsewhere were intrigued to hear that candidates for posts had to spend three months in the Centre before their appointments were ratified, and that during this probationary period they had to be accompanied by their wives, both wife and husband being kept under observation. A difficult and discontented wife can cause a lot of trouble in an isolated research institution.

In October 1970, Borlaug was awarded the Nobel Peace Prize. The award of a *peace* rather than a scientific prize is interesting. Nobel scientific prizes are usually given for research which adds substantially to knowledge and opens up new scientific vistas, and the Nobel Committee may have felt that the creation of new cereal strains by already familiar techniques did not fall into this exalted category. On the other hand, the Committee may also have felt that the giving of a Peace Prize would convey the idea that the work accomplished would influence the future stability and well-being of mankind.

Led by its Director, the Centre in Mexico has carried out what he has called "two decades of aggressive research". As might be expected, the results in Mexico itself have been particularly impressive. The production of wheat rose from 1190 million tons in 1960 to 2100 million tons in 1970. Mexico has become self-sufficient in wheat for the first time. This increase has not adversely affected the production of other foods. Beans are a traditional food in Mexico; some of the species of beans now grown in many countries were originally domesticated by neolithic communities in this part of the world. The Mexicans have not abandoned their favourite food (an important source of protein), because of abundance of wheat; according to figures issued by the U.S. Department of Agriculture, the production of beans has increased substantially during the last decade, and at the same time livestock production has gone up by 40 per cent. Mexico was, of course, in a particularly good position to benefit from the research carried out within its own borders. Many young Mexican scientists who took part in the programme of the Centre were available to help Mexican farmers to make use of its findings.

For countries outside Mexico wishing to introduce the "wonder seeds", special arrangements were necessary, which are described by Borlaug in his Nobel Lecture. Centres with programmes and objectives similar to those of the Mexican "Improvement Centre" have been brought into existence in different parts of the world—in the Philippines, Columbia, Nigeria, India and Pakistan, some of these being assisted financially by U.S. foundations. In the Philippines the "International Rice Research Institute", concerned with the world's other major cereal food, has been highly successful. A network of contacts and communication between the centres in Mexico and the Philippines and centres elsewhere has facilitated the dissemination of the new strains of wheat and rice, and their adjustment to local conditions by local research workers. Agricultural scientists in Pakistan evolved a cross between a wheat strain produced in Mexico and a local strain, which they called: "Mexi-Pak"; this gave excellent yields until it was replaced by something better. Borlaug believed in using, from time to time, research workers immersed in the details of plant physiology to educate ignorant farmers in methods of cultivating new strains, thereby forcing the research workers to realise the real troubles of the cultivator. This policy of closely associating research with what the Americans call "extension" services, has proved most successful in several countries.

In 1965 there were poor harvests resulting from drought, notably in India and Pakistan, and in India, as we have seen, what threatened to be a calamitous famine in Bihar was averted only by the import of large quantities of American surplus wheat. After droughts there are usually abundant rains and bumper crops and this happened after the bad years of the mid-sixties. But something else also happened, namely the dissemination of the "wonder-seeds". The dwarf varieties of wheat began to be extensively grown, not only in India and Pakistan, but also in Afghanistan, Turkey, Lebanon,

Morocco and other countries. A "production explosion" ensued. In India, for example, the production of wheat rose by over 50 per cent in a few years, and there was much the same order of increase in West Pakistan, which soon became self-sufficient. Wheat production figures for the last 12 years in the "Far East" (mainly India and Pakistan) as reported in the latest FAO review, "The State of Food and Agriculture, 1972", are as follows:

Wheat Production (*million metric tons*)

1960	14·71	1964	14·57	1968	23·62
1961	15·32	1965	17·43	1969	25·99
1962	16·61	1966	14·06	1970	28·14
1963	15·4	1967	16·35	1971	30·28

FAO[2] reports that "a number of new high-yielding wheat varieties with better consumer acceptability, short growing season and adaptability over a wider area were released in these countries during 1971 for irrigated and dryland farms".

Two points in this statement are of special interest. The first is the reference to "consumer acceptability". At one time it was being said that the new strains made unpalatable bread. The other is the reference to "dryland farms", suggesting that strains less dependent on abundant irrigation are being evolved.

The increase in rice production in some countries in Asia has been almost equally dramatic. For example, production in Ceylon has increased by 34 per cent. In the early 1960s the Philippines imported a million tons of rice annually. The country is now self-supporting and will soon become rice-exporting. Japan, where basic pioneer work on high-yielding dwarf varieties of rice was done, now has a troublesome rice surplus. Overseas markets for rice are shrinking.

All this is hopeful and encouraging, but in his Nobel Peace Prize lecture Borlaug expressed resentment at statements on the part of critics that the Green Revolution has created more problems than it has solved, pointing out that it is better to be faced by problems of plenty than those of scarcity. It has certainly created problems—agricultural, economic and social. The new varieties will at first benefit mainly the larger farmers with some capital who possess good irrigated land and storage facilities, and can buy the necessary fertilisers and pesticides. They will be of less benefit to small-holders

and landless agricultural workers. Landless labourers, a large group
in countries like India and Pakistan, will be driven in increasing
numbers off the land by unemployment into cities which lack industries, and are not ready to receive them. But this seems to be too
simple a view of the situation. An authoritative report said in 1969:
"In some areas in India wholly new phenomena are being observed;
farmers looking hard for labour and complaining they cannot get it;
wages at least doubled since 1957; and many more jobs outside
farming too, as the farmers spend their new wealth. Similarly, rising
incomes from farm exports are soon spent on goods that require
more *industrial* workers to make them."[3]

But agronomical problems abound. The new seeds need heavy
dosing with nitrogen fertilisers, and India and Pakistan do not yet
produce nearly enough of these. But a unit weight of nitrogen
fertilisers, applied to the new crops, gives a return in terms of protein,
the chief constituent of which is nitrogen, twice as large as that given
by indigenous varieties. Local parasites may launch a vigorous
attack on the wonder crops, but Borlaug believes that the original
dwarf varieties from Mexico carry a wider spectrum of disease resistance than the local types they have replaced. Some new Indian
varieties are very resistant to parasites. Storage accommodation for
harvested grains, pesticides, fertilisers and seed is at present inadequate in the poor countries. The most basic need of all is for
more water. It is encouraging to learn that in parts of India where
the new crops are now being grown, large numbers of tube wells
have been sunk.

In a later lecture, given in November 1971 at the sixteenth session
of the FAO conference, Borlaug strongly criticised current efforts to
check the use of D.D.T. and other pesticides, and went so far as to
call his lecture "Mankind and civilisation at another crossroad".*,[4]
He said that conservationists and environmentalists, both in and out
of government, together with only partially informed people in the
communications media, have embarked on a crusade designed to
end the use of agricultural chemicals such as pesticides and fertilisers.† "They give no thought," he said, "to the end results of such
actions—the eventual starvation and political chaos that will

* 1971 McDougall Memorial Lecture. Frank McDougall was one of the
Founding Fathers of FAO.

† As had previously happened, in the Scandinavian countries, the use of
D.D.T. was made illegal in the U.S.A. in 1971.

plague the world." He also commented sourly that "sedentary conservationists on vacation from the cities, who know little about real farming or the countryside, are the most strident opponents of chemical pesticides and fertilisers".

If some crop suddenly gives much greater yields, this usually means that farmers will, if they can, plant more of it, displacing for the moment other crops with a constant out-turn. But greater abundance of any crop is likely to mean a fall in its selling price with less incentive to cultivate it. The introduction of the new varieties of wheat and rice will involve considerable adjustments in agriculture in Asia and elsewhere. Land will be freed for growing other vegetable crops and for the greater production of livestock. From the standpoint of human nutrition, these are changes in the right direction. But planning will be needed to ensure that long term results are favourable. At the moment agronomists are puzzled because the cultivation of the high-yielding varieties of wheat has been followed, at least in some areas (but not in Mexico), by a fall in the cultivation of legumes or pulses, foods of importance in the diet of peoples living largely on cereals because of their richness in protein. If this tendency continues, steps to check it will be necessary.

The Green Revolution promises further substantial increase in world cereal supplies. But these were already increasing before the Revolution dawned, and cereals are only one of the many foods that sustain mankind. There was indeed a period in the mid-1960s when food production seemed to be falling behind the growth of population, especially in Asia where the food situation is most precarious. Weather conditions were adverse and the prophets of Doom were able to enjoy themselves. Things picked up again, until once more, in 1972, the world was faced with extensive droughts leading to heavy calls on its food stocks (Chapter 20). But apart from such climatic vagaries, trends in food production have on the whole been favourable in the last two decades, though indeed the world production of fish has not grown in accordance with earlier hopes. Everywhere, or almost everywhere, agriculture and animal husbandry, guided by science, have become more efficient. Knowledge of genetics is increasingly applied both to crops and livestock. Farm machinery is being steadily improved. Fertilisers and pesticides are produced in larger quantities at lower prices. Modern methods of grass management and the replacement of hay by silage are important new developments, contributing, along with numerous other improvements in care and feeding, to the better health and greater size of livestock, and also to larger milk yields. The effects of technical progress are strikingly shown in the reduction in the man-power needed to produce a given quantity of food. In some technic-ally-advanced countries the point has been reached at which one man engaged in farming is able to supply the food requirements of some thirty families.[5]

The provision to poor countries of what is nowadays called "tech-nical assistance" is nothing very new. The imperial and colonial powers gave technical assistance, in agriculture and other fields, to dependent territories, though not very generously. Some countries, such as Japan, learned modern scientific procedures from technic-ally-advanced countries without being taught. But it is only since the second world war that "technical assistance" has become one of the world's major pre-occupations. "Experts" and funds have been made available to poor countries on a large scale, mainly through the United Nations and its Agencies. Not all this earnest effort has been successful; there are experts and experts and some coun-tries are difficult to assist. But by and large it has had substantial results.

The production of food is enormously and increasingly influenced by science and its vigorous application, but this is only one part of the story. What is called food technology is in certain respects as im-portant as production. In early days human beings consumed, more or less directly, the grain, meat, fish and fruit which the earth pro-vided. Now, at least in the developed countries, almost every in-gredient in the human diet passes through intricate processes before it reaches the table; it is subject, that is to say, to the operations of modern food technology. This vast subject cannot be adequately discussed here, since food technology affects food supplies in a host of ways. One obvious way is effective preservation and the elimina-tion of waste. If, as may happen, there is a loss, from various causes, of 10 per cent of a food-crop between maturing, harvesting and consumption, the prevention of this loss is as valuable, in terms of total supplies, as an increase of 10 per cent in production.

Among the triumphs of food technology are substances such as margarine which we eat without knowing what they are made of, and "fruit juices" rich in synthetic vitamin C which never saw fresh fruit. It can confer edibility and palatability to foods and food mixtures which would not otherwise be eaten by human beings.

Some of the protein-rich food mixtures, which are proving so valuable in famine relief, fall into this category. Vitamins have been manufactured in bulk from non-edible materials, after their identification and synthesis. So have essential amino acids which enhance the nutritive value of proteins present in cereals and other common foods. The large-scale manufacture of vitamins is a peculiarly remarkable modern phenomenon. It is surprising to be shown, when visiting a large pharmaceutical factory, stocks of vitamins in powder form sufficient to supply the daily needs of millions of people for several years. Bread, in England and the United States, is "enriched" with several synthetic vitamins. The deficiency disease beri-beri, due to lack of a vitamin called vitamin B_1 or thiamine, was once very common in South and East Asia, including Japan. Today the Japanese make large quantities of pure vitamin B_1 in modern factories; they swallow this powder in various ways and no longer suffer from beriberi. They also export it in large quantities to other countries in South and East Asia.

Like vitamins, protein, fat and carbohydrate—the "energy-yielding" nutrients—can be synthesised from non-food sources, especially coal and petroleum. But in general such synthesis is at present a laborious and expensive process and has not yet reached the stage of large-scale commercial development. During the second world war, German chemists made edible synthetic fat from coal, to the delight of Hitler, but not in sufficient amounts to make a significant contribution to German food supplies. Formaldehyde, an inexpensive product derived from petroleum or natural gas, can be made to yield glucose and other sugars, which in turn can be built up into sucrose, starch and other carbohydrates. But the commercial manufacture in this way of starch, the principal carbohydrate in human diets, would scarcely be feasible. "Starch synthesised from sugars, themselves made from formaldehyde—even assuming that such synthesis can be worked up into an industrial process—will always be more expensive under normal circumstances than natural starch from cereals or roots."[6]

The principal constituents of proteins, the amino acids, can and have been synthesised, and some have been made in bulk in pharmaceutical factories. Special attention has been given to lysine, in which cereal proteins are relatively deficient. The addition of lysine to cereal foods increases their nutritive value for animals and man. The same effect could be produced by the selective breeding of grains containing protein with a high lysine content, a problem to which attention is now being given.

The United Nations has published a report called "International Action to Avert the Impending Protein Crisis".[7] This report states that "it is essential that the United Nations family urgently take action aimed at closing the present gap between world protein needs and protein supplies and at preventing even more widespread protein deficiency in future generations". To fill the gap, more "conventional" proteins, i.e. proteins from animals, fish and plants, are required. But account must also be taken of the so-called "unconventional" proteins; these include proteins in oil-seed residues left after the oil has been expressed, which are in fact widely used in making protein-rich mixtures distributed for famine relief. "Most developing countries", the report says, "have enough oil-seeds, if properly processed, to meet the present protein needs of children." Soya bean and cotton seed are important sources of such protein. Other unconventional protein sources are fish protein concentrates, protein from green leaves, and so-called "single-cell" proteins. "Single-cell" proteins are obtained from suitable strains of yeast grown on waste carbohydrate material such as molasses, or, more significantly, on petroleum. The quantity of petroleum needed to provide enough protein for a million people by this means would amount to a negligible fraction of total petroleum supplies. However, "single-cell" proteins have not yet proved convenient or acceptable either for animal or human consumption.

It would be foolish to claim that advancing food technology—by no means confined to the affluent countries—can of itself solve the world's great food problems. But it can do much, as the synthesis of essential vitamins from inedible materials shows, vitamins being foods according to any reasonable definition of the term. It would indeed be equally foolish to minimise what modern food technology has already achieved, and still more its potential achievements. It is a new factor in the world food situation, likely to have remarkable consequences.

Chapter 18

More People and Fewer People

IF food supplies are rigidly limited and the population steadily grows, starvation is inevitable. World food production, as we have seen, is increasing all the time. The major questions are: Can production continue to increase fast enough? Can population growth be slowed down before it outstrips the utmost efforts to expand food production?

A whole library of books, conference reports and articles on these subjects is available. Publications found especially valuable in writing this Chapter are listed in the references [1-6].

Some modern writers have called speculation about population and food supply "The Numbers Game". The inventor of the numbers game in this context was Thomas Robert Malthus, who in 1798 published the first edition of his *Essay on the Principle of Population*.[6] Malthus formulated his law that food production increased at most by "arithmetical progression" (1, 2, 3, 4, 5), leading to doubling in twenty-five years, while population increased by "geometrical progression" (1, 2, 4, 8, 16), a formidable addition of numbers during the same period. It has been remarked that this "law", often solemnly restated, has little foundation in fact and was indeed something that Malthus made up out of his own head. But in his last work, *A Summary View of the Principle of Population*, he was at some pains to justify both "progressions", particularly the second. In simple terms, he argued that improvement in living conditions will lead to increase in population which will far exceed in scale any possible increase in food supplies. Population growth *must* inevitably be checked by war, starvation and pestilence. His ideas served as a counterblast to Utopian writers who foresaw a splendid future for man through social and political transformations born of the French Revolution, and the advance and application of science. He emphasised, for the first time, the dangerous and powerful factor of population growth. Later in the 19th century his writings were a source of valuable concepts to Darwin and Wallace when the theory of natural selection was being formulated.

It is worth noting that in the presence context "population" is often an emotional word, which may account for the bad temper of some of those who write about it. A fact which lends acerbity to debate is that at present the most rapidly-growing populations are in the poor countries. There are some who feel that the inhabitants of these countries have too many children because they are too fond of copulating—"They breed like rabbits, don't they?"—forgetting that the highest birth rates on record were reported in some Western countries in the 19th century. (During that century the population of Victorian England quadrupled.) The very titles of certain current books and articles on population sound a note of strident alarm, or even of hysteria: *The Population Bomb; The Closing Circle; The End of the Population Explosion; The Hunger to Come; The Hungry Future; The Hungry Planet; The Modern World at the Edge of Famine; Famine–1975.* Incidentally, expressions such as "explosion" and "bomb", based on an analogy between a chemical or physical reactions and vital statistics, obscure the issue.

A typical doomsday statement, which does not take cognisance of the Green Revolution, is as follows:

"Every year food production in underdeveloped countries falls a bit further behind burgeoning population growth and people go to bed a little hungrier. While there are temporary or local reversals of the trend, it now seems inevitable that it will continue to its logical conclusion in mass starvation."

Even a normally well-balanced author, namely C. P. Snow, writes about population in terms of awe and extreme pessimism. "I have been nearer", he says, "to despair this year, 1968, than ever in my life. Many millions of people in the poor countries are going to starve to death before our eyes—or we shall see them doing so upon our television sets."[7]

The population of Western countries began slowly to mount about the middle of the 18th century. In Asia, where the expectation of life was lower, a similar increase did not begin until a century later.

In underdeveloped communities a very high birth rate of perhaps 45 per 1000—about the highest of which the human species is capable— has been necessary to provide enough people to survive the dangers of the environment and to produce the next generation. Such a high birth rate demands the complete specialisation of women as childbearers and child-rearers. Their situation in society has been well described by Davidson and Passmore:[5]

"It was necessary that every adult woman should be as fertile as possible. The organisation of society in all countries, both in the East and in the West, was such as to encourage fertility. In this, all the great religions of the world, Confucianism, Hinduism, Judaism, Christianity and Mohammedanism, have co-operated. An early marriage and a large family were the avowed aim for every girl. Those who achieved this aim received both social and religious approval. This attitude to women was all but universal until 200 years ago. Under the circumstances it was sensible—indeed, essential—if mankind was to survive. However, now under very different circumstances, it still persists to some extent in all countries and in many it remains the dominant concept of woman's role in society."

The Psalmist assures the righteous man:

"Thy wife shall be as a fruitful vine by the sides of thine house; thy children like olive plants round about thy table."

Psalm 128, 3

Throughout most of history the olive plants have been troublesome to rear. Recently we have been told of a newly-discovered ancient civilisation in north-east Iran—Sharh-I-Sokhta—which is dated at about 3000 B.C.* Through the ages the site has been covered by a hard crust of salt, sand and clay, beneath which lie the relics of a busy urban civilisation. One part of the crust has concealed an enormous graveyard with perhaps 21,000 graves. These have still to be explored, but by December 1972, sixty had been opened, to show that over a half contained the skeletons of children under nine years of age. At the very dawn of civilisation the growth of population was strongly checked by ignorance of child care and child feeding, and consequent high infant and child mortality.

Until quite recent times child life has been as precarious as it was in Sharh-I-Sokhta in 3000 B.C. There was indeed a slow rise in population after the middle of the 18th century, to which more "law and order", at least in some countries, no doubt contributed, together with a small amelioration in living conditions. But it was not until a hundred years later that developments in medicine and

* *The Times*, 11 December 1972.

public health—particularly the latter—began seriously to affect the death rate and population growth, and in due course entirely changed the demographic picture. The subsequent spurt in population has been due almost entirely to these factors, so potent that they can bring death rates tumbling down among illiterate communities who are satisfied with the services of the local witch doctor or his equivalent. Health services can operate effectively in countries which are not being "developed" to any large extent in other ways. Paul Erlich[8] has coined the phrase "exporting death control" which is ignoble if it implies that the export of penicillin, D.D.T., vaccines and baby foods to poor countries should be restricted until they have mastered birth control procedures. Louis Pasteur and Ronald Ross would have strongly objected to it. Actually, experience shows that the spread of some methods of death control will take place of its own momentum, without strong encouragement on the part of doctors and public health workers. Death control should not be thought of exclusively, or even primarily, in terms of the eradication of major epidemic diseases such as yellow fever, smallpox and plague, or of the prevention of malaria, though this has been one of the greatest "death control" triumphs of the 20th century. In Ceylon the death rate was halved and the population doubled in a period of twenty years by malaria control. Less spectacular measures have greatly influenced population growth and here one thinks especially of the steady fall in infant and child mortality which is now taking place in nearly all developing countries. Professionally one of my tasks has been to try to improve the feeding of infants and children in poor countries, thereby helping more of them to survive and to become parents themselves in due course. It has been disconcerting to be told, from time to time, that I was doing harm. My critics were, of course, unfamiliar with the idea that parents must feel assured of the survival of at least three healthy children before they will consider preventing births.

"It is abundantly clear", comments a despondent journalist, "that it is the doctors who, unwittingly, have condemned the third world to poverty. It is the importation of advanced medical science into an economy that is anything but advanced that, by sharply reducing infant mortality and lengthening life expectancy, has created a problem for which there is no civilised solution." To which most doctors reply, in their simple way, that the prevention of suffering and death, and the rearing of healthy citizens, are wholly beneficent aims. They cannot tolerate any suggestion that medicine and public health should be withheld from human beings anywhere because of fear of the population explosion.

The rate of growth of the world's population in the 20th century is nonetheless altogether without precedent, and there are no signs of slackening. According to United Nations forecasts, world population, now (1973) about 3630 million, may reach something between 5970 and 7100 million by A.D. 2000, the range depending on fertility and other factors. Some writers feel that statements such as "A million more people are being added to the planet every five days" are particularly impressive though they may mean little to most readers. But no one can question the formidable nature of the population figures however they are presented. It is often insisted that the Green Revolution gives the world but a short breathing space; it will not feed the 7100 millions figuring in the UN charts for the year 2000.

Population increase depends, of course, on the balance between the birth rate and the death rate. In the 1960s the general world rate of increase was about 1·9 per cent per annum—about 2·5 per cent or more in the developing countries, and about 1·0 per cent in the affluent countries. One of the reasons why the developing countries are in the lead in this respect is that they are experiencing the first impact of modern preventive medicine, which acts more strongly on "unhealthy" populations than on those which have already benefited from it for some years. The general figure of 1·9 is something new in human history; moreover, as United Nations experts point out, there is likely to be still more rapid growth in the 1970s and 1980s, because of the larger number of females surviving and passing into the child-bearing age. In most of the developing countries, the fall in the death rate during the present century has been very considerable, but the birth rate is falling much more slowly. In India, for example, the death rate is now 16·7 per 1000, while the birth rate was 42 in 1971.

Death can be prevented or postponed by mass measures such as malaria control and proper drains, but birth is the concern of individuals. The large family, desired by most parents in poor countries for psychological, social and economic reasons, is rooted in ancient customs and traditions which change slowly.

Food production has been running steadily ahead of population growth, but with a smaller lead in the developing than in the affluent countries. The world food situation, however, deteriorated somewhat in the 1960s. Population continued to grow, but agriculture had some poor years in the earlier part of the decade, particularly in East and South Asia. This was the period when the doomsday prophets were most vociferous. Some of the heat was taken off by the Green Revolution, and by the prevention—without too much difficulty—of a great famine in Bihar in 1967 (Chapter 15). At the United Nations' "Conference on the Human Environment" in Stockholm in 1972, "pollution" pushed "starvation" a little off the centre of the stage. But—to change the metaphor again—the pursuing ogre is lightly wounded, not killed.

Two interrelated factors are involved in population growth and its control. The first is motivation, i.e. the attitude of men and women towards the bearing and rearing of children. Do they *want* a quiverful of children, none at all, or something in between? The second is the means of preventing the birth of children, covered, though not completely, by the term "birth control". The factor of motivation will be considered first.

Communities may fail to reproduce themselves because they lack the urge to do so. Early in this century some Melanesian islands in the Pacific were almost depopulated because the inhabitants, deprived of an exciting traditional culture by the white man, lost the will to live. The same has happened to other conquered peoples, such as the North American Indians. Negro slaves in the Caribbean failed to reproduce themselves, and the replacement of numbers, during the centuries of sugar-slavery, depended on carrying new ship-loads of slaves across the Atlantic by the dreadful Middle Passage. In the United Kingdom in the 1930s, during a dreary period of widespread unemployment, the birth rate fell to the lowest point ever recorded, so that the population was failing to reproduce itself; what was called the "reproductive index" was below 1. Modern industrial civilisation was designated by thoughtful people a "biological failure", since it did not provide people with incentives to keep the race alive. But with the reduction in unemployment in the late 1930s, the emotional stimulus of the second world war and the subsequent creation of the Welfare State, the birth rate began to rise again. There was a post-war boom in babies and forebodings about "biological failure" were soon forgotten.

This was an astonishing and unusual episode in the annals of human reproduction, but it does show how sensitive the birth rate

The monsoon soaking desiccated land, India 1973.

8a Famine relief work: stone breaking, Maharastra 1973.

8b Protein-rich food mixture for children: 400 calories daily. Maharastra 1973.

can be to the current social and economic environment. Normally a falling birth rate is associated with a rise in the standard of living rather than with economic recession, particularly if the rise is accompanied by improvement in maternal and child health. If child life becomes safer—if the mortality rate in infants and young children is drastically reduced, as nowadays it can so readily be— parents in poor countries do not need to bring so many children into the world to ensure against the danger of being left alone and unsupported in old age. But a rising standard of living usually makes a quiverful of children a liability rather than an asset. This is particularly evident on farms where child labour, essential in the past, is now less needed because of modernisation and mechanisation. The fewer the children, the better the education they can be given and the better their start in life.

It is regarded as axiomatic that rising levels of living and lower infant and child mortality lead to a decline in the birth rate. Ward and Dubos[1] say that "the change of the whole context of people's lives into the more modern context of higher education, female emancipation, rapid industrialisation, productive modernised agriculture and city life" offers "a complex but already fairly successful solution to the problem of excessive population growth". This is encouraging but perhaps a little optimistic.

Postponement of the age of marriage, associated to some degree with improved living standards, has a very definite effect on the birth rate. In primitive societies girls are usually married soon after puberty, at an age when fertility is highest in the human female. The emancipation and higher education of women rapidly change this practice, as is abundantly evident today in some developing countries. Sometimes, as in India, the old custom of early marriage may be maintained, but young married women may proceed with their education and take university degrees before they begin to raise families. The late marriages of Ireland, which have helped to keep the population in check since the famine, are a different phenomenon. Their main purpose and effect have been to prevent the breaking up of farms into fragments below a reasonable size.

The next question to be asked is whether the physical means now available for controlling the number of births are effective and adequate. Most methods of "birth control" aim at preventing the union of the sperm and the ovum, or the development *in utero* of the

M

embryo resulting from their union. There are other methods which do not fall into those categories; for example, induced abortion, which means removing a homunculus from the womb and dropping it into a bucket; and female infanticide by exposure, an ancient method of controlling population numbers, which disposes of a fully formed and viable human being.

An increasingly used means of preventing conception without interfering with the sexual act is sterilisation, which usually involves cutting, by simple surgery, the ducts through which the sperm or the ovum pass on their way to implantation in the wall of the uterus. In some countries today adult males who submit to the cutting of the *vas deferens* receive a substantial reward. In others it is illegal. It is a method of contraception widely practised in India.

Until recently birth control, depending mainly on so-called "barrier" methods, has been a crude, messy and embarrassing business, more so for women than for men. Few doctors, physiologists or sociologists studied the subject in its various aspects scientifically. Married couples received little guidance and were left to master the difficulties themselves, with some help from Margaret Sanger and Marie Stopes. Birth control was frowned on by the authorities, particularly church authorities, and in a number of countries the sale of contraceptives was prohibited by law, as indeed it is to this day.

The advent of "the Pill" (which deserves to be spelt with a capital), evolved since the second world war mainly in the United States, has changed the situation. A description of the pill by A. S. Parkes,[3] himself a leading authority on sexual physiology, may convey little to the average reader, but will show that this field has not been neglected by scientists:

"It remained", he says, "for Pincus and Rock about ten years ago (1956) to exploit the pituitary-depressing activity of the newly-prepared orally active progesterone-like substances and so introduce oral contraception in a practicable form. Thus was born 'the pill' which consists of one or other of several different orally active progestagens, usually with a small mixture of oestrogen. It is necessary, of course, not merely to postpone ovulation, but to suppress it altogether and for this purpose medication is required during the greater part of the inter-menstrual period, from day 5 to day 25 of the cycle. This technique of conception-control is remarkably effective—so effective, in fact, that the effects of the exogenous progestamen on the endometrium and cervical mucus are probably supplementary anti-fertility factors which prevent conception even in the event of a break-through ovulation as diagnosed by a rise in pregnanediol excretion."

Doctors and scientists may have been largely responsible for the population explosion, but with the creation of the pill they have done something to make amends.

The pill, in its original or slightly modified forms, is the most convenient and effective means of contraception so far discovered. Women taking it regularly run no risk of becoming pregnant. Its side-effects are usually no more than slightly unpleasant and very rarely dangerous. It must indeed be swallowed daily for twenty days in each month and this calls for conscientiousness on the part of the swallower. It is now produced on a very large scale at a low cost, and is the most widely-used contraceptive in the affluent countries. Its distribution in developing countries is also rapidly growing and it is now being used in "family planning"* programmes in many countries outside Europe and North America, with a variety of bodies contributing to the cost. It is, of course, also used by women who pay for it.

The next most popular method of birth control at the present time is known as "the inter-uterine device" or "I.U.D.". The I.U.D. is a suitably-shaped slip of plastic or other material inserted into the cervix of the uterus, thereby preventing the uterus from closing and from snugly retaining the growing embryo. I.U.D.s can be made in thousands for almost nothing, and are widely used, particularly in Asia. They have the disadvantage (from the standpoint of cost) that a moderately skilled and trained worker is needed to insert them. They sometimes cause bleeding and slip out of position. On the other hand, their continued effectiveness, unlike that of the pill, depends on inaction and not action on the part of the woman.

* The expression "family planning" was introduced a few years ago as a euphemism for "birth control", a term invented by Margaret Sanger. It is intended to convey the idea that larger as well as smaller families may sometimes be desired by husbands and wives, and medical treatment for sterility may be needed. But in practice it has rarely been used in this sense. "Planned Parenthood" is a dignified alternative, appearing in the title of the leading organisation for promoting birth control—IPPF, the "International Planned Parenthood Federation."

Modern contraceptive methods are steadily increasing in number and efficiency and more records are being kept of results. The growing literature shows that the subject is no longer neglected by research workers; in fact it is becoming one for devoted specialists. This is something new, but a more important departure is that governments, United Nations organisations and powerful non-official bodies have begun to support "family planning" programmes in many parts of the world. The educated public, while worried by all the fuss about over-population, and the prospect of there being more and more people to be fed, is not yet aware of what is being done to reduce the rate of increase.

The attitude and activities, in this field, of the United Nations and some of its Agencies, have been described, in some detail, by Richard Symonds and Michael Carter, in their book *The United Nations and the Population Question*.[9] One of the earliest international workers to insist on the dangers of overpopulation was the biologist Julian Huxley, the first Director-General of UNESCO. In 1946 the UN Population Commission was established, reporting to the Economic and Social Council. The "population projections" sponsored by the UN Population Division, which served the Commission, have been of far-reaching importance. These alarming projections dramatised the situation, showing for example, that world population might double between A.D. 1960 and 2000. There were indeed "high", "medium" and "low" projections, based on different figures with respect to fertility, but even the lowest called for a tremendous increase in world food supplies. After presentation to the World Population Conference in 1954, they have dominated subsequent literature on world population.

But this was only a beginning for the United Nations. Step by step it has become involved in programmes to check population growth. Here the position of WHO has been of interest. The League of Nations avoided any public discussion of birth control which it defined (in 1932) as a practice "abhorrent to a large section of religious belief and contrary to the national laws of certain countries". The Health Committee of the League—in a sense the predecessor of WHO—was instructed to withdraw a report containing references to birth control; ultimately the report was accepted after some passages had been deleted. Equally, WHO was at first prevented by some of its member governments, notably that of the Catholic Republic of Ireland, from including anything resembling birth control and family planning in its programme. But times have changed. WHO's Brazilian Director-General has recently stated:

"In response to requests from Member States WHO provides advice and guidance on the patterns of organisation, administration and management essential to the efficient conduct of family health services including family planning. Specifically, WHO sees as its role the development of family planning activities within the general health services, in direct relationship to the maternal and child health component or other relevant services. The merit of this arrangement is that the health protection afforded by such integrated services induces confidence in parents that their children will survive and thus inclines them more readily to family planning practice."

WHO strongly emphasises the relation between maternal and child health services and family planning. Most countries undertaking family planning programmes agree with WHO, and their newly-created "Department of Family Planning" or its equivalent, is attached to the Ministry of Health. Clearly the approach to mothers through child welfare clinics is desirable and convenient. But here we must bear in mind the paucity of doctors and welfare clinics in the poor countries generally. In such circumstances the establishment of at least elementary health services is the first necessary step.

Within the last decade the United Nations has become more and more concerned with encouraging family planning action programmes. The United Nations Fund for Population Activities (UNFPA), established in 1968 as part of the United Nations Development Fund, is the largest UN body in this field. In 1972 it was supporting family planning in 74 countries, with a budget of 44 million dollars, and expectations that the annual budget would soon exceed 100 million dollars. The money came from both governments and non-official donors. The Fund is helping to organise a World Population Conference in 1974. Two other important organisations need mention here. The International Planned Parenthood Federation (IPPF), with headquarters in Lower Regent Street in London, was founded in 1952, with a small staff and a budget of a few thousand pounds. Its budget in 1972 was over 25 million dollars; it has 5 regional offices in various parts of the world and family planning associations in some 79 countries are linked with it. The IPPF is not a United Nations body, but its connections with UN are close. Significantly its Secretary-General, Miss Julia Henderson, was formally Director of the UN Bureau of Social Affairs. Then there is the "Office of Population" part of "The U.S. Agency for International Development", which provided 95 million dollars in 1971 for approximately similar objectives. This organisation has made extensive studies of the progress of family planning, and recently issued a publication on this subject which will be used in the next chapter.

United Nations and other agencies not lacking in funds can supply money, information, pills and specialised personnel. They can support centres where subordinate workers destined to approach women in their homes can be trained. They can encourage national planned parenthood associations. But governmental family planning departments and programmes, indicating an awareness on the part of governments that something needs to be done, are more important than outside aid. According to IPPF, some forty governments now organise and finance family planning, needless to say on a widely varying scale. An important aspect of current family planning activities is the establishment of "mobile units" which teach mothers how to limit their families, and supply them with the means of doing so. Popular education, sometimes including sex education in schools, is part of the movement. Sterilisation, with rewards for the minor operation required, is practised in a few countries, while the expression "abortion legal on medical grounds" can be liberally interpreted. Large families may be officially discouraged in other ways. The Government of Singapore recently announced sharply that maternity and family allowances would cease beyond the third child. Better educational opportunities for young women and their employment in offices and light industry will postpone the age of marriage—a long-recognised method of reducing the birth rate. Some governments have set themselves targets, i.e. to reduce the country's birth rate to a much lower level by a given date. For example, Egypt, assisted by a number of foreign organisations and relying principally on the pill, aims at 30 per 1000 by 1978. The present birth rate is 44 per 1000 and the death rate 16·5, so that the growth rate of the population is 2·5 per cent annually.

Given the extent of the movement, it will be relevant to comment briefly on the attitude of the great religions of the world towards family planning. Buddhism is quite indifferent. Procreation and family life are of little interest to the followers of the Buddha, seeking emancipation from worldly affairs and the attainment of *nirvana*. Moslem theologians have no objections, though children are regarded as the greatest blessing provided by Allah. The Koran does not forbid *coitus interruptus*—the only method of birth control known when it was written—and a classical authority specifically stated that the practice was justified to preserve a wife's health and to allay the worries caused by numerous children. In 1937 the Mufti of Egypt declared, in simple language, that it was permissible for husband and wife, by mutual consent, to take measures to prevent semen entering the uterus, in order to prevent conception. In 1972 a conference of Moslem savants from twenty-four countries, meeting in Morocco, expressed approval of what it called "balanced procreation", but strictly prohibited abortion after the fourth month of pregnancy, unless it was for saving the mother's life. The conference was indeed unhappy about abortion at any stage of pregnancy.

The Jews do not seem to have adopted any positive attitude towards birth control, one way or the other, though it is possible that family size was a serious question in over-crowded ghettoes. It was noted in the last century that Jewish infants in England were healthier than English infants, with a lower mortality, probably because of better food and hygiene. Jewish infants did not often suffer from rickets. In modern Israel concern has been expressed at the low Jewish birth rate as compared with the Arab, and at the fact that Jews from underdeveloped countries tend to have larger families than Jews from Europe. But no "policy" regarding birth control has as yet emerged.

To the Hindu, the begetting of a son is a religious duty. The caste structure of Hindu society lends primary significance to the family of parents, grandparents, children, uncles, aunts and cousins, and beyond this to the extended or joint family. Widows who can no longer contribute children are regarded with opprobrium, and in the old days were encouraged to burn themselves alive on the funeral pyres of their husbands. To the outside observer, Hindus seem highly sexed, and Hindu religious art is unique in its portrayal of the human sexual act and its postural potentialities. Again, Hindus appear to be obsessed with family occasions and obligations. But there is little formal objection to family planning in

India on the grounds that it runs counter to custom and religion. Contraception is not linked with the destruction of life, prohibited by some sections of Hinduism. The sperm and the ovum are invisible. Sterilisation which does not interfere with the sexual act is surprisingly acceptable.

The New Testament, apart from the Ten Commandments the chief moral authority for Christians, has little to say about procreation. The Fathers of the Church exalted celibacy to a place in the Christian ethos which it has to some extent retained ever since. But marriage is an honourable estate, preferable to celibacy except for those with special vocations. The Christian attitude towards marriage and its privileges and obligations is described in the magnificently-worded Anglican marriage service. Its first purpose, the Prayer Book says, is the procreation of children, its second the avoidance of sin and fornication, and its third "mutual society, help and comfort". Interference with the primary purpose of marriage is unnatural and sinful. The governing principles were stated by Pope Pius XI in 1930 in the following terms:

"Any use whatsoever of matrimony exercised in such a way that the act is deliberately frustrated in its natural power to generate life is an offence against the law of God and of nature."

Both Catholic and Protestant churches have frowned upon birth control, but during recent years the Protestant laity has taken little personal account of ecclesiastical bans. The same seems to be broadly true of the Roman Catholic laity, since in many Catholic countries the birth rate has declined at much the same rate as in neighbouring Protestant countries, even when the sale of contraceptives is prohibited by law. The Catholic attitude towards birth control may, however, restrain the governments of some Catholic countries from taking action to promote it. Its influence on the programme of WHO has been noted. Family planning programmes in certain countries, for example Mauritius and the Philippines, have concentrated on the so-called "rhythm" method, acceptable to the Roman Church, since it merely means restricting copulation to a period in the monthly cycle when the union of the sperm and the ovum is least likely to take place. But this method is not very effective. In predominantly Catholic Latin America a number of governments support family planning, but in general official hostility is still fairly strong. Programmes run by voluntary bodies are however often tolerated, these being presented as measures for family health and welfare and not for population limitation.

The population of China is somewhere between 650 and 700 million, which represents about one-fifth of the human race. Chinese attitudes towards birth control are therefore important on a world basis. The Chinese are essentially a non-religious people, though they may render pious respect to their ancestors. Nor are they a highly-sexed people. According to tradition, the Chinese man of wisdom lives frugally and does not take much interest in women. The Chinese seem ready to respond to the teachings of their Communist government with regard to family limitation and its importance to China. The Chinese peasant has always desired large families for the pragmatic reason that he needed sons and daughters to work on the family holding and to look after him and his wife when they are old. The better organisation of agriculture and the development of collective farming has reduced this need. The more sophisticated townsman agrees with the dictum of the authorities— even if he does not always follow it—that a man should not think about marriage before the age of 28.

A few governments are swayed more by the modern religion of nationalism than by traditional faith. The Government of Libya, for example, will have nothing to do with family planning and encourages increase in population, in so far as this is possible. The same ideas exist in a few other new African countries. Africa is underpopulated in comparison with other continents and pressure of population on available resources of land and food is as yet scarcely evident.

Family planning is not simply a matter of setting up clinics staffed by trained nurses and offering convenient contraceptives or subsidised sterilisation. Actually it bites deeply into the fabric of society and has strong associations with religion in the broad sense of the term, so that motivation is in the long run more important than birth control techniques. The considerable group of enthusiasts who promote family planning in different parts of the world do not always give sufficient weight to these facts.

Chapter 19

Family Planning

As we have seen, there are two kinds of famine: one, the catastrophe from which man has suffered periodically since the dawn of history; the other, starvation caused by the world's failure to produce enough food to feed too many people. Most of this book has been about the first kind—the famine of the Litany due to drought or flood, pests, disorder and war. Such famine has had much in common everywhere in the world. The grim picture of a famine-stricken population has been the same in all ages and places.

The second kind of famine is still only a threat—the threat that numbers of people will outstrip any possible increase in world food supplies. It will be considered in this chapter, with special reference to factors making for retardation in population growth.

The movement to reduce the birth rate is unquestionably gaining momentum in a large part of the world. The Office of Population, Agency for International Development, U.S.A., has recently (1971) gone on record as follows:[1]

"Although population programs are of recent origin in many countries, not yet apparent in some, and the bulk of work needed to solve the world demographic crisis still lies ahead, there is reason for optimism that the major part of this work will be accomplished by the end of this decade.

In other words, it is now possible to think in terms of the world —by 1980—being well on the road towards finding positive solutions to its problem of excess reproduction and population growth.

This optimism is based upon the emergence and confluence of a number of favourable trends and developments:

The concept of fertility control—that improved control of fertility confers large benefits upon individuals and nations—has been broadly disseminated in an increasingly receptive world.

Many countries have removed or modified laws that restricted

178

the availability and use of the most effective means of birth control.

Resources available for development of population and family planning programs have increased rapidly.

International organisations have greatly increased their activities in the population and family planning field.

Key breakthroughs in fertility control technology have occurred ahead of schedule.

Many countries are developing increasingly effective family planning programs.

Recent census and other demographic data indicate a more favourable world population picture than had been projected from earlier data."

Such general statements, though they may help to calm the terrors of the disciples of Paul Erlich, are not fully convincing. They lack a sufficient foundation of vital statistics. But some encouraging figures are available. For example, substantial recent falls in the birth rate of certain affluent countries, whose vital statistics are reliable, have been reported. In December 1972, the Census Bureau in Washington, D.C., announced that a sharp fall in the U.S. birth rate had taken place in the previous five years, and that the estimate of population for A.D. 2000 should be reduced by 22 million. In England, in the same month, the Office of Population Censuses and Surveys reported that the 1971 census had given a population figure lower than the expected one. Projections of growth in numbers during the next forty-years therefore needed revision. It was estimated that in the year 2011—forty years ahead—the number of births would be 170,000 less than had previously been anticipated. The 1971 figure may, of course, represent only a beginning in the decline of the birth rate.

The same process is also taking place in West Germany, the richest country in Western Europe. Relying on research carried out by the recently established "Federal Institution for Population Research", the West German government has reported that in 1972 deaths exceeded live births by 29,000, and has estimated that the country's "native" population will fall by nearly a million by the year 2000. Their present birth rate is one of the lowest in the world. The total population continues to rise because of the steady influx of foreigners to do the country's donkey work. At present one in four of German women use the pill. In East Germany, the richest country in eastern Europe but with a completely different economic system, much the same thing appears to be happening.

The pill and induced abortion are unquestionably contributing to falling birth rates in affluent countries where economic and social circumstances and the good health of infants and children favour small families. Such a fall is likely to take place in all affluent countries. This does not imply that the same thing is about to happen in poor countries, where conditions for the mass of the population are very different. But the fall does suggest that the birth control methods currently practised on the three countries referred to above are remarkably efficient and likely to succeed elsewhere in the world.

Outside the technically-advanced regions there are countries—small countries—where the birth rate is definitely declining because of birth control or family planning. Examples are Singapore, Hong Kong, Taiwan, South Korea, Puerto Rico and Barbados. In Hong Kong the birth rate decreased from 35·5 per 1000 in 1961 to 18·9 per 1000 in 1970. Barbados is of rather special interest. In this small island, with a population of about 250,000, the infant mortality rate, less than 30 years ago, was 150 per 1000 live births (it had been 400 in 1920). But because of a high birth rate (38) the population continued to increase. Then a progressive medical officer of health set up half a dozen infant welfare centres at which mothers were given instruction about the care and feeding of their children, and minor diseases were relieved. By 1970 the infant mortality rate had fallen to 40, and there was also a decrease in deaths in early childhood. Other things being equal, this would have meant a considerable increase in the density of the island's population. But simultaneously mothers were taught methods of birth control and in recent years have been supplied with the pill, so that by 1970 the birth rate had fallen to 21. The prospects of "standing room only" in this Caribbean island are now remote.

While useful lessons may be drawn from such small samples of humanity, the world's major population problems lie in great countries with many million inhabitants. In Asia the situation is dominated by two massive concentrations of population, in China and India, which together contain about 1400 million people, more than one-third of the world total, and over one-half of that of Asia. Japan and Indonesia, with estimated populations in 1970–71 of

104 and 121 million, are other countries of considerable size in the Asian region.

China, now officially called the People's Republic of China, is the largest country in the world. In 1971 its population was estimated at 685 million, which may be out by many millions either way. The highest authorities in the country, including Chairman Mao, are aware of the need for controlling population growth and a national family planning programme is taking shape. A good deal of information about that programme is available, and, though some doubts about its accuracy are unavoidable, most of it seems to bear the stamp of truth. The most extensive report on the subject was produced by two Japanese workers, Mr Tameyoshi Katagiri and Professor Takuma Terao, who visited China in 1972 on behalf of IPPF.[2] At the invitation of the Chinese Medical Association, they spent three weeks in the country and were given all possible help in their enquiries. The shortness of their visit suggests that the information they obtained was provided by their hosts and not based on what they saw for themselves. Much of what they reported has, however, been corroborated by other foreign observers.

In 1952 Chairman Mao was disconcerted by figures emerging from the census of the previous year, and by forecasts that China's population would reach 1000 million in 1980. He was told that about 14 million extra people were being added each year. Previously Mao had felt that birth control and family planning were opposed to Chinese Confucionist traditions, but he abandoned this attitude, and the Communist government decided to launch a birth control campaign in 1958. At the same time the marriage age was raised to 20 for men and 18 for women. It was taught that 32 and 25 were the ideal marriage ages for men and women respectively. The family planning campaign survived the Cultural Revolution and emerged in 1970 more vigorous than ever. While the initiative came from the government, it is claimed that there is no element of compulsion behind the movement and that it rests on the wishes of ordinary Chinese men and women themselves. People in towns and cities have some understanding of the population problem and like discussing it. National tasks come first, they say, and a man should not think of marriage before 28. A family of three children should be the aim. As has previously been suggested, the Chinese are not highly sexed in the western sense of that expression. The dictum of St Paul about marriage and burning would not appeal to them and

they admit that they have never been able to make head or tail of
Freud.

Many different methods of contraception are used, including
"pills", sterilisation (for both sexes), and I.U.D.s, as well as condoms
and other old-fashioned contraceptive devices familiar to Marie
Stopes. While it is reported that contraceptive "pills" of the modern
type are manufactured and distributed in China, quantitative facts
are not available. Abortion is legal and is often carried out by a
"vacuum aspiration" technique said to have been invented by
Chinese doctors. Family planning services are free.

Over 80 per cent of the population live in rural areas and are
engaged mainly in food production. These are obviously more
difficult to reach and influence than urban or semi-urban communities, either for the introduction of health measures or the encouragement of family planning. To bridge the gap, China has created an
unusual corps of health workers called "barefoot doctors" who with
their assistants number about 3 million. The barefoot doctors are
young men and women educated to the secondary school level and
given a brief and simple training which enables them to perform
useful medical services, in addition to their ordinary daily work.
They deal as best they can with public health problems and emergencies, helping qualified doctors where these exist. Of importance
in the present context is that they are involved in the family planning programme. They carry "pills" and other contraceptives with
them for immediate and direct distribution, sometimes supplying
these to women actually at work in the fields. They are trained to
insert I.U.D.s—not a very difficult thing to do.

To support the whole campaign, older children in schools, at
least in towns and cities, are taught something about family planning and the need for it. Such teaching can scarcely have as yet
been extended far into rural areas. In 1967 primary education was
available for only 60 per cent of children.

No one really knows, or can know for some years to come, what
effect all these activities are having on the birth rate and the size
of the population. Chairman Mao admitted in 1970 that family
planning in rural China was making slow progress. But at least it
can be said that Chinese thinking about population is optimistic;
some observers believe that the population growth is even now less
than 2 per cent and that the goal of a 1 per cent rate by A.D. 2000
will be achieved. Early in the present century the Chinese, then

powerless, were sometimes called the Yellow Peril, because their huge and growing numbers seemed a threat to the rest of the world. A China with a population held in restraint will be more potent in world affairs.

In neighbouring Japan the population is increasing at a lower rate (1·1 per cent per annum) than in any other country in Asia.[1] Birth control was introduced into Japan by Margaret Sanger as long ago as 1922, but in the 1920s and 30s was frowned upon by the government because of the desire to have plenty of men for military purposes. Population pressure—the need for *lebensraum*—could be regarded as an excuse for belligerency. After the war the return of the army was followed by a steep rise in the birth rate, and at the same time Japan's colonial territories were restricted by defeat. At this period induced abortion to reduce family size became common, and was made legal in 1947. The people in general realised the desirability of keeping numbers down.

Government health authorities, however, believed that induced abortion damaged the health of mothers, and authorised and encouraged the sale of sixty "contraceptive chemicals" as a counter attraction. Actually both abortion and conventional contraceptives have been increasingly used and between them keep numbers under control. Family planning, centred in the health services and in particular those concerned with maternity and child welfare, has become an accepted part of family life. It is curious that I.U.D.s and the pill are little used and in fact illegal.

The birth rate in Japan, with its population (1970) of some 104 million, is 17·0, which is considerably lower than that in the United States. Japan subscribes liberally to IPPF and the IPPF Western Pacific Regional Pacific Office is in Tokyo. She advises countries in Asia on family planning programmes and supplies them with educational material. The control of population numbers has coincided in Japan with the achievement of remarkable material prosperity and the possession of one of the "hardest" currencies in the world.[3,1]

Apart from China and Japan, and from India which will be considered at some length later, brief reference must be made to two comparatively large countries in east and south Asia, namely Indonesia (Pop. 121 million) and Thailand (Pop. 34 million). All that is possible here, with respect to these countries, is to draw attention to IPPF reports on their family planning activities. The latest report for Indonesia,[4] with some unimportant textural changes, reads as follows:

Birth rate	1965–70	**48·3**
Death rate	1963–70	**19·4**
Population growth rate per cent	1963–70	**2·8**

There has been an official family planning programme since 1968. The target is 6 million "acceptors" and 2450 family planning clinics by 1976. A national Family Planning Association was founded in 1957, which was affiliated to IPPF in 1967. There are now (1971) 1954 family planning clinics and 530,000 "acceptors", of whom about 50 per cent receive the pill, and 44 per cent are fitted with inter-uterine devices (I.U.D.s). Abortion is legal on medical grounds. Education in family planning is being developed. Assistance is provided by IPPF, UNFPA (United Nations Fund for Population Activities), the Population Council, the Ford Foundation, CWS (Church World Service), SIDA (Swedish International Development), USAID (United States Agency for International Development) Japan, Oxfam, Netherlands, WAY (World Assembly of Youth), the Rockefeller Foundation and the Pathfinder Fund.

(The Pathfinder Fund, somewhat unexpectedly in view of its name, specialises in Inter-Uterine Devices and the testing of their efficiency. Based on Boston, Massachusetts, it operates in forty countries and has published seven volumes on "IUD Performance Patterns".)

A very similar programme is reported for Thailand where, it is said, there were over 3500 clinics and some 400,000 "acceptors" in 1971, and the pill is the most widely used contraceptive agent. The aim is to have over two million "acceptors" by 1976. Family planning in Thailand is the responsibility of the Ministry of Public Health.

Geographically speaking, Egypt is part of Africa, but its demographic situation is akin to that found in many Asian countries. Largely dependent on food grown in the narrow Nile valley, as in the days of Joseph, Egypt has a population of about 34 million to which 800,000 are added annually. With a high birth rate and a falling death rate (44 and 16 respectively in 1970) the population has been increasing rapidly. The pill is the most popular contraceptive; it is distributed through some 3500 family planning clinics, with assistance from UN bodies and interested foundations. Public health and other officials believe that a substantial fall in the birth rate is now taking place. Population control is of special significance in Egypt since the great Aswan dam, as well as providing power for industry, will bring large new areas of land under cultivation. A relentlessly increasing population would neutralise its effects on per caput food consumption.[1]

In comparison with most of Asia and Egypt, Africa South of the Sahara is sparsely inhabitated. It has nearly a quarter of the earth's surface and less than one-tenth of its inhabitants, so that at first sight no problem of over-population appears to exist. But the birth rate is high—47 per 1000 in 1970—and in some African countries the death rate is falling steadily as a result of sanitary and public health measures. The doctors—expatriate and native, but in recent years more of the latter than the former—are busily at work as usual. The old expression, "the White Man's Grave", is long since obsolete, and black babies are avoiding the grave in increasing numbers.

In over half the countries of Africa there is no organised family planning. This is, however, rarely due to active hostility on the part of governments. If these do not support it themselves, they are usually ready to allow international and non-governmental organisations to do so. The United Nations has established an Economic Commission for Africa (ECA), of which nearly all independent African States are members. ECA has an expanding population programme, supported by the "UN Fund for Population Activities" (page 173), with a "Center" located in Addis Ababa in Ethiopia. The Center helps governments to organise family planning programmes and to train workers to help in these, and also to prepare reports and undertake demographic studies. An African Population Conference was organised in Ghana in December 1971, by ECA in association with a body not previously mentioned, the International Union for the Scientific Study of Population (IUSSP), and IPPF. But the movement has not yet gone very far in Africa. The sums donated for work in this field are small in comparison with those donated in other continents. Only a few countries like Algeria and Libya are hostile. President Boumediene of Algeria said in June 1969: "I take this occasion to say—on the subject of what some are pleased to call the population explosion—that we are not in favour of false solutions such as birth control . . . we are, on the contrary, in favour of positive solutions, such as the creation

N

of new jobs, of schools for children, and better social conditions."
The estimated population of Algeria is 14 million, the birth rate 49,
and the rate of natural increase (1970), 3·3 per cent.

In some French-speaking African countries, laws restricting the
sale of contraceptives are operative.

In most of Africa, there is no obvious density of population,
except perhaps in the urban conurbations which are coming into
existence here as in other continents. Maternity and child welfare
services, the usual basis of family planning, have as yet scarcely
been developed, though in some areas they are working successfully.
It is understandable that African governments do not put family
planning high on their list of priorities.[4]

The most rapid population growth in the world is at present in
south and central America. The term "Latin America" covers most
of this region, the population of which is increasing by 3 per cent
per year. According to a UN estimate, numbers are likely to swell
from 290 million in 1970 to 756 by the year 2000. Characteristic of
Latin America is the spread of urbanisation, on a scale beyond
that of other developing regions. The growth rate of many urban
areas is about 7 per cent per year, and living conditions in the
so-called shanty towns which surround the principal cities are
dismal and unhealthy. In these marasmus and kwashiorkor and
associated conditions are common and infant and child mortality
high. The "bands of misery" around Latin American cities grow
thicker every year as rural people leave heavily-populated country
areas in search of better living conditions.

Some governments in Latin America support family planning,
but not very enthusiastically. Politically, the issue is a sensitive one,
though within recent years the church has become less hostile. Here
as elsewhere, there is little governmental objection to the efforts of
outside agencies, and most of the familiar bodies, such as IPPF,
USAID, the Population Council and the Ford Foundation, provide
technical advice and financial assistance. The usual contraceptive
methods are taught, with emphasis on the pill and I.U.D.s. Abortion
is illegal in much of Latin America and is regarded as a menace
to public health. Family planning is defended on the grounds that
it offers a better and safer way than abortion of limiting family size.

In some five countries in the region ministries of health have
adopted a favourable attitude towards family planning. Family
planning associations provide services in about fourteen countries,

nearly all operating in urban communities. Only in Chile and Columbia is an attempt being made to cover the whole country. Any optimistic assessment of progress achieved is scarcely justifiable. All that can be said is that a beginning has been made and some resistance broken down.

Problems of population are world-wide, but it is in India that increasing numbers seem most dangerous, and catastrophe most imminent. India is always prominent in the minds of those who bewail mankind's coming doom from excessive population. It is therefore necessary to give special attention to the situation in that country.[5,6]

India has about 550 million inhabitants as compared with China's 685 million; that makes her the second largest country in the world, with 14 per cent of the world's population inside her borders. The great majority of her people are Hindu. With a birth rate of about 37·5 and a death rate of 16·0, some 13 million people are added to the population every year, and at the present rate of increase numbers will be doubled by A.D. 2000. The advances in public health responsible for this phenomenon are more remarkable than is generally realised. Up to 1920 the infant mortality rate was about 220 per 1000 live births; it is now about 113, equivalent to the rate in England and Wales in the year 1915. The general death rate fell from 27 to 16 between 1950 and 1970.

India is keenly aware of her population problem. The country is making great efforts to climb out of the abyss of poverty and to play a leading part in the modern world. Four Five-Year Plans, the first beginning in 1952, have contributed substantially to progress. A wide range of industries, heavy and light, has been developed, and most essential consumer goods are now produced within the country. Agriculture has not been neglected, and the Green Revolution has been at least a partial success. But the Government of India and the educated Indian public feel that these achievements are being neutralised by the inexorable increase in numbers. This applies especially to food production. The solution of "abstinence" from copulation, advocated by Mahatma Gandhi, could scarcely be accepted by a modern state.

Family planning activities in India were initiated in the early 1920s, when birth control clinics were opened in Poona and Mysore. The official governmental programme began in 1950, and at first made little headway; progress was delayed by a trial of the so-called "rhythm method", which here as elsewhere was found to be value-less. But increasing sums were allotted to family planning through each successive Five-Year Plan as follows:

Budget allocation (Rs/–)

1st Five Year Plan, 1951–56	3 million Rupees	
2nd „ „ „ 1956–61	49·5 „	„
3rd „ „ „ 1961–66	270 „	„
4th „ „ „ 1969–74	3000 „	„

The Fourth Plan lays down a target birth rate of 32 per 1000 by 1974 and 25 per 1000 by 1978–79.

The Ministry of Health, Family Planning and Urban Development in the Central Government includes, as its name indicates, a Department of Family Planning. Responsibility for action in the fields of health and family planning rests largely with State Governments, but for family planning the Central Government disburses the funds. A "National Institute of Family Planning", headed by the Minister of Health, and including State Health Ministers, has the task of guiding policy and co-ordinating the activities of Central and State Governments. It is assisted by a Family Planning Commissioner. The Central Government's organisation to limit population growth extends downwards through state family planning bureaux, district family planning bureaux, urban family planning centres, rural family planning centres, rural sub-centres, mobile units and hospitals, to reach the philoprogenitive masses.

Side by side with state-supported family planning, there is a non-official programme, smaller in scope, promoted by The Family Planning Association of India. The Association, which obtains funds from the International Family Planning Federation, the Government of India and some of the usual foundations, runs model clinics, mobile units and training centres for subordinate staff. It claims that its educational programme reaches between 4 and 5 million people. It has hired a commercial advertising train to spread information on family planning. For the past nineteen years it has published bulletins and periodicals. More recently it has produced educational films. Abundant help is provided by non-Indian foundations and agencies. The IPPF[4] lists twenty-one of these.

What has been jocularly called the "cafeteria approach" has been generally adopted in both government-supported and non-official family planning programmes in India. That is to say, the customers —married couples—are free to choose the method of birth control they prefer. At present they are choosing—in that order—conventional contraceptives, sterilisation and I.U.D.s. Few oral contraceptives (the pill) are distributed, though these are bought by the well-to-do in the big cities. The use of I.U.D.s has somewhat declined in the last few years, but sterilisation has increased in popularity. "Acceptors" of I.U.D.s and sterilisation are paid something for their acquiescence; the average compensatory sum, which varies from place to place, is about Rs 30/-.

Over 60,000 people are employed in the government family planning campaign, and as many more village midwives (dais) have been given some elementary training in birth control methods.* Some optimistic authorities believe that a real effect on the national birth rate was produced between 1961 and 1970, and point to certain areas where a decline seems evident. It has been reckoned that the family planning movement prevented 2·2 million births in 1970–71, and some 7·4 million previous to that year. According to the latest records, about 9 million sterilisations have been performed. Whether the target laid down in the Fourth Five-Year Plan of a birth rate of 32 per 1000 by 1974 and 25 per 1000 in 1978–79 remains to be seen.

Critics point out that in a poor country the system of paying individuals a substantial sum for a minor operation is liable to abuse. Claims for reimbursement can readily be exaggerated by subordinate officials. But at least it can be said that the seriousness of the population problem has been realised by responsible people in India and that the problem is being confronted. We may recall that within the last ten years two famines have been faced by Indian administrators (Chapters 15 and 16).

Family planning programmes throughout most of the world are sustained by public education and propaganda. A common type of educational poster contrasts a happy family of four with a large miserable family of eight or more. The Indian family planning symbol, to be seen everywhere in India, is four stylised heads— mother, daughter, son, father—which somehow convey a sense of smug satisfaction; the family of eight is too familiar to need representation. A poster from Hong Kong demonstrates rather

* The dais are not eager to reduce their means of livelihood.

3 Family planning poster, India. *The ideal family of four.*

4 Family planning poster, Hong Kong. *Wording on the poster as circulated reads "Plan your family before it is too late".*

5 Family planning poster, Thailand. *The wording reads "Happier homes come from family planning".*

obviously the burden of a large family. The charming poster from Thailand speaks for itself.

Most of the advertising material in support of family planning issued in the developing countries is pleasing and polite. But some birth control slogans devised in the United States are more provocative: "Stop at two"; "suppress your local stork"; "stop people pollution"; "make love, not babies".[7]

Chapter 20

The Immediate Future

No final judgment can yet be made on the possibility of controlling the world's population. But, as the last chapter showed, a beginning has been made and the signs are hopeful. The impulse is there and the knowledge is available. If birth rates can be reduced in Europe, they can be reduced in Asia and in Central and South America.

The danger of famine of the traditional type is another matter. Here we are on more familiar ground and in a better position to make sensible forecasts. It can be said firmly that the prospects of eliminating this ancient human calamity are good, although at the time of writing (mid-1973) the world food situation is rather precarious. Apart from effective relief, we have reached the point at which famine should not be allowed to occur at all. This means in the first place more food either produced within the country where the danger exists, or obtainable from elsewhere in the world. It also means early warnings, and there is now little possibility that a famine situation will arise unheeded, as in Bengal in 1943. Governments are ready to report the occurrence of food shortage. Apart from governments, international organisations are on the alert. As we have seen, the United Nations and its agencies have responsibility for the early detection of food shortage and famine. Journalistic reports of imminent famine tend to be made without full justification. Famine is news.

Some facts about the current world food situation will be given here. FAO's reports on "The State of Food and Agriculture" are the most reliable sources of information. The 1972 report[1] disappointed expectations, though it was less despondent than some reports in the early 1960s. In 1971 agricultural production in the developing countries rose by only 1 to 2 per cent, as against a hoped-for annual expansion of 4 per cent. In the developed countries, on the other hand, the increase in output was large: 9 per cent in North America, 5 per cent in Western Europe and 3 per cent in Oceania, giving an overall figure of 6 per cent. Wheat is the most important human food, and an encouraging phenomenon was the increase in world wheat production, which was estimated as 353 million tons in 1971, 11 per cent greater than the 1970 figure. The Canadian wheat crop was almost 60 per cent higher than in 1970 and the U.S. crop was a record. Nearly all the wheat-producing countries were involved, but not China and Russia. India, thanks to the Green Revolution, established buffer stocks of over 7 million tons in 1972 and proudly but prematurely proclaimed herself self-sufficient in wheat.

The Good Lord felt that this was rather too good to be true. The first country to tell the world about serious food shortage was the U.S.S.R. In 1972 the Russian wheat harvest was 30 million tons below the target figure, mainly because of bad weather in the Ukraine. Crop failure was due to sub-zero temperatures during the winter of 1971–72, with not enough snow to protect new shoots, followed by drought and a long heat wave. Russia was obliged to turn to the U.S.A. for supplies of food, buying at full commercial prices 11 million tons of wheat, about 20 per cent of the U.S. crop. This was a purchase of unprecedented size. Though the weather was probably enough to account for the Russian shortfall, evidence of disorganisation and incompetence came to light, and the Minister of Agriculture was sacked. Agriculture has always been a weak spot in the U.S.S.R., so successful in some other technical fields. Some think that the country has never recovered from the massacre of its most competent farmers, called Kulaks, in 1929. It is significant that the U.S.S.R., proud of her doctors and public health experts, is an enthusiastic member of the World Health Organisation. But she has consistently declined to join FAO, feeling, perhaps, that in the sphere of agriculture she has little but defects to show the world.

Almost simultaneously China announced that her wheat harvest in 1972 was poor because of drought, smaller than the 1971 harvest by some 10 million tons. As a result, she had to buy 6 million tons of wheat from Australia, Canada and the U.S.A.

Then came trouble in India. In 1972 there was serious drought affecting a population of perhaps 10 million people in the State of Maharastra, which includes the cities of Bombay and Poona. This followed abnormally low rainfall in the previous two years. At the end of 1972 the land in the affected area was completely dessicated, with no prospect of rain until the middle of 1973 (Plate 5). An itinerant Oxfam employee reported that he swallowed so much dust on one day that he could scarcely speak for the next two days. After a visit to the area the invincible Indira Gandhi decided that it would be necessary for India to buy 2 million tons of wheat in the United States at the full commercial price. During the Bihar crisis of 1967 (Chapter 15), wheat had been purchased on a concessional basis, but because of a subsequent diplomatic quarrel between India and the U.S.A. about Bangladesh, honour made it necessary for India to pay the dollars for this later consignment in full. The cost was equivalent to about 20 per cent of India's precious foreign exchange reserve. The afflicted population needs water as well as food, and this means transporting drinking water by truck and digging wells which will provide water both for human beings and for crops.

Plates 1a, 1b, 5, 7, and 8a are Oxfam photographs of this famine. They show vividly the effect of long drought: the parched land; the remains of water in a river bed; the distribution of drinking water from a truck; the feeding of the people; breaking stones for road making in return for relief payment.

Nor can Bangladesh, with a population of perhaps 75 million, be overlooked. In 1972 food grains were imported into Bangladesh on a large scale, 900,000 tons being supplied by India alone. But India, stricken by drought, could not do the same again in 1973. A UN expert mission, which visited Bangladesh in the autumn of 1972, reported that import requirements in 1973 would be 2·5 million tons, 500,000 tons of this to be set aside for building up reserve stocks. In most of Bangladesh rice rather than wheat is the preferred cereal. The cost of imports on this scale would amount to more than a half of the country's funds for foreign exchange. In effect, determined action by her government will be needed to carry Bangladesh through 1973 and 1974 on the basis of her own reduced food output, supplemented by perhaps half a million tons of cereals from abroad.

In January 1973, the Dutch Director-General of FAO, Dr A. H. Boerma, made an important statement at a press conference in Rome, a synopsis of which follows:

The world food situation, he said, was causing considerable alarm. There had been a series of unusually bad harvests in many countries due mainly to drought. The world's reserve stocks of food were being depleted to a lower level than had been the case for a number of years. While there was not an immediate threat of widespread famine, there were food shortages in several countries. He advised governments whose countries were likely to need supplies to make their arrangements in good time. World prices of wheat had risen by 70 to 80 per cent since the middle of 1972, imposing a heavy burden on the financial reserves of countries forced to buy cereals abroad.

The governments of some of the key countries had already adopted measures to increase food production. The United States had lifted some of its controls on grains and rice acreage in order to encourage farmers to grow larger crops from the spring of 1973. In Canada, the Minister of Agriculture had called on farmers to grow all the wheat they could this spring. India, too, had embarked on an intensive campaign to boost its spring harvest. The Soviet Union was planning to try and make up for last year's crop losses by increasing its investment in agriculture by 10 per cent.

However, early weather reports from several important areas— including the Soviet Union—were far from reassuring. The situation was not helped by the fact that there was at present a shortage of fertilisers which had led to higher prices for them and which would accentuate the difficulties of several important countries.

Speaking emotionally for a Dutchman, the Director-General then said:

"The possibility that I have envisaged of a world shortage of cereals later this year or next year may not materialise. But, in the name of reason, can this world of the 1970s, with all its scientific prowess and its slowly growing sense of common purpose, go on enduring a situation in which the chances of enough decent food for millions of human beings may simply depend on the whims of one year's weather. Is this a tolerable human condition? Emphatically not."[2]

In June 1973 the Council of FAO was warned that things were little better and in the following month a similar warning was given to the Economic and Social Council of the United Nations (ECOSOC). The possibility of a world-wide grain shortage in 1974 was now admitted. The situation was, of course, subject to constant change and uncertainty.

In Maharastra the drought ended in the traditional fashion in June. Plate 6b shows the dramatic coming of the rains, and Plate 7 the soaking of the land. Before a new harvest can be reaped the wet soil must be broken up and seeds sown, by people who are weak after a long period of underfeeding, and are in need of famine rations for several months after the rains have arrived. Stone-breaking was an important famine relief task (Plate 8a), done in return for payment. Food distribution to children in this famine followed much the same lines as in Bihar in 1968 (Chapter 15), though perhaps its scale was less liberal. The condition of children receiving supplementary protein-rich foods improved as it has done in other recent famine emergencies (Plate 8b).

The ending of the drought was followed by tremendous floods in parts of northern India and Pakistan in July and August 1973. The rains came in superabundance, and there was much destruction of crops, stores and dwellings. Several thousand people in the Indus valley were drowned. Generous relief was needed to offset the effects of too much water. The Indian peninsula is not fortunate in its climate.

Meanwhile large areas in Africa were hit by drought. These were mainly new countries lying to the west and south of the Sahara—Chad, Mali, Mauretania, Niger, Senegal and Upper Volta, falling into what is sometimes known as the Sahelian zone. The drought also extended to parts of Ethiopia, leading to a serious food shortage. Relief measures in the Sahelian zone were initiated by the United Nations. It is perhaps not surprising that meteorological pundits have begun to talk of the "Decline of the monsoon" induced by large-scale world climatic changes.

The FAO *State of Food and Agriculture, 1973* was issued to the public in September 1973. In a Foreword the Director-General repeated earlier forebodings:[3]

"The world food situation in 1973 is more difficult than at any time since the years immediately following the devastation of the second world war. As a result of droughts and other unfavourable weather conditions, poor harvests were unusually widespread in 1972 . . . Mainly because of massive purchases contracted by the U.S.S.R. in 1972 world stocks of wheat have been drawn down to the lowest level for 20 years. Rice is also in very short supply. There is thus little if any margin against the possibility of another widespread harvest failure in 1973.

"A number of governments, including those of such major producing countries as Canada, China, India, the United States and the U.S.S.R., have taken special measures to increase food production in 1973. The effect of all these measures depends on the weather, however, and it is still too early to form any reliable picture of the likely outcome. Some developing countries are facing additional difficulties in 1973 as a result of the current shortages and high prices in world fertiliser markets."

But in spite of numerous uncertainties, FAO did not regard the "production outlook" for 1973 as unfavourable. It believed that most indications pointed to larger harvests in the developed countries. Normal weather and good harvests were probable in Western and Eastern Europe. In Great Britain, after alarmist reports in June and July, the cereal harvest was an excellent one. In European Russia—the main grain-producing area of the U.S.S.R. —the winter cold was relatively mild and the heavy losses of the previous year were not repeated. The weather in the Near East was mildly unfavourable, verging on drought in some countries. In South America Argentina's important wheat crop was expected to make a strong recovery after the poor harvest of 1972.

Clearly the immediate world food situation in 1973 was disturbing, in that stocks of food had fallen to an unusually low level. But it was by no means catastrophic, unless quite abnormal weather continued for another year or more. The great food-producing countries were engaged in rebuilding their stocks as quickly as possible. Canada, the United States, Australia and other countries will no doubt continue to produce surplus foods, especially wheat, for which there is a continuing world demand. They will not allow their cupboards to become bare, and they are, of course, capable of producing more food than they do at present. Throughout most of the world, apart from periodic climatic setbacks, and bad years like 1972, food production is increasing all the time (Chapter 17). It has become fashionable to decry the Green Revolution, which has in fact been remarkably successful, though its achievements in India have been overshadowed by the economic and social disruption accompanying the creation of Bangladesh, and by a grim drought in Western India. The buffer stocks of wheat which India amassed were all too quickly depleted. It is generally admitted, of course, that the Green Revolution cannot by itself solve the world problem of population and food supply. Borlaug himself believes that it will provide a breathing space of perhaps twenty years during which the menace of over-population can be vigorously attacked. Other Borlaugs may extend the breathing space by other discoveries. Research designed to increase supplies of staple foods is likely to become highly popular during the next few decades, attracting the best scientific brains. One Nobel Prize may lead to another.

Famine of the familiar historical type, a periodic calamity with baneful effects on groups of human beings, can now be strongly counteracted. Mankind possesses assets which greatly facilitate its prevention. Especially there is now the United Nations and its machinery, enabling threats of famine to be detected at an early stage, and effective action to be promptly initiated. (But as the Epilogue on the recent famine in Ethiopa shows, disastrous delays in detection and action may still occur.) Use can be made of the knowledge of methods of relief feeding gained within recent years. Children, the most vulnerable group in a famine-stricken population, can be given protein-rich food supplements with consequent improvement in their health. Should we find ourselves witnessing, together with Lord Snow (page 164), scenes of famine on our television screens we are likely to see, not emaciated corpses, but children receiving some improved form of supplement and beginning to thrive.

On a different plane, the cereal wheat is a tremendous asset to humanity. The seeds of wheat, it has been said, were the seeds of civilisation. The earliest human settlements in Western Asia, and the civilisations of which they became the base, lived mainly on wheat as their staple food. For perhaps 8 millennia wheat has been pre-eminent among cereals, though of course other cereals, such as maize and rice, have supported successful civilisations in some parts of the world. During this long period, man has improved methods of growing wheat and preparing it for consumption, and in various forms it is now acceptable to people everywhere. It is possible to produce wheat in much greater quantities than at the present time, and its distribution to those in need presents no material difficulties. Almost complete technical mastery of one of its varieties, *Triticum vulgare*, has been achieved.[4]

What has been done in conquering famine in its traditional manifestations gives hope that man will successfully master the broader problem of adjusting world food supplies and world population.

Epilogue

Famine in Ethiopia

As we have seen, great progress in famine relief operations has been made during the present century. But these have not been equally successful everywhere. Some countries, such as India, have shown themselves capable of handling emergency famine situations threatening millions of people, and of making good use of foreign aid, while others are less able to counter the disaster and are in special need of help from wealthier and technically more advanced countries and international and charitable organisations. A brief account of the recent famine in Ethiopia will illustrate these matters, and also some of the measures for famine relief discussed in earlier chapters.

Ethiopia is prone to severe periodic droughts. In the 1970s two large mountainous provinces, Tigre and Wollo, north and north-east of the capital, Addis Ababa, were afflicted with drought which began early in 1971, after preceding seasons of poor rainfall. The population of the two provinces put together is from 5 to 6 million people. About 85 per cent of the land under cultivation is devoted to cereals, including wheat, barley, sorghum, maize and teff (*Eragrostis abyssinica*). Of these teff, a cereal confined to Ethiopia, is grown in the greatest quantities. Its small pin-head-sized grain contains 9 per cent of protein, which has an amino acid composition reasonably well suited for meeting human amino acid requirements.

In normal times the area supports some cattle and other domestic animals, but the drought led to heavy losses of livestock, pressing hard on nomads, of whom there are many in this part of Ethiopia. Cattle suffered severely, while camels and (as usual) goats showed greater capacity for survival.

Some deaths took place early in 1973, and by the middle of that year thousands of people were dying, with children in the majority. It was estimated that from 50,000 to 100,000 people died in Wollo province alone—perhaps 500 per day—when the famine was at its height. Disease, especially diarrhoea, but also pneumonia, bronchitis, measles and typhus, contributed substantially to mortality. An epidemic of measles took heavy toll. Marasmus and kwashiorkor were prevalent in infants and young children, the former being the more common.

There was unfortunately some delay in the official recognition of the famine. Perhaps it was felt invidious to bother the old emperor, head of the Organisation of African Unity, about a local catastrophe, and without his fiat no action could be taken. However, there were organisations in Addis Ababa ready to take the initiative. One of these was the "Ethiopian Nutrition Institute" established a few years ago, financed largely by Sweden, and employing Swedish experts in nutrition and related fields. Another was the Unicef Area Office, also located in Addis Ababa, which serves a group of countries in north-east Africa as well as Ethiopia. With the help of various organisations including Oxfam, a famine relief programme, for which the Government of Ethiopia was nominally responsible, took shape in 1973. The principal measure was the establishment of primitive relief camps which provided monotonous cooked meals to people from the surrounding countryside and special food mixtures to children. Thirteen relief camps in Wollo province gave shelter, food and some medical assistance to 30,000 people, and also provided some help to a further 25,000 for whom there was no room in the camps. Even in the camps themselves some children were so weak that they could not crawl to the feeding centres and remained hidden in corners waiting to die. One of the larger camps, Dessie in Wollo, accommodated 3500 people, mainly children; when the famine was at its worst, about thirty people were taken in daily at this camp, which had a daily mortality rate of about eighteen. Bad sanitary conditions in the camps fostered disease. Many camps were short of water. Indian efficiency in running refugee camps was not equalled in Ethiopa.

In October 1973 a film was made in Dessie for British television by Jonathan Dimbleby, a member of the distinguished family of broadcasters. This excellent film stimulated the collection of funds for relief. Over £1,500,000 was donated by the British public in a short time, to be used by Oxfam, Christian Aid, Save the Children and other agencies. Teams of keen volunteers supervised by doctors, undertook and enjoyed the relief work, though disconcerted by the plethora of flies and fleas in Ethiopa. Apart from the non-govern-

o

mental agencies, the "World Food Program" participated, supplying 10,000 tons of grain, and the Swedish, Swiss and British governments made substantial contributions.

In a few months the situation in the famine area greatly changed for the better. Wheat, distributed to the bulk of the population by Ethiopian officials, assuaged hunger; some 500 g per head was issued daily. Especially valuable in rescuing children were certain supplementary foods: "faffa"; wheat flour mixed with soya; and "Disco". "Faffa" is based on ground teff, a usual formula being as follows:

	per cent
teff	57
soya	18
chickpea	10
sugar	8
skim milk	5
with vitamins and minerals	2

This mixture, manufactured under the supervision of the Ethiopian Nutrition Institute, was given in the form of porridge, 50 g of which was fed daily to children. Usually this led to a rapid improvement in physical condition. A mixture of wheat and soya was almost equally effective.

Disco, described as a "high energy food" and devised by the Dunn Nutritional Laboratory, Cambridge, is a simple mixture consisting largely of vegetable oil and skim milk powder, with some essential mineral elements. Children are given several mouthfuls of "Disco" five times a day—in some cases they have to be tube fed. "The great advantage of Disco", a nutritionist wrote, "is that it can be used for all conditions ranging from severe protein malnutrition (kwashiorkor) to starvation (marasmus). This means that it can be administered by relatively untrained staff. I would say that the success rate has been fairly phenomenal. Some children admitted in an apparently dying state were on their way home within only three weeks. Instead of merely maintaining their nutritional state, as often happens with normal feeding programmes, the children were catching up on the weight and strength they had lost. From a nutritionist's point of view the results were very, very good."

The famine in Ethiopia was not a great famine, though a death toll of perhaps over 100,000 is by no means negligible (and inexcusable at this stage in the history of famine). Effective measures were initiated only after much of the damage had been done. When vigorous action was undertaken by international and voluntary agencies the picture quickly changed, and with so much aid available it is unlikely that further famine mortality will take place even if drought continues through 1974. The existence of these agencies is an important safeguard against the worst manifestations of famine. An encouraging aspect of the episode in Ethiopia was the most successful use of protein-rich dietary supplements to save and rehabilitate grievously-ill children. Here knowledge and experience gained in recent years proved invaluable, while observations made in Ethiopia may be most useful for famine relief work elsewhere.

References

Introduction

1. Keys, A., Henschel, A., Michelson, O. and Taylor, H. L. (1950) *The Biology of Human Starvation*. Minneapolis. University of Minnesota Press.
2. Walford, C. (1879) *Famines of the World, Past and Present*. E. Standford, London.
3. Loveday, A. (1914) *The History and Economics of Indian Famines*. G. Bell & Sons Ltd.

Chapter 2

1. Famine Inquiry Commission. (1945) *Report on Bengal*. Government of India.
2. Porter, A. (1889) *The Diseases of the Madras Famine of 1877–79*. Madras.
3. Donovan, D. (1848) Dublin Medical Press, Vol. 19, 67.
4. Woodham-Smith, Cecil. (1962) *The Great Hunger, Ireland 1845–9*. Hamish Hamilton, London.
5. Scrimshaw, N. S., Taylor, C. E. and Gordon, J. E. (1968) *Interactions of Nutrition and Infection*. WHO Monograph Series No. 57.
6. Report of the Commissioners appointed to enquire into the famine in Bengal and Orissa in 1866. Vol. 1, published 1868.

Chapter 3

1. Edwards, E. S. (1947) *The Pyramids of Egypt*. Penguin Books, Harmondsworth.
2. Keys *et al*. *The Biology of Human Starvation*. loc. cit. Chapter 1.
3. Vaudier, Jacques. (1936) *La famine dans l'Egypte ancienne*. L'Institut Français d'archéologie orientale.
4. Keller, Wegner. (1956) *The Bible as History*. Trans. from German by William Neil. Hodder and Stoughton, London.
5. Grollenberg, L. H. *et al*. (1956) *Atlas of the Bible*. Nelson, London.

Chapter 4

1. *The Great Famine: Studies in Irish History, 1845–52.* (1956) Editors: R. Dudley Edwards and T. Desmond Williams. Brown and Nolan Ltd, Dublin.

2. Woodham-Smith, Cecil. (1959) *The Reason Why.* Hamish Hamilton, London.

3. Woodham-Smith, Cecil. (1963) *The Great Hunger, Ireland 1845–9.* Hamish Hamilton, London.

4. Freeman, T. W. (1957) *Pre-famine Ireland: A study in historical geography.* Manchester University Press.

5. *The Works of William Makepeace Thackeray.* (1878) Vol. xviii. Smith, Elder and Co., London.

6. Nicholson, Asenath. (1934) *The Bible in Ireland.* Hodder and Stoughton, London.

7. Smith, Adam. (1776) *The Wealth of Nations.* Vol. 1, Chapter xi.

8. Somerville-Large, Peter. (1972) *The Coast of West Cork.* Gollancz, London.

9. *Transactions of the Central Relief Committee of the Society of Friends during the Famine in Ireland in 1846 and 1847.* (1852) Hodges and Smith, Dublin.

Chapter 5

1. Loveday, A. (1914) *The History and Economics of Indian Famine.* G. Bell and Sons, London.

2. Indian Famine Inquiry Commission Reports. 1880, 1888, 1898, 1901. Published by the Government of India.

3. Piggott, Stuart. (1950) *Prehistoric India to 1000 B.C.* Penguin Books, Middlesex.

4. Woodruff, Philip. (1954) *The Men who Ruled India,* Vol. II. *The Guardians.* Jonathan Cape, London.

5. Hickey, William. (1923) *Memoirs.* Vol. III, p. 105.

6. Quoted in the Report of the Indian Famine Commission, 1880.

7. Trevelyan, Humphrey. (1973) *The India We Left.* Macmillan, London.

8. *The Imperial Gazetteer of India.* (1907) Vol. 3. Oxford.

9. Passmore, R. (1951) "Famine in India. An Historical Survey". *The Lancet.* 18 August 1951, p. 303.

10. Berg, Alan. (1971) *Famine Contained: Notes and Lessons from the Bihar Experience.* From: "Famine. A symposium dealing with nutrition and

relief operations in times of disaster". The Swedish Nutrition Foundation, Uppsala.

Chapter 6

1. Kipling, Rudyard. (1900) *The Day's Work*. Macmillan, London.
2. Kipling, Rudyard. (1937) *Something of Myself*. Macmillan, London.
3. Ramalingaswami, V., and others. (1971) *Studies of the Bihar Famine of 1966–67*. From: "Famine. A symposium dealing with nutrition and relief operations in times of disaster". The Swedish Nutrition Foundation, Stockholm.

Chapter 7

1. Stephens, Ian. (1966) *Monsoon Morning*. Ernest Benn, London.
2. Famine Inquiry Commission. (1945) *Report on Bengal*. Government of India Press.

Chapter 8

1. Mallory, W. H. (1926) *China, Land of Famine*. American Geographic Society, New York
2. Naval Intelligence Division, Geographical Handbook Series (1942). Vol. 2.
3. FAO. (1970) *Lives in peril. Protein and the child*. Rome.
4. Yao, Shan Yu. (1941) *Chronological and Seasonal Distribution of Floods and Droughts in Chinese History, 206 B.C. to A.D. 1911*. Harvard *Journal of Asiatic Studies*, Vol. vi, p. 273.
5. Yao, Shan Yu. (1943) *Geographical Distribution of Floods and Droughts in Chinese History, 206 B.C. to A.D. 1911*. Far Eastern Quarterly, August 1943.
6. King, F. M. (1911) *Farmers of Forty Centuries*. Jonathan Cape, London.
7. Ross, E. A. (1923) *Standing Room Only*. Century Company, New York.
8. Malthus, Thomas Robert. (1798) *An Essay on the Principle of Population*.

Chapter 9

1. Troyat, Henri. *Tolstoy*. Published in France in 1965. Published in England in 1968 by W. H. Allen, London. (Translated from the French by Nancy Amphoux.)

2. Asquith, Michael. (1943) *Quaker Work in Russia 1921–23*. Oxford University Press, London.

3. Muggeridge, Malcolm. (1934) *Winter in Moscow*. Eyre & Spottiswoode, London.

4. Curtis, Norah, and Gilbey, Cyril. (1944) *Malnutrition. Quaker Work in Austria 1919–24 and Spain 1930–39*. Oxford University Press, London.

5. Medical Research Council. (1932) *Vitamins: A Survey of Recent Knowledge*. Special Report Series No. 167.

Chapter 10

1. *Malnutrition and Starvation in the Western Netherlands. Part I. September 1944/July 1945*. (1948) General State Printing Office, The Hague.

2. Ditto, Part II.

3. Dols, M. J. L. and Van Arcken, D. J. A. M. (1946) "Food Supply and Nutrition during and immediately after World War Two". *Millbank Memorial Fund Quarterly*, Vol. XXIV, No. 4.

4. Pyke, Magnus. (1970) *Man and Food*. World University Library. Weidenfeld and Nicolson, London.

Chapter 11

1. *Encyclopædia Britannica*. (1972) Article: "Famine". Vol. 9.

2. FAO. (1972) *The State of Food and Agriculture, 1972*. Rome.

3. *Food and Nutrition Procedures in Times of Disaster* (1967) FAO Nutritional Studies No. 21. (Author: G. B. Masefield.)

Chapter 12

1. *The Oxfam Story*. (1964) Pergamon Press, Oxford.

2. Gill, Peter. (1970) *Drops in the Ocean. The Work of Oxfam, 1960–1970*. Macdonald Unit, London.

3. Fuller, Edward. (1956) *Eglantyne Jebb (1876–1928)*. Booklet issued by the Save the Children Fund, London.

Chapter 13

1. Scrimshaw, Nevin S. (1968) *Early Malnutrition and Brain Damage*. PAG Bulletin, No. 8.

2. Protein Advisory Group. (1972) *Statement on Relationship of Pre- and Post-Natal Malnutrition in Children to Mental Development, Learning and Behaviour*. PAG Bulletin, Vol. 11, No. 2.

3. FAO. (1970) *Lives in Peril. Protein and the Child*. Rome.

Chapter 14

1. Lowenstein, Frank W. (1962) *An Epidemic of Kwashiorkor in the South Kasai, Congo.* Bulletin of the World Health Organization, 27, 751.

2. Ganz, Bruno. (1969) "A Biafran Relief Mission". *The Lancet,* 29 March 1969, p. 660.

3. *Study Mission to Biafra.* (1970) Senator Charles E. Goodall. Washington, D.C.

4. Omololu, A. (1971) *Nutrition and Relief Operations—the Nigerian Experience.* From: "Famine. A symposium dealing with nutrition and relief operations in times of disaster". The Swedish Nutrition Foundation, Stockholm.

5. Aall, Cato. (1970) *Relief, Nutrition and Health Problems in the Nigerian/Biafran War.* Journal of Tropical Pediatrics, 16, 2, 19.

Chapter 15

1. Ramalingaswami, V., Deo, M. G., Guleria, J. S., Malhotra, K. K., Sood, S. K., Prakash, O. M. and Sinha, R. V. N. (1971) *Studies of the Bihar Famine of 1966–67.* From: "Famine. A symposium dealing with nutrition and relief operations in times of disaster". The Swedish Nutrition Foundation, Stockholm.

2. Verghese, George. (1967) *Beyond the Famine.* Published by the Bihar Relief Committee.

Chapter 16

1. Galbraith, John Kenneth. (1971) *The Role of the Voluntary Organisations in Man-Made Disaster; and a Proposal.* The 1971 Gilbert Murray Memorial Lecture. Published by Oxfam.

2. Scrimshaw, Nevin S. (1971) *Statement to Subcommittee to Investigate Problems connected with Refugees and Escapees.* Committee of the Judiciary, U.S. Senate. 30 September 1971.

3. Oxfam (1971) *The Testimony of Sixty on the Crisis in Bengal.* October 1971.

Chapter 17

1. Aykroyd, W. R. and Doughty, J. (1970) *Wheat in Human Nutrition.* FAO Nutritional Studies, No. 23. FAO, Rome.

2. FAO. *The State of Food and Agriculture, 1972.* Rome.

3. Ditchley Foundation. (1969) *Population Growth.* Ditchley Paper No. 17.

4. Borlaug, Norman E. (1971) *Mankind and Civilisation at Another Crossroad.* McDougall Memorial Lecture. FAO, Rome.

5. Clarke, Colin. (1971) *Starvation in Plenty.* Secker and Warburg, London.

6. Pyke, Magnus. (1970) *Synthetic Foods.* John Murray, London.

7. United Nations. (1968) *International Action to Avert the Impending Protein Crisis.* Report to the Economic and Social Council of the Advisory Committee on the Application of Science and Technology to Development. New York.

Chapter 18

1. Ward, Barbara and Dubos, René. (1972) *Only One Earth. The Care and Maintenance of a Small Planet.* André Deutsch, London.

2. Maddox, John. (1972) *The Doomsday Syndrome.* Macmillan, London.

3. Parkes, A. S. (1966) *Sex, Science and Society.* Oriel Press, Newcastle-upon-Tyne.

4. Symposium Annales Nestlé, *Humanity and Subsistence.* Vévey, 1960.

5. Davidson, S. and Passmore, R. *Human Nutrition and Dietetics.* Fourth Edition, 1970. E. & S. Livingstone, Ltd, Edinburgh.

6. Malthus, Thomas Robert. (1798) *Essay on the Principle of Population.*

7. Snow, C. P. (1971) *Public Affairs.* Macmillan, London.

8. Erlich, Paul R. (1968) *The Population Bomb.* Ballantine Books.

9. Symonds, R. and Carter, M. (1973) *The United Nations and the Population Question 1945–1970.* Chatto & Windus for Sussex University Press.

Chapter 19

1. Agency for International Development, Office of Population, Washington, D.C. (1971) *Population Program Assistance.* U.S. Government Printing Office.

2. International Planned Parenthood Association. (1972) *Medical Bulletin. Family planning in the People's Republic of China. Report on first official IPPF visit.* Vol. 6, No. 2, June 1972. Stephen Austin, Hertford, England.

3. Maramatsu, Minora. (1969) Institute of Public Health, Tokyo. Chapter in *"National Programmes in Family Planning, Achievements and Problems".* Edited by Bernard Berelson, University of Chicago.

4. International Planned Parenthood Federation. (1972) *Family Planning in Five Continents.* London.

5. International Planned Parenthood Association. (1972) *Situation Report, India.* London.

6. Chandrasekhar, S. (1967) *India's Population. Facts, Problems and Policy.* Meenakshi Prakashan, Meerut, India.

7. Chisholm, Anne. (1973) *Philosophers of the Earth. Chapter on Paul Erlich.* Sidgwick & Jackson, London.

Chapter 20

1. FAO. (1972) *The State of Food and Agriculture, 1972.* Rome.

2. FAO. (1973) *FAO House News.* Vol. XV, No. 2. Rome.

3. FAO. (1973) *The State of Food and Agriculture, 1973.* Rome.

4. Aykroyd, W. R. and Doughty, Joyce. (1970) *Wheat in Human Nutrition.* FAO Nutritional Studies, No. 23. Rome.

Index

Aall, Dr Cato, 133
Africa, 4, 121–2, 124, 128–34, 177, 197; and family planning, 184–6
Algeria, 185–6
America, Latin: and family planning, 186–7; wheat crop, 198
America, United States of: Irish emigration to, 40–41, 44–5; Irish Relief Committee, 41; food for Bihar, 137, 140; Peace Corps, 138; birth-rate decline, 179; wheat supplies, 194, 195
Amery, L. S., 78
amino acids, 122, 125, 127, 161
Amos, Book of, 9
anaemia, 19, 136
Argentina, 198
Arnhem, 99
Asquith, Michael, 92
Aurangzeb, Emperor, 51, 52
Austria, 94–6

'Balahar', 139, 146
Bangladesh, 69, 119, 143–9, 195
Barbados, 180
Benedict XV, Pope, 118
Bengal: 1943 famine, 8, 11, 12, 20, 49, 55, 60, 63, 69–80, 193; earlier famines, 52; death rate, 55, 74–5, 77; rice crop, 73–4, 141; mistakes and failures of relief measures, 76–7, 78–80, 141
Bernadotte, Count, 107
Bhutto, Z. A., 144, 149
Biafra, 130–4
Bible in Ireland, The (Nicholson), 32

Bihar: averted famine of 1966–67, 20, 57, 63, 66, 114, 135–42, 146, 147, 156, 168, 195; 1770 famine, 52, 135; Hastings' granary in, 52, 87, 135 and *pl.* 2a; 'Panic Famine' (1873–74), 55, 135; massive relief operation (1966–67), 137–42, 146, 147, 197
Biology of Human Starvation, The (Keys *et al.*), 1
birth control, 168–73. *See also* family planning
Black Death, 5, 20
Boerma, Dr A. H., 109, 195–6
Borlaug, Dr Norman E., 155, 156, 157, 158 and *pl.* 6a
'British Association' (for Irish famine relief), 41
British Medical Research Council, 96
Buddhism, and family planning, 175

Calcutta, 69, 72, 75, 76 and *pl.* 3a
Canada: Irish migration to, 40–41; wheat production, 194, 196
cancrum oris, 22
cannibalism, 16, 50, 83, 93
CARE (Co-operation for American Relief Everywhere), 113–14, 139, 148
Caritas, 131
Carrington, C. E., 68
Carter, Michael, 172
Catholics, and family planning, 176
Ceylon, 157, 166
Chick, Dame Harriette, 96